Clinical Respiratory Physiology

LUKE HARRIS

MB, BS (LOND), MRCP (EDIN)
Consultant Chest Physician
and Consultant in Charge
Respiratory Physiology Laboratory
Aintree Unit, Fazakerley Hospital,
Liverpool

Consultant Chest Physician
Newsham General Hospital,
East Liverpool University Hospital Group

BRISTOL
JOHN WRIGHT & SONS LTD
1975

ISBN 0 7236 0374X

PRINTED IN GREAT BRITAIN BY HENRY LING LTD.
AT THE DORSET PRESS, DORCHESTER
A SUBSIDIARY OF JOHN WRIGHT AND SONS LTD.

PREFACE

The purpose of this short text is to try to clear up some of the difficulties which a succession of Housemen and Registrars have asked me to explain. I have therefore stressed the practical aspects of applied respiratory physiology together with those theoretical concepts that I feel are necessary for proper understanding. The book will, I hope, meet the basic requirements of junior doctors working in respiratory units and those studying for higher qualifications. It should be of value to technicians in respiratory laboratories, and to General Physicians wishing for a brief review of the subject. It may even stimulate an interest in senior medical students, whose knowledge of respiratory physiology is regrettably often precarious.

I have deliberately refrained from cluttering up the text with references. Indeed to quote them all would at least double the size of the book. Instead I have included a bibliography at the end. The books listed have been of great value to me over the years and contain many hundreds of references. The really interested reader of my little book will undoubtedly wish to turn to them.

L.H.

November 1974

TO MY WIFE AND CHILDREN
IN GRATITUDE FOR THEIR ENCOURAGEMENT

CONTENTS

SYMBOLS AND ABBREVIATIONS

Ventilatory

PRIMARY

V	=	volume
$\dot{V}$	=	volume/unit time
P	=	pressure
F	=	fractional concentration
R	=	respiratory exchange ratio (without subscript) and also resistance (with subscript)
T_L	=	transfer factor
G	=	conductance
C	=	compliance
S	=	specific
D	=	diffusing capacity

SECONDARY

I	=	inspired
E	=	expired
A	=	alveolar
T	=	tidal
D	=	dead space
B	=	barometric
L	=	lung
AW	=	airway
M	=	membrane

LUNG VOLUMES

IRV	=	inspiratory reserve volume
TV	=	tidal volume (normal quiet breathing)
VC	=	vital capacity
FVC	=	forced (or fast) vital capacity

FEV = forced expiratory volume (with subscript for time, e.g. 0·75, 1·0, 3·0)
ERV = expiratory reserve volume
FRC = functional residual capacity
RV = residual volume
TLC = total lung capacity
MBC or
MVV = maximum breathing capacity or maximum voluntary ventilation
MEFR = maximum expiratory flow rate
MIFR = maximum inspiratory flow rate
PEFR = peak expiratory flow rate
FMF or
MMF = maximum mid-expiratory flow rate (with subscript for portion measured, e.g. 25–75%, 200–1, 200 ml.)

OTHER
f = respiratory frequency
kCO = diffusion coefficient

Blood

PRIMARY
$\dot{Q}$ = volume per unit time
C = gas concentration (content)
S = saturation
P = pressure
D = pressure difference

SECONDARY
a = arterial
v = venous
$\bar{\text{v}}$ = mixed venous
c = capillary
s = shunt
t = total

NB: The 'p' in 'pH' does *not* stand for pressure but is a conventional symbol for negative logarithm. A capital italic '*P*' should always be used for pressure, e.g. $P\text{CO}_2$ (*see* Chapter 11).

Chapter One

Ventilatory Capacity (Timed Spirometry)

Expiratory Measurements

A number of measurements can be made from a fast (or forced) expiratory trace, and each may be used as an index of expiratory airways obstruction (provided that restriction of ventilation can be excluded).

FEV_1 = forced expiratory volume in the first second (other FEV times are sometimes used, e.g. 0·75 sec, 3 sec, but FEV_1 has become the accepted standard in general).

FVC = forced vital capacity (this may be less than the vital capacity (VC) performed slowly, especially if there is premature collapse of larger airways).

$(FEV_1/FVC) \times 100$ (sometimes expressed as FEV per cent) distinguishes between obstructive and restrictive conditions. The normal ratio is >80 per cent at age 20, >75 per cent at age 40, >70 per cent at age 60. In obstructive airways diseases FEV_1/FVC is reduced. In restrictive conditions the ratio is normal, even though FEV_1 and FVC are individually reduced.

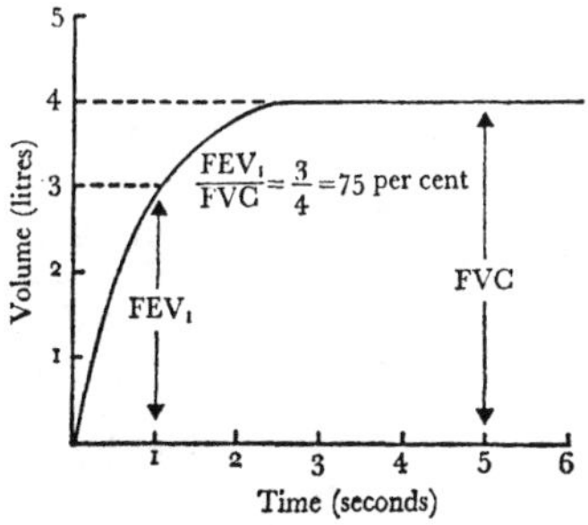

This is a normal trace (as obtained on the popular type of dry spirometer) for a 40-year-old man, 1·82 m in height.

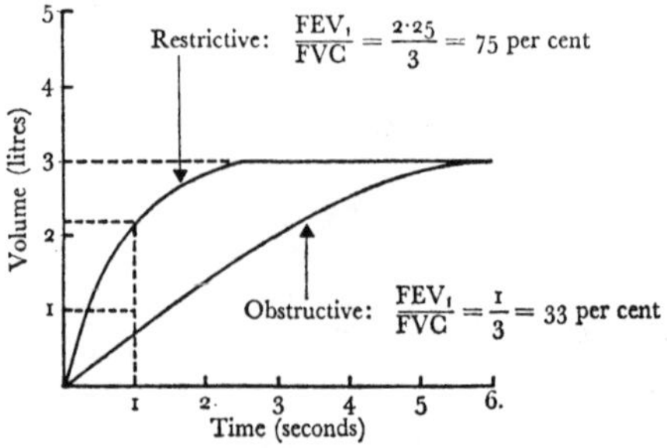

These traces (for men of same age and height as above) indicate the distinction between obstructive and restrictive patterns.

The usual method of obtaining the forced expiratory tracing is to ask the subject to take in the biggest breath he can and then breathe out into the machine as hard and fast as he can, i.e. maximum inspiration followed by recording maximum rapid expiration.

Other indices which can be obtained from the trace offer doubtful advantage over a carefully performed FEV_1 and FVC, although some workers claim that they are more sensitive, as they are less dependent on the initial part of expiration which is influenced by subject co-operation.

MEFR = maximum expiratory flow rate measured in litres per min. over 1 litre after expiration of the first 0·2 litres (i.e. from 0·2 to 1·2 litres).

FMF (or MMF) = maximum mid-expiratory flow measured in litres per min. over the middle 50 per cent of the FVC.

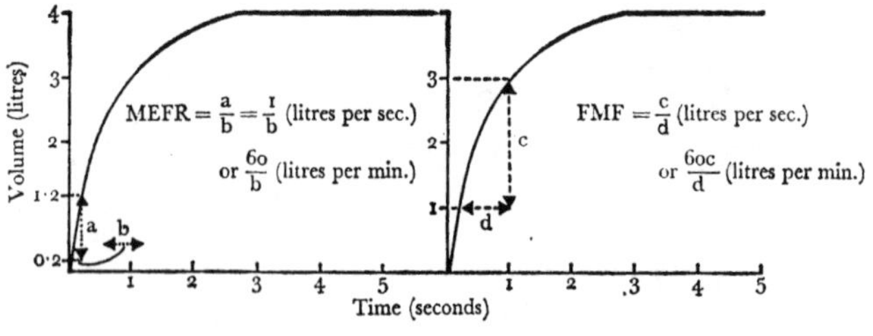

PEFR = peak expiratory flow rate, is a widely used measurement, being read from the dial of a peak flow meter. It does not distinguish between obstruction and restriction.

MVV = maximum voluntary ventilation, which is obtained by measuring the volume expired with the subject making the greatest possible respiratory effort for 15 seconds and then multiplied by 4 to give the rate in litres per min. This has largely been abandoned in favour of the other methods already described.

Reversibility of expiratory airways obstruction can be assessed by measuring FEV_1 before and after administration of a bronchodilator (Note: FEV_1 and FVC may change proportionately or disproportionately either way, therefore change in FEV/FVC per cent does *not* measure reversibility). Expiratory airways obstruction should not be labelled irreversible until it has been shown that there is a lack of response to—

1. A sympathomimetic β_2-adrenergic stimulator, e.g. isoprenaline, salbutamol etc.
2. A compound of theophylline, e.g. proxyphylline, aminophylline, etc.
3. A corticosteroid or corticotrophin.

A clinically significant response is a 20 per cent increase in FEV_1 over the resting value (although some workers accept 15 per cent).

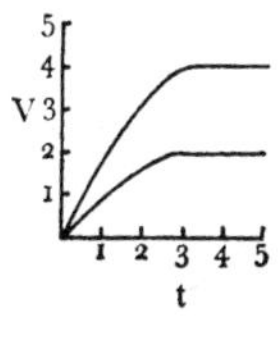

Post-bronchodilator	FEV_1	2·0	FEV_1 increase
	FVC	4·0	$\frac{(2-1)}{1} \times 100 = 100$ per cent.
	FEV per cent	50 per cent	
Pre-bronchodilator	FEV_1	1·0 L	
	FVC	2·0 L	FEV per cent. No change
	FEV per cent	50 per cent	

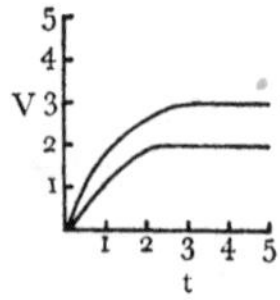

Post: FEV$_1$ 2·0 L; FVC 3·0 L; FEV per cent 67 per cent — FEV$_1$ increase $\frac{(2-1)}{1} \times 100 = 100$ per cent

Pre: FEV$_1$ 1·0 L; FVC 2·0 L; FEV per cent 50 per cent — FEV per cent increased

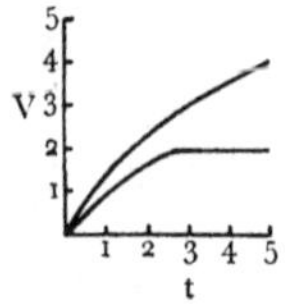

Post: FEV$_1$ 1·5 L; FVC 4·0 L; FEV per cent 37·5 per cent — FEV$_1$ increase $\frac{(1·5-1)}{1} \times 100 = 50$ per cent

Pre: FEV$_1$ 1·0 L; FVC 2·0 L; FEV per cent 50 per cent — FEV per cent decreased

Inspiratory Measurements

The equivalent of the forced expiratory measurements may be made during inspiration also viz:

FIV = forced inspiratory volume
MIFR = maximum inspiratory flow rate
PIFR = peak inspiratory flow rate

FIV and MIFR can be obtained with a fast moving drum water-filled spirometer, but not from the commonly used dry spirometer. PIFR requires a specially modified peak flow instrument.

Some workers consider that impaired inspiratory flow rates reflect restrictive disorders. It has also been suggested that comparison of inspiratory and expiratory flow rates e.g. FIV_1/FEV_1 or MIFR/MEFR or PIFR/PEFR may help to distinguish between asthma and emphysema (on the grounds that the ratio is high in asthma, but normal in emphysema) and restrictive conditions (low ratio).

E.g. Normal young man

MIFR	300 litres per min	ratio 0·75
MEFR	400 litres per min	

Asthmatic

MIFR	250 litres per min	ratio 1·25
MEFR	200 litres per min	

Emphysematous

MIFR	150 litres per min	ratio 0·75
MEFR	200 litres per min	

Diffuse fibrosis

MIFR	200 litres per min	ratio 0·5
MEFR	400 litres per min	

It has further been suggested that the FVC correlates best with the inspiratory indices.

In practice they are seldom used because the FEV_1, FVC and FEV per cent ± bronchodilator usually give sufficient information for clinical purposes.

Predicted values for FEV_1 based on Age, Height and Sex

Values ± 0·45 litres of predicted value may be considered as being within normal range, i.e. within 3 diagonal grid lines on either side of predicted.

(*See* next page)

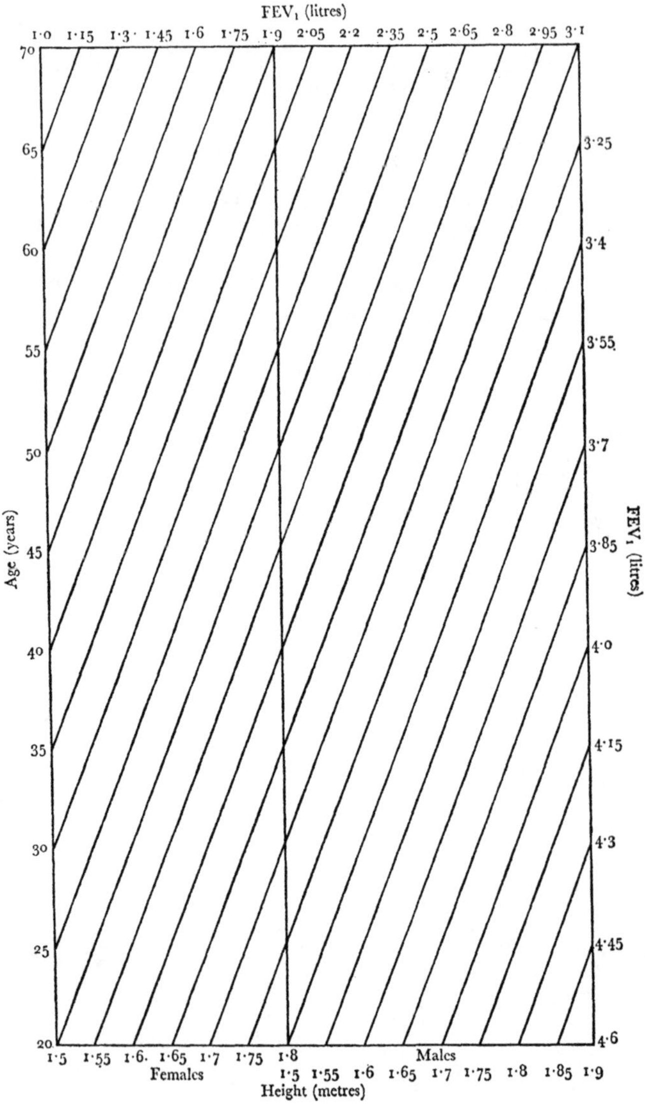
FEV₁ (litres)
1·0 1·15 1·3 1·45 1·6 1·75 1·9 2·05 2·2 2·35 2·5 2·65 2·8 2·95 3·1
70 65 60 55 50 45 40 35 30 25 20
Age (years)
3·25 3·4 3·55 3·7 3·85 4·0 4·15 4·3 4·45 4·6
FEV₁ (litres)
1·5 1·55 1·6 1·65 1·7 1·75 1·8
Females
Males
1·5 1·55 1·6 1·65 1·7 1·75 1·8 1·85 1·9
Height (metres)

Chapter Two

Lung Volumes

Measurement of lung volumes is of little intrinsic value. The measurement of residual volume is necessary, however, for measuring pulmonary transfer (diffusion) factor by the single breath carbon monoxide method, and for obtaining total lung capacity whereby the emphysema pattern of impaired diffusion can be distinguished from the restrictive pattern. It is no longer thought that the ratio of residual volume to total lung capacity is of diagnostic value.

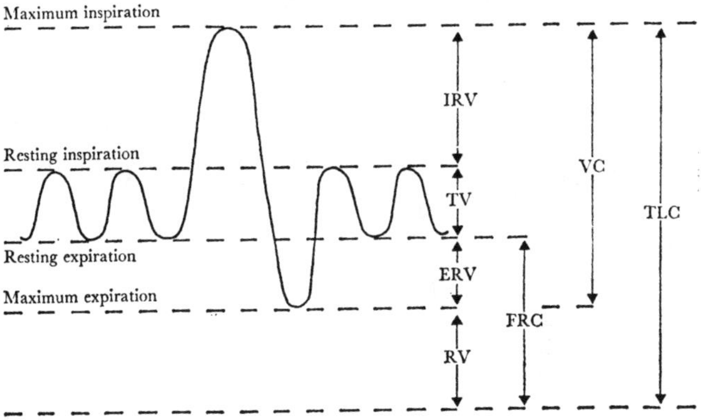

IRV	=	inspiratory reserve volume
TV	=	tidal volume (normal quiet breathing)
ERV	=	expiratory reserve volume
RV	=	residual volume
FRC	=	functional residual capacity
VC	=	vital capacity
TLC	=	total lung capacity

VC, IRV, TV and ERV are obtained from simple spirometry with a slow moving drum spirometer. TLC is obtained either by measuring FRC by a gas dilution method, subtracting ERV from this to obtain RV and adding this to VC to obtain TLC, or by measurement of total thoracic gas volume by whole-body plethysmography.

Closed Circuit Helium Dilution Method for FRC

This is a widely used method because it can so readily be combined with measurement of single breath transfer factor and because it does not suffer from the defect of the open circuit nitrogen method of being very sensitive to small errors of analysis.

The basic principle is as follows:

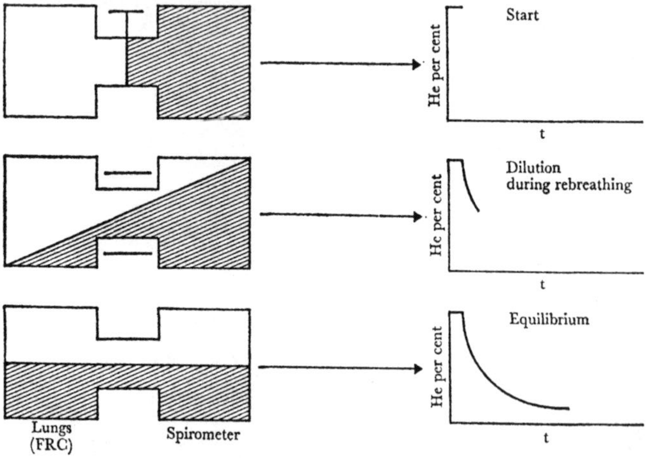

If initial helium concentration was 10 per cent in a spirometer volume of 3 litres, the amount of helium would be:

$$\frac{10}{100} \times 3 = 0{\cdot}3 \text{ litres}$$

At the end of equilibration this amount of helium is distributed equally between spirometer and lungs FRC (subject having been switched into rebreathing circuit at end of a normal expiration). Suppose, then, that final helium concentration is 4 per cent, we can say that:

$$\frac{4}{100} \times (3 + \text{FRC}) = 0{\cdot}3$$

$$\therefore 3 + \text{FRC} = \frac{0{\cdot}3 \times 100}{4} = 7{\cdot}5$$

$$\therefore \text{FRC} = 7{\cdot}5 - 3 = 4{\cdot}5 \text{ litres}$$

In practice allowance has to be made for apparatus dead space, and for change in volume due to oxygen consumption (which is usually done by adding O_2 to circuit during rebreathing at such a rate that the spirometer tracing is kept level).

The rate of dilution of helium, i.e. plotting helium per cent (on a log scale) against time in 30-second intervals may be used to derive an index of the uniformity or non-uniformity of ventilation (mixing efficiency) e.g.:

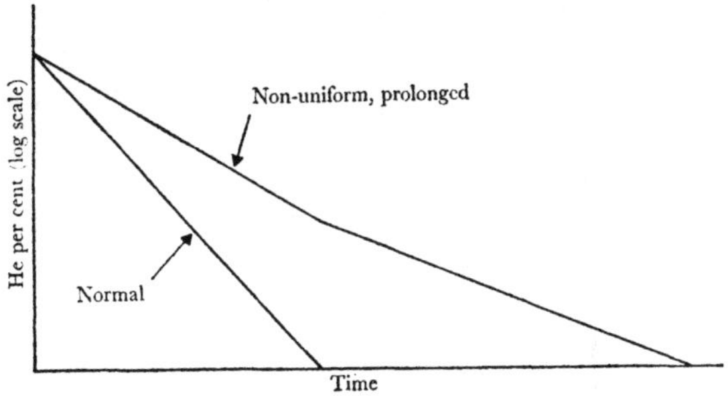

Note: The slow spirometry tracing may demonstrate air trapping during the VC manœuvre viz:

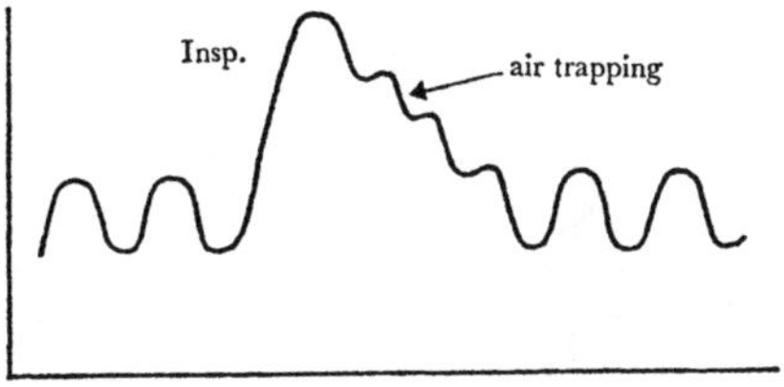

Open Circuit Nitrogen Washout Method

As already mentioned this is not recommended if other methods are available, because the calculation is very sensitive to small errors in N_2 analysis. Mixing efficiency can also be measured in this method.

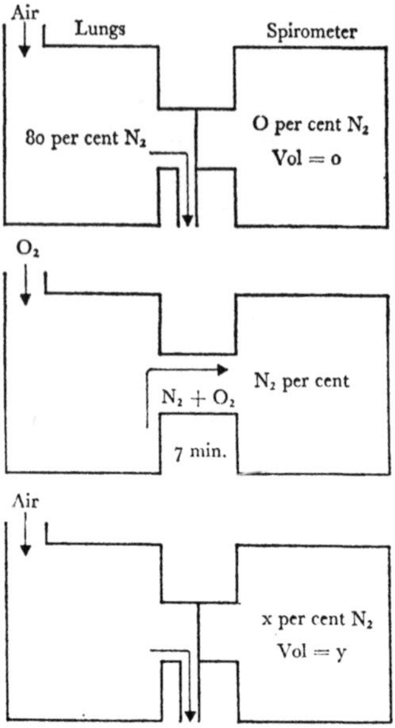

If N_2 concentration at end of 7 min. is 5 per cent and volume is 50 litres this gives the quantity of N_2 as $\frac{5}{100} \times 50 = 2{\cdot}5$ litres

This must all have come from the lungs (at FRC) which started with a concentration of 80 per cent N_2.

Therefore $\frac{80}{100} \times \text{FRC} = 2{\cdot}5$ L

$\therefore \text{FRC} = \frac{2{\cdot}5 \times 100}{80} = 2{\cdot}125$ L

➡ $\text{FRC} = \frac{(x) \times (y)}{80}$

In practice correction has to be made for N_2 washed out from blood and turns into alveolar gas due to lowering of nitrogen pressure (P_{N_2}).

Whole-body Plethysmography Method

This method measures thoracic gas volume, i.e. ventilated and non-ventilated areas (e.g. emphysematous cyst). If there are non-ventilated areas it will give a higher value than the FRC measured by closed circuit helium dilution. The principle upon which it operates is based on Boyle's law. $P_1V_1 = P_2V_2$ if temperature is kept constant. It is an easy, rapid method but the apparatus is very expensive.

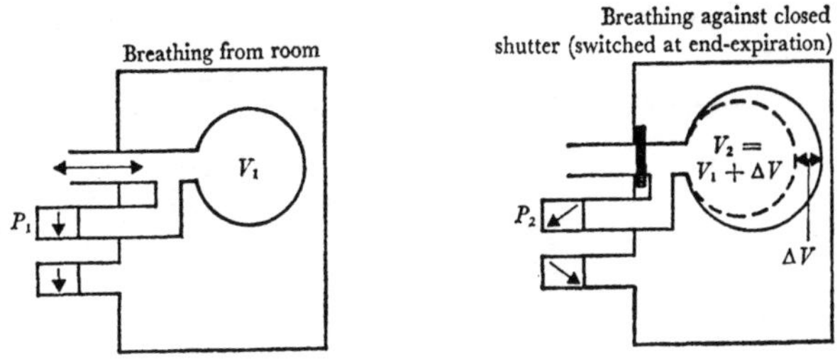

$$P_1 V_1 = P_2 (V_1 + \Delta V)$$

Measure P_1; P_2 and ΔV obtained from plethysmograph pressure change (apparatus having previously been calibrated so that $\Delta P/\Delta V$ is known). Then $V_1 = \dfrac{P_2 . \Delta V}{P_1 - P_2}$ (V_1 = FRC).

Total Lung Capacity based on Height for Males and Height and Age for Females

Normal range for : males = predicted value ±0·9 litres
females = predicted value ±0·5 litres.

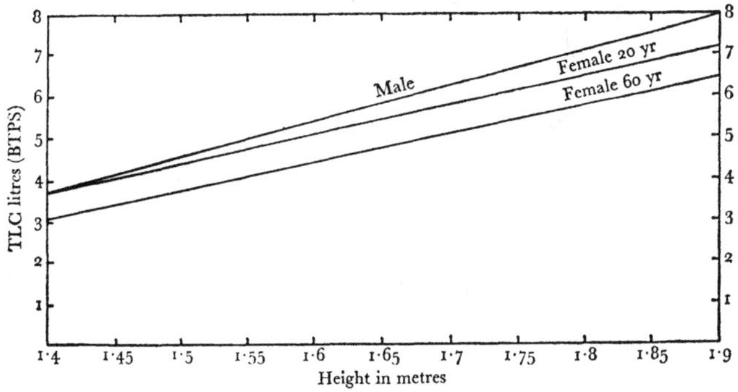

Residual Volume as Percentage of Total Lung Capacity

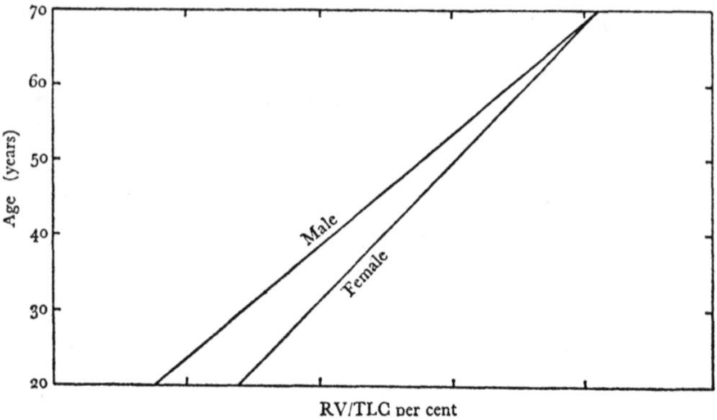

Chapter Three

Ventilation

Pulmonary ventilation can be assessed as minute ventilation. The volume of expired air collected over a period of time expressed in litres per minute is called the expired minute volume or $\dot{V}_E$. This is equivalent to tidal volume (V_T) multiplied by frequency of breathing (f) i.e. $\dot{V}_E = V_T \times f$. If measured as inspired minute volume (which is sometimes more convenient) it is given the symbol $\dot{V}_I$. $\dot{V}_I$ can be converted to $\dot{V}_E$ if expired nitrogen concentration F_{EN_2} is known. Since N_2 is not metabolized, $\dot{V}_I \times F_{IN_2} = \dot{V}_E \times F_{EN_2}$, where F_{IN_2} = inspired N_2 (i.e. 79·04 per cent), hence $\dot{V}_I = \dot{V}_E \times F_{EN_2}/F_{IN_2}$, $\dot{V}_E = \dot{V}_I \times F_{IN_2}/F_{EN_2}$. In general testing $\dot{V}_E$ by itself is of little clinical help, but its relationship to oxygen consumption ($\dot{V}_{O_2}$) is useful. This ratio $\dot{V}_E/\dot{V}_{O_2}$ is known as the oxygen ventilation equivalent. It is remarkably stable in man, and the normal range is 25 ± 5. A higher figure means that ventilation is disproportionate to oxygen consumption, i.e. overventilation. (This distinguishes it from increased ventilation which is in proportion to increased metabolic needs.)

The part of ventilation which is 'effective' in ventilating the alveoli is known as alveolar ventilation ($\dot{V}_A$), the portion which is not so used is called dead space ventilation ($\dot{V}_D$), i.e. $\dot{V}_E = \dot{V}_A + \dot{V}_D$.

$\dot{V}_A$ and $\dot{V}_D$ can be calculated from knowledge of expired carbon dioxide tension (P_{ECO_2}), arterial carbon dioxide tension (P_{aCO_2}) and $\dot{V}_E$.

$$\dot{V}_D = \dot{V}_E \cdot \left(1 - \frac{P_{ECO_2}}{P_{aCO_2}}\right) \text{ or } \dot{V}_D/\dot{V}_E = 1 - (P_{ECO_2}/P_{aCO_2})$$

$$\dot{V}_A = \dot{V}_E \cdot \left(\frac{P_{ECO_2}}{P_{aCO_2}}\right)$$

It should be understood that the same expired minute volume can give different degrees of alveolar minute volume, or the same alveolar minute volumes can be obtained from different expired minute volumes depending on the amount of dead space ventilation at a given time in a given patient.

In practice $\dot{V}_D/\dot{V}_E$ is often calculated as an index of 'wasted' ventilation, an increased ratio indicating a larger proportion of dead space ventilation and a decrease in alveolar ventilation. $\dot{V}_D/\dot{V}_E$ is spoken of as dead space: tidal volume ratio; the normal ratio is less than 0·3 (or 30 per cent).

During artificial ventilation tidal volume (V_T) per breath and frequency (f) of breathing are often used in setting the apparatus, but the ultimate aim is maintenance of near normality of blood gas and pH ($\dot{V}_E = \dot{V}_T \times f$).

Normal values for these indices at rest are very approximate. The following figures are only a guide:

$\dot{V}_E$	6–10 litres per min.
$\dot{V}_A$	4–7·5 litres per min.
$\dot{V}_D/\dot{V}_E$	0·2–0·3
f	12–20 cycles per min.
$\dot{V}_T$	about 0·5 litres

$$\dot{V}_E = \dot{V}_D + \dot{V}_A$$

1.

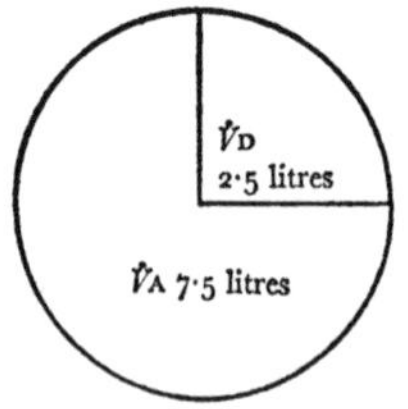

$\dot{V}_E = 2·5 + 7·5 = 10$ litres $\dot{V}_D/\dot{V}_E = 2·5/10 = 0·25$

2.

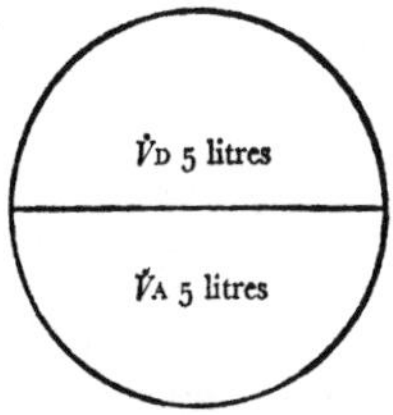

$\dot{V}_E = 5 + 5 = 10$ litres $\dot{V}_D/\dot{V}_E = 5/10 = 0{\cdot}5$

3.

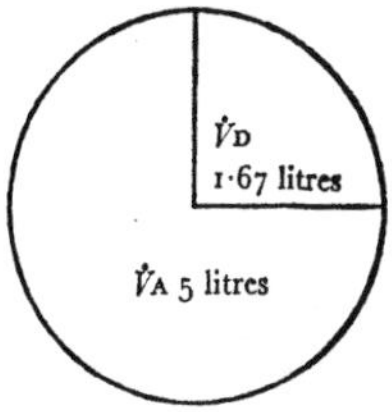

$\dot{V}_E = 1{\cdot}67 + 5 = 6{\cdot}67$ litres $\dot{V}_D/\dot{V}_E = 1{\cdot}67/6{\cdot}67 = 0{\cdot}25$

4.

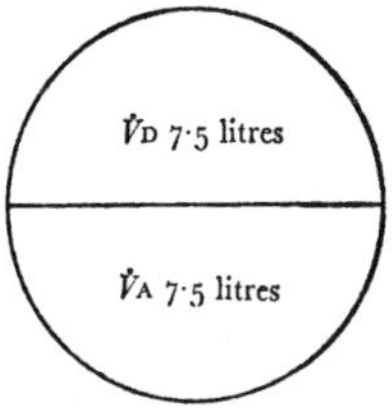

$\dot{V}_E = 7{\cdot}5 + 7{\cdot}5 = 15$ litres $\dot{V}_D/\dot{V}_E = 7{\cdot}5/15 = 0{\cdot}5$

1. and 2. have same $\dot{V}_E$ but different $\dot{V}_A$ and $\dot{V}_D/\dot{V}_E$
1. and 3. have same $\dot{V}_D/\dot{V}_E$ but different $\dot{V}_A$ and $\dot{V}_E$
2. and 4. have same $\dot{V}_D/\dot{V}_E$ but different $\dot{V}_A$ and $\dot{V}_E$
1. and 4. have same $\dot{V}_A$ but different $\dot{V}_E$ and $\dot{V}_D/\dot{V}_E$
2. and 3. have same $\dot{V}_A$ but different $\dot{V}_E$ and $\dot{V}_D/\dot{V}_E$

Illustration of Inter-relationship between $\dot{V}_E$, $\dot{V}_D$ and $\dot{V}_A$

These measurements are much more valuable when recorded during exercise since artefacts due to the subject's anxiety, unfamiliarity with procedure, consciousness of nose clip and mouthpiece become insignificant in relation to the increase in ventilation due to exercise itself.

The relationship between minute volume and oxygen consumption remains constant during mild to moderate exercise (25 ± 5). During severe exercise the $\dot{V}_E/\dot{V}_{O_2}$

ratio increases (35 ± 5). Variations with age and sex are small and may be ignored for clinical purposes.

Mild exercise is that producing an oxygen uptake ($\dot{V}O_2$) of about 1 litre per min., moderate exercise $\dot{V}O_2$ 1·5 litres per min., severe exercise 2 litres per min.

(If $\dot{V}E$ alone is measured; it can be related to work load (in kp. m. per min. or watts) on the approximation that 300 kp. m. per min or 50 watts will produce $\dot{V}O_2$ of 1 litre per min; 600 kp. m. per min or 100 watts will produce $\dot{V}O_2$ of 1·5 litres per min.)

Raised figures for $\dot{V}E/\dot{V}O_2$ indicate a disproportionate ventilatory response to exercise.

Chapter Four

Oxygen Consumption and Carbon Dioxide Output

Oxygen consumption ($\dot{V}O_2$) and carbon dioxide output ($\dot{V}CO_2$) may be expressed in litres per min or ml per min. They are measured by analysis of expired air. This may be performed in a number of ways:

1. Collection of expired air
   a. Douglas bag and one-way low resistance valve
   b. Tissot spirometer
   c. Continuous analysis from mouthpiece
2. Analysis for O_2 and CO_2 together
   a. Micro Scholander apparatus
   b. Haldane apparatus
   c. Mass spectrometer
3. Analysis for O_2 and CO_2 separately
   a. O_2—rapid O_2 analyser or paramagnetic O_2 analyser
   b. CO_2—rapid CO_2 analyser or Micro-Scholander or Campbell-Haldane apparatus (or any other variety of Haldane apparatus).

The ratio $\dot{V}CO_2/\dot{V}O_2$ is known as the respiratory exchange ratio (R). Under basal conditions this is the same as the respiratory quotient (RQ) used in metabolic studies.

Under normal resting conditions R is approximately 0·85. Correction has to be made for this in relating inspired to expired volumes. During exercise R increases to approximately 1·0 which greatly simplifies the use of the alveolar air equation under those conditions (*see* Chapter 10).

The importance of $\dot{V}O_2$ in relation to $\dot{V}E$ has been discussed in Chapter 3.

A higher $\dot{V}CO_2$ on exercise (and hence $R>1$) would imply an excessive ventilatory response. A low $\dot{V}CO_2$ (and $R<1$) on exercise would imply that a ventilatory limit had been reached.

$\dot{V}CO_2$ or $\dot{V}O_2$ are required for calculation of cardiac output by the Fick principle (*see* Chapter 6).

Normal resting $\dot{V}O_2$ is 0·25 to 0·3 litres per min
$\dot{V}CO_2$ is 0·20 to 0·24 litres per min
R is 0·85

Normal exercise	medium	moderate	severe
$\dot{V}O_2$	1 litre per min	1·5 litres per min	2·0 litres per min
$\dot{V}CO_2$	1 litre per min	1·5 litres per min	2·0 litres per min
R	1	1	1

$\dot{V}O_2 = (\dot{V}I \times FIO_2) - (\dot{V}E \times FEO_2)$ corrected for difference between $\dot{V}I$ and $\dot{V}E$.

When FIO_2 = inspired O_2 concentration as a fraction
FEO_2 = expired O_2 concentration as a fraction
$\dot{V}CO_2 = \dot{V}E \cdot FECO_2$ with correction for valve box dead space,
where $FECO_2$ = expired CO_2 concentration as a fraction.

Chapter Five

Diffusion

Diffusion is the process of transfer of gas from alveolus to blood. Since it involves more than simply physical diffusion across a membrane it is better to use the term Transfer Factor (T_L). Although it is oxygen transfer which really concerns us, for convenience we measure carbon monoxide transfer. This is because the partial pressure of CO in blood can be taken as zero for practical purposes owing to the high affinity of CO for haemoglobin.

$$\text{Diffusion} = \frac{\text{Rate of uptake of gas}}{\text{Pressure gradient across membrane}}$$

$$= \mathring{V}_{CO}/P_{ACO} - P_{aCO}$$

but $P_{aCO} = 0$ thus $T_{LCO} = \mathring{V}_{CO}/P_{ACO}$

The various methods for measuring transfer factor differ in the techniques for obtaining the data needed for this calculation.

Steady State Methods

A gas mixture containing approximately 0·1 per cent CO is breathed by the subject. Expired gas is collected for one minute and analysed for CO, O_2 and CO_2. This provides the data for $\mathring{V}_{CO}$.

$$\mathring{V}_{CO} = \mathring{V}_E \left[\left(\frac{F_{EN_2}}{F_{IN_2}} \cdot F_{ICO}\right) - F_{ECO}\right]$$

Alveolar CO tension is calculated by assuming that the dead space/tidal volume ratio derived from P_{CO_2} measurements is the same for CO.

$$\frac{\dot{V}D}{\dot{V}E} = \frac{PaCO_2 - PECO_2}{PaCO_2} = \frac{PACO - PECO}{PACO - PICO}$$

from manipulation of which we get:

$$PACO = PICO - [(PICO - PECO).\ PaCO_2/PECO_2.]$$

It has, of course, been assumed that arterial and alveolar CO_2 pressures are equal (Riley's concept of ideal alveolar gas).

The main disadvantages of the method are that the pattern of breathing may affect the results, and it has been calculated that small errors in estimation of CO or CO_2 may lead to large errors in calculated T_L, in the resting state. This does not apply to exercise (maximum diffusing capacity).

The main advantages are that the method can be used in even severely disabled subjects and it can be used during exercise. Arterial puncture need be no deterrent since ear lobe samples are reliable (*see* Chapter 10).

(Methods involving collection of expired alveolar gas for PCO, or end-tidal sampling for P_{CO_2} are not reliable in patients with respiratory disease).

Single Breath Method

This involves inspiring a gas mixture containing approximately 0·3 per cent CO, 14 per cent He in air. The breath is held for approximately ten seconds and an alveolar sample then collected, after washout of dead space. From analysis of inspired and expired CO and He, the volume inspired and the breath holding time, together with residual volume (measured separately) it is possible to calculate the transfer factor.

$$T_L = \frac{160\ (V_I + RV)}{\text{time (seconds)}} \times \log_{10}\left[\frac{F_ICO \times F_EHe}{F_ECO \times F_IHe}\right]$$

The advantages of this method are that it is bloodless, readily repeatable, independent of breathing pattern and standardized so that results from different laboratories are comparable.

The disadvantages are that it is not suitable for very dyspnoeic subjects, is affected by the lung volume at which measurement is made (but usually measured from FRC) and cannot be performed during exercise.

Rebreathing Method

In many ways this is similar to the single breath method. The mixture rebreathed contains a low concentration of CO and the calculation is as for the single breath method. A separate measurement of residual volume is required for patients with respiratory disability.

It has the advantage that it can be performed by a patient unable to hold his breath for ten seconds. On the other hand it has the disadvantage of needing the co-operation of the subject in breathing at a rate of 25 per min, and taking measurements after 10 sec and 30 sec rebreathing adds technical complications.

Normal range can be read from the graph.

For example: female, age 35, height 1·4 m, rebreathing method:

a. From graph: age and height give T_L 21
b. Female, so subtract 10 per cent giving $21 - 2{\cdot}1 = 18{\cdot}9$
c. Rebreathing so subtract 2 giving $18{\cdot}9 - 2 = 16{\cdot}9$
d. Range therefore $16{\cdot}9 \pm 5 = 11{\cdot}9$ to $21{\cdot}9$ ml per minute per mm Hg.

Effect of impaired T_L on blood gases is to produce hypoxaemia without hypercapnia, because the diffusibility of CO_2 is about twenty times that of O_2 and fatal anoxaemia would develop before diffusion defect could possibly affect CO_2.

Initially the hypoxaemia may only occur on exercise, later it may be found at rest (at which stage a fall in saturation as well as pressure will often be demonstrable on exercise).

Diffusion Coefficient (kCO)

Transfer factor may be related to lung volume by the ratio T_L/V_A, where V_A = alveolar volume in litres. This is called diffused coefficient (kCO). The single breath method then becomes simplified and separate measurement of RV is no longer required. The calculation then becomes—

$$\text{kCO} = 160/t \times \log_{10}\left[\frac{F_{ICO}}{F_{ECO}} \times \frac{F_{EHe}}{F_{IHe}}\right] \text{ ml per min per mm Hg per litre}$$

kCO less than 3·0 ml per min per mm Hg per litre indicates marked impairment of transfer and such figures are found in emphysema and diffuse fibroses.

Prediction formulae for kCO are:

Men: kCO = 0·646 − 0·0327 × age (years)
Women: kCO = 5·869 − 0·0098 × age (years)

In emphysema kCO is usually less than 45 per cent of predicted whereas in chronic bronchitis it is usually greater than 70 per cent.

Transfer Factor (T_L) based on Age and Height

1. Range for any given age and height is ±5
2. Males : read direct from graph
   Females : subtract 10 per cent of graph reading
3. Single breath : read direct from graph
   Steady state : subtract 4
   Rebreathing : subtract 2

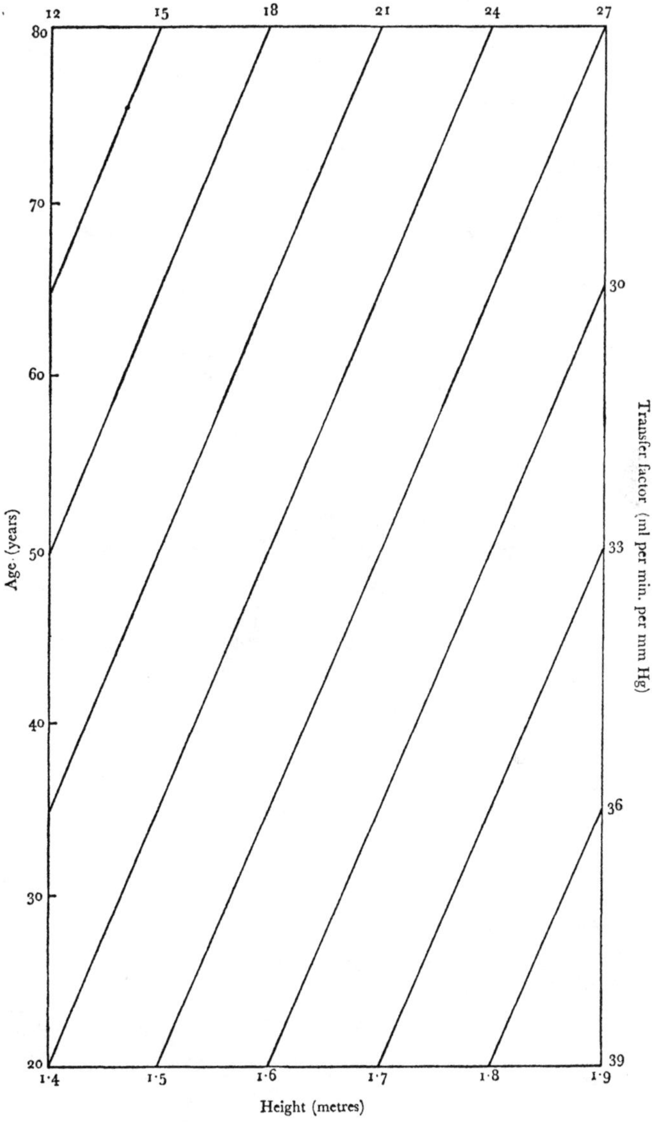
12
15
18
21
24
27
80
70
60
50
40
30
20
Age (years)
30
33
36
39
Transfer factor (ml per min. per mm Hg)
1·4
1·5
1·6
1·7
1·8
1·9
Height (metres)

Chapter Six

Cardiac Output (Pulmonary Blood Flow)

In the absence of left-to-right heart shunts cardiac output is equal to pulmonary blood flow. Impaired cardiac output ($\dot{Q}t$) may be the limiting factor in exercise in some patients, and changes in pulmonary blood flow will alter ventilation–perfusion ratios (*see* Chapter 7).

Direct Fick O_2 Method

This is calculated from the formula:

$$\dot{Q}t = \dot{V}O_2 / CaO_2 - C\bar{v}O_2$$

(cardiac output is in litres per min; oxygen uptake is in ml per min; arterial and mixed venous oxygen content is in ml per litre).

The method necessitates cardiac catheterization and arterial puncture (or ear lobe samples). It is equally valid at rest as well as exercise. O_2 content can be obtained from PO_2 from the tables of Kelman and Nunn (1966).

Indirect Fick CO_2 Method

This is calculated from the formula:

$$\dot{Q}t = \dot{V}CO_2 / C\bar{v}CO_2 - CaCO_2$$

(CO_2 output in ml per min; mixed venous and arterial CO_2 contents in ml per litre).

Cardiac catheterization is not required since mixed venous PCO_2 can be obtained by the rebreathing technique both at rest and on exercise; CO_2 content can then be obtained from the tables of McHardy. Ear lobe samples can be used for PCO_2 ('arterial') and arterial puncture avoided.

At rest this method is not altogether reliable because of the (normally) small veno–arterial CO_2 content difference. On exercise, however, it is a valid method and compares well with other methods.

Body Plethysmograph Method

The principle of this method is that N_2O is inhaled by the patient inside the body-box. As the N_2O becomes dissolved in blood flowing through pulmonary capillaries, the pressure in the box decreases. From the knowledge of the pressure changes, alveolar N_2O pressure, solubility of N_2O and alveolar volume it is possible to calculate pulmonary capillary flow. Alveolar volume is itself measured by the body-box method (*see* Chapter 2).

This method has the advantage of not requiring cardiac catheterization, does not require blood samples and no injections are needed. It cannot, however, be used on exercise because of problems of water vapour and temperature in the plethysmograph. The apparatus plus suitable manometers etc. is very expensive.

Dye Dilution Method

Cardiac output can be measured by dilution of an injectable substance—indocyanine green, coumassie blue, ^{131}I-labelled human albumin, or cold saline. Indocyanine green has the advantage of being measurable by spectrophotometry, usable on exercise, repeatability, does not require steady state for measurements and is independent of arterial oxygen content. Coumassie blue can be detected with an ear oximeter; ^{131}I requires a scintillation counter. Cold saline method measures temperature changes with a thermistor.

Normal values are frequently expressed as cardiac index, i.e. cardiac output/body surface area in litres/min/square metre. The mean normal resting value is 3 litres per min per m^2.

(= 5·5 litres per min in average male of 1·8 m^2).

Table 1. EXERCISE VALUES FOR CARDIAC INDEX (LITRES PER MIN PER M^2)

	MALES		FEMALES	
	<40	>40	<40	>40
Mild	7·5	6	6·5	7·5
Moderate	9·5	8·5	8·0	8·0
Severe	11·5	11	9·0	9·5

± 20 per cent of stated values should be considered as within normal range.

Chapter Seven

Ventilation–Perfusion Ratios

More important than either the distribution of ventilation alone, or the estimation of pulmonary blood flow alone, is consideration of the relationship between them, since the state of the blood gases is determined by this relationship. It is, of course, possible to measure the two factors separately and obtain an overall ratio for the two lungs together—the $\mathring{V}/\mathring{Q}$ ratio. (Alveolar minute ventilation is obtained as in 'lung volume', pulmonary blood flow as in 'Cardiac Output' and the ratio is then $\mathring{V}_A/\mathring{Q}_T$.) The normal ratio is 0·8 (average $\mathring{V}_A$ 4 litres per min, average $\mathring{Q}_T$ 5 litres per min). It is now possible to measure simultaneous ventilation and blood flow by the use of radioactive gases.

Radioactive Xenon Method

The gas is inhaled and the dissolved gas injected intravenously. Ventilation and blood flow are displayed on a chart as the radioactivity is detected by suitably placed counters. In this way regional differences in ventilation–perfusion ratios can be demonstrated.

Studies in normal subjects have shown that $\mathring{V}/\mathring{Q}$ ratios are not uniform throughout the lungs. As one moves from apex to base ventilation decreases and perfusion increases, i.e. $\mathring{V}/\mathring{Q}$ ratios are higher at the apex and lower at the base.

Although this is probably the best method of determining regional differences in $\mathring{V}/\mathring{Q}$, it does involve handling radioactive material and expensive scanning apparatus.

Other indirect methods for assessing abnormalities of perfusion, and of $\dot{V}/\dot{Q}$ ratios are therefore often adopted.

Anatomical Shunt (Oxygen test)

The principle of this test is that if 100 per cent oxygen is breathed for long enough (20 min) all the nitrogen will be washed out of the lungs and the $P\text{O}_2$ will be maximal.

Under these conditions arterial oxygen pressures will be maximum no matter what the pathology of the lung (and oxygen content will be maximal) except for any blood which has by-passed the alveoli.

DETECTION OF SHUNT

The simple detection of anatomical shunting is most sensitively obtained by measurement of arterial $P\text{O}_2$ while breathing 100 per cent O_2. Alveolar $P\text{O}_2$ will then be $P\text{B} - P\text{H}_2\text{O} - P\text{A}\,\text{CO}_2$ (e.g. 760 − 47 − 40 = 673). Under these conditions there will be no alveolar to end-capillary gradient and arterial $P\text{O}_2$ which is less than this indicates that some blood must have by-passed ventilated alveoli. Dissolved O_2 exerts a pressure of 100 mm Hg for each 0·3 ml per 100 ml; a fall in O_2 content of as little as 0·1 ml per 100 ml will, therefore, lower pressure by 33 mm Hg. The latter is the normal amount of shunt (2 per cent) so normal $P\text{aO}_2$ on 100 per cent O_2 is 640.

MEASUREMENT OF SHUNT

This is done in the same way but, in addition, mixed venous oxygen has to be measured (*see* Chapter 10). The calculation uses O_2 content which can be measured directly or (possibly with greater sensitivity) derived from pressure measurements. The shunt is often recorded as a fraction of the cardiac output i.e. $\dot{Q}\text{s}/\dot{Q}\text{t}$ per cent, but if cardiac output is also measured $\dot{Q}\text{s}$ can be given in absolute terms.

$$\frac{\dot{Q}\text{s}}{\dot{Q}\text{t}}\ \text{(per cent)} = \frac{C\text{cO}_2 - C\text{aO}_2}{C\text{cO}_2 - C\bar{\text{v}}\text{O}_2} \times 100$$

where, $\dot{Q}s$ = shunt, $\dot{Q}t$ = cardiac output,
Cco_2 = pulmonary capillary O_2 content (assumed to be O_2 capacity of Hb plus maximum dissolved, i.e. 2 ml. per 100 ml)
Cao_2 = arterial O_2 content,
$C\bar{v}o_2$ = mixed venous O_2 content.

Physiological Shunt and Venous Admixture Effect

If the same shunt calculation is carried out with the subject breathing room air, the so called 'physiological shunt' will be estimated. This includes the anatomical shunt plus venous admixture effect. If the oxygen procedure is also carried out to measure anatomical shunt, the venous admixture effect may be obtained by subtraction.

The venous admixture effect represents that portion of the blood flow acting as if it were perfusing non-ventilated alveoli, i.e. as a shunt.

The 'venous admixture effect' actually includes not only alveoli with blood flow and no ventilation, but also alveoli with normal ventilation and markedly increased blood flow, and alveoli with varying degrees of underventilation in relation to perfusion.

Physiological shunt normally does not exceed 7 per cent of cardiac output. Venous admixture effect is normally less than 2 per cent in young subjects, less than 4 per cent in elderly.

Physiological Dead Space

The method of calculating this and normal values are given in Chapter 3.

It includes anatomical dead space (which can be measured by a technique involving rapid continuous analysis of N_2 after a single inhalation of O_2), alveoli with no blood flow, alveoli with normal or increased ventilation and reduced blood flow, grossly overventilated alveoli with normal blood flow.

Single Breath CO_2 Test

Expired air is analysed continuously for CO_2. If alveolar CO_2 rises significantly during expiration different areas of the lung must have different CO_2 tensions at the end of inspiration (= uneven $\mathring{V}/\mathring{Q}$ ratios) and be emptying at different rates, i.e. uneven $\mathring{V}/\mathring{Q}$ ratios and uneven distribution of ventilation.

On the other hand constant CO_2 during alveolar expiration cannot be taken to mean normal distribution of $\mathring{V}/\mathring{Q}$ ratios. Uneven $\mathring{V}/\mathring{Q}$ ratios plus even distribution of ventilation give the same effect, since, if emptying is uniform in rate the streams of different alveolar CO_2 levels will mix evenly and the expired alveolar CO_2 will remain constant.

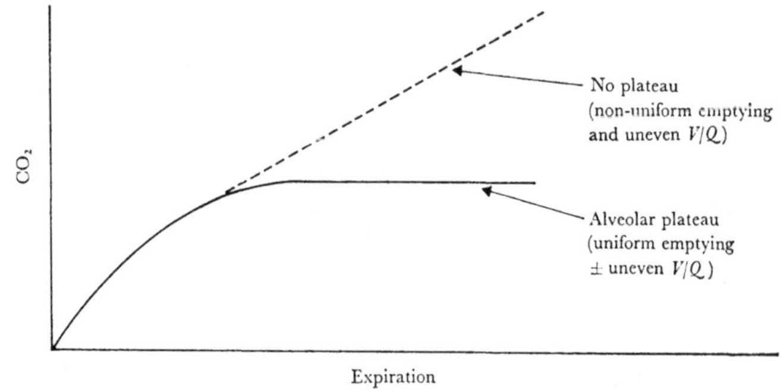

Alveolar-arterial O_2 Difference (A − aDO_2)

The alveolar air equation will be mentioned in Chapter 10. However, for calculation of alveolar–arterial O_2 difference (A − aDO_2) the full equation may be used:

$$P_{AO_2} = F_{IO_2}(P_B - 47) - \frac{P_{aCO_2}}{R} + \left[\frac{P_{aCO_2}}{R} \times F_{IO_2}(1 - R)\right]$$

(but if $R = 1$ the term in square brackets becomes 0; if

R = 0·8 it only becomes 2 mm Hg! Variation in P_{IO_2}, i.e. ($F_{IO_2} \times (P_B - 47)$) with atmospheric pressure, however, could make 9 mm difference between P_B 740 and P_B 780).

An increase in $A - aDO_2$ may be due to—

1. Uneven $\dot{V}/\dot{Q}$ ratios
2. Generalized underventilation
3. Anatomical venous to arterial (R → L) shunts
4. Impaired transfer factor

The three latter (2, 3 and 4) can be excluded by appropriate tests and (1) established by exclusion.

Arterio-alveolar CO_2 Difference ($a - ADCO_2$)

This has been advocated as a measure of uneven ventilation in relation to perfusion, particularly with pulmonary embolism.

Its use is very limited because:

1. It is difficult to be sure that an alveolar sample is really representative (particularly if there is any chronic lung disease)
2. Compensatory mechanisms come into play diverting circulation to ventilated alveoli
3. Actual infarction will abolish the effect (which results from continued ventilation of under or non-perfused alveoli)

   e.g. 1/5 of lung non-perfused ($\dot{V}/\dot{Q} = \infty$) → $P_{CCO_2} = 0$, $P_{ACO_2} = 0$.

   4/5 of lung normal ($\dot{V}/\dot{Q} = 0{\cdot}8$) → $P_{CCO_2} = 40$, $P_{ACO_2} = 40$ then (*a*) mixed arterial P_{CO_2} will all be derived from normal portion → P_{aCO_2} 40.

   (*b*) Mixed alveolar P_{CO_2} will be 1/5 from non-perfused and 4/5 from normal →

$$\frac{(1 \times 0) + (4 \times 40)}{5} = 33$$

thus $a - ADCO_2 = 40 - 33 = 7$.

Diagrammatic Representation of Effects of Changes in Ventilation–perfusion Ratios

	Ideal	Shunt	Dead Space	Under-ventilation	Over-perfusion	Over-ventilation	Under-perfusion

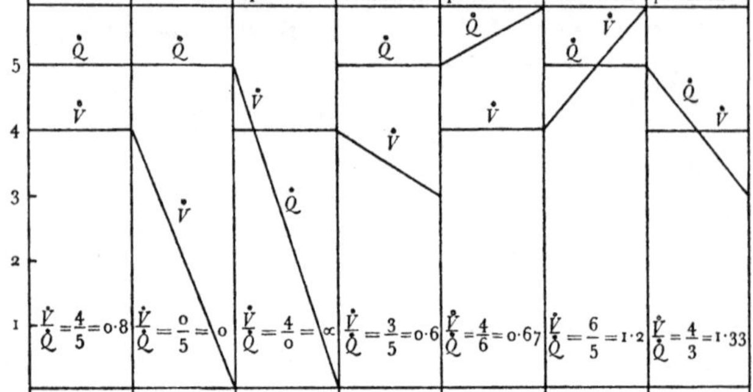

	Ideal	Shunt	Dead Space	Under-ventilation	Over-perfusion	Over-ventilation	Under-perfusion
P_{AO_2}	Normal	0	Inspired	Lowered	Lowered	Raised	Raised
P_{ACO_2}	Normal	0	Inspired	Raised	Raised	Lowered	Lowered
P_{aO_2}	Normal	Venous	0	Lowered	Lowered	Normal	Normal
P_{aCO_2}	Normal	Venous	0	Raised	Raised	Lowered	Lowered

There is evidence that in chronic obstructive lung diseases with reversibility of obstruction (asthma and chronic bronchitis with asthma) there is a compensatory mechanism whereby perfusion is reduced to underventilated alveoli.

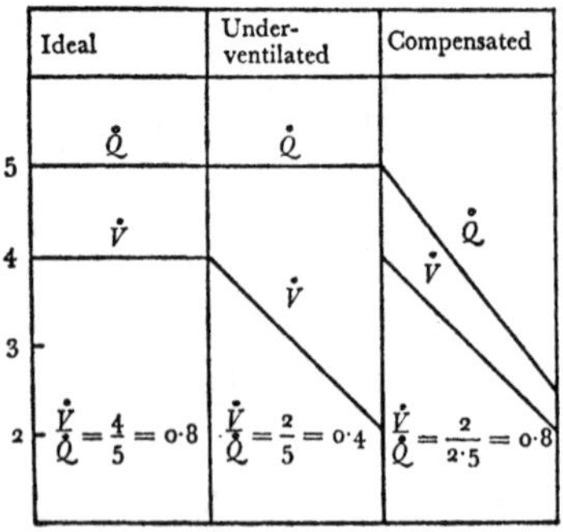

This is a highly idealised diagram and compensation is never as complete as depicted.

It is known that low P_{AO_2} or high P_{ACO_2} may produce pulmonary vasoconstriction, and it has been suggested that this is the mechanism of the homeostatic effect. β-adrenergic bronchodilators may disturb this mechanism by producing a disproportionate increase in perfusion and hence lower P_{O_2}.

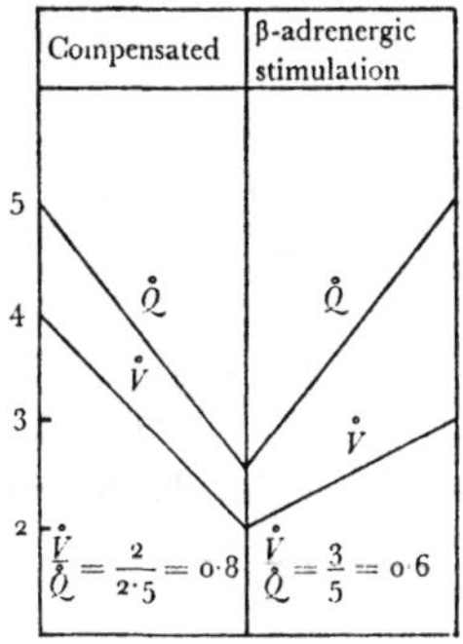

The mechanism of β-adrenergic bronchodilator induced hypoxaemia

BRONCHOSPIROMETRY

With a double lumened catheter in the trachea the ventilation, oxygen uptake (and also, if desired, CO_2 output, volume and carbon monoxide uptake) can be measured separately for each lung.

Chapter Eight

Compliance and Work of Breathing

Compliance is a measure of elasticity—the distensibility or stiffness respectively of the lungs. It is defined as the volume change per unit pressure change under static conditions. (So-called 'dynamic' compliance is a misnomer. It refers to a method of measuring compliance during a series of breaths, but measurements are nevertheless taken at points of nil-flow, i.e. static points.)

Pressure changes are obtained by using intra-oesophageal tube or balloon. The subject inspires from the end of a normal expiration (i.e. FRC) a measured volume, holds his breath, and the pressure is measured. This is repeated several times with different inspired volumes.

A pressure-volume curve can then be constructed, the slope of which gives the compliance of the lungs.

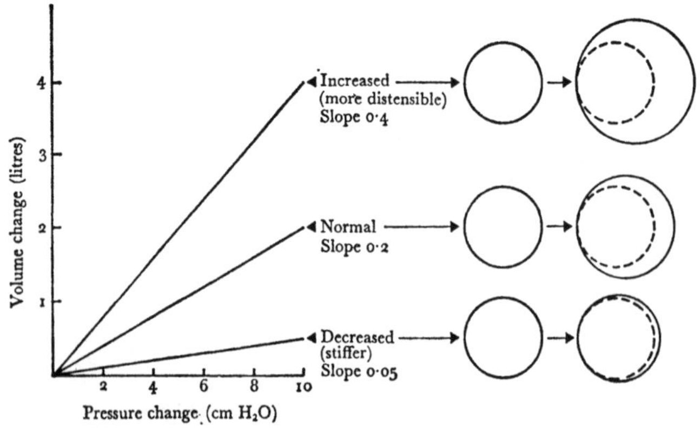

To be meaningful compliance should be related to the lung volume (specific compliance) at which measurements were taken, i.e. to FRC. Unfortunately few published data have related compliance to FRC and many of the conclusions concerning the significance of changes in compliance are of dubious value.

Normal values related to FRC are: 0·038 to 0·07 litres per cm H_2O per litre (mean 0·05).

Uncorrected normals are:

(0·343 × height in metres) − 0·425

± 40 per cent of predicted value

or

0·08 to 0·23 litres per cm H_2O.

One effect of decreased compliance will be to produce uneven $\mathring{V}/\mathring{Q}$ relationships and hence hypoxaemia.

Increased compliance on the other hand will lead to overdistension and increased physiological dead space.

Work of Breathing

The main components of the work of breathing can be derived from the pressure-volume curve obtained during quiet breathing.

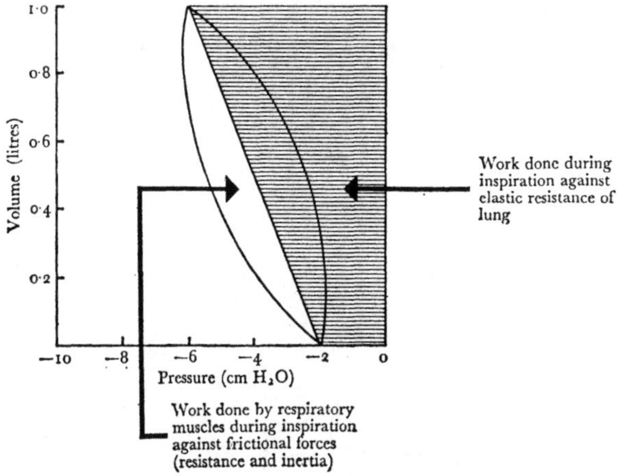

The energy cost of breathing, i.e. O_2 consumption of respiratory muscles, can be estimated by the increase over resting O_2 uptake on voluntary or stimulated (e.g. by CO_2 inhalation) increase in respiration or breathing through an added resistance.

i.e. $\mathring{V}O_2$ respiratory muscles $=$ $\mathring{V}O_2$ overventilating $-$ $\mathring{V}O_2$ resting.

This is approximately 0·5 ml O_2 per litre ventilation on quiet breathing rising to about 1·2 ml per litre on moderate exercise. The energy cost of breathing is high in chronic obstructive lung disease, pulmonary fibrosis and thoracic cage immobility. Further respiratory stimulation in such patients could theoretically lead to a situation where the O_2 requirements of respiratory muscles for the increased ventilation is greater than the extra O_2 absorbed by the increased ventilation.

Respiratory Frequency and Work of Breathing

As rate increases, depth decreases (assuming a standard alveolar minute ventilation) which decreases elastic forces, but increases resistive forces.

The normal compromise is a respiratory frequency of about 15 cycles per min.

Patients with decreased compliance have rapid shallow respiration which minimizes the elastic factor.

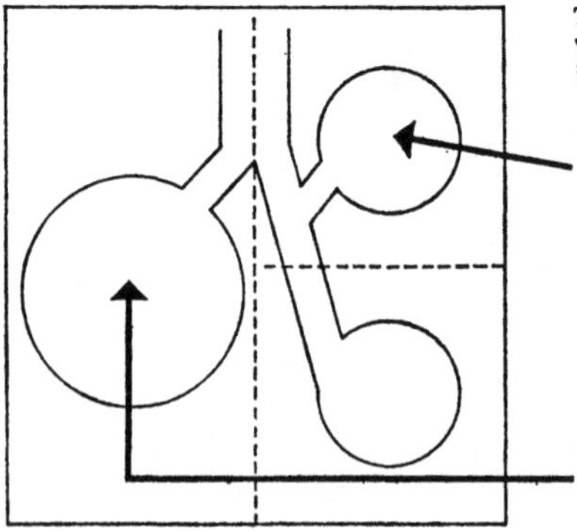

This does not mean 1 lung is less compliant than 2, or 1 lobe less compliant than 1 lung. If, however, the compliance values are related to volume, sense is restored, e.g.:

Volume of both lungs = 4 litres

$$\rightarrow C = \frac{0{\cdot}2}{4} = 0{\cdot}5 \text{ litres per cm } H_2O \text{ per litre}$$

Volume of 1 lung = 2 litres

$$\rightarrow C = \frac{0{\cdot}1}{2} = 0{\cdot}5 \text{ litres per cm } H_2O \text{ per litre}$$

Volume of 1 lobe = 1 litre

$$\rightarrow C = \frac{0{\cdot}05}{1} = 0{\cdot}5 \text{ litres per cm } H_2O \text{ per litre}$$

Chapter Nine

Airway Resistance

Resistance equals driving pressure over flow, thus airway resistance (RAW) is obtained from the formula:

$$R\text{AW} = \frac{\text{alveolar} - \text{atmospheric pressure (cm } H_2O)}{\text{velocity of air flow (litres per min)}}$$

expressed as cm H_2O per litre per min. In clinical practice measurements such as FEV_1, are used as indices of resistance (*see* Chapter 1).

Airway resistance can be measured by:

1. *Pressure-flow method.* This is similar to the method of measuring compliance (q.v.) except that flow is plotted against pressure difference between oesophagus and mouth. This is a tedious and inconvenient method.

2. *Interrupter method.* The basic assumption here is that when airflow is interrupted by a shutter, equalization of pressure occurs throughout the respiratory tract and mouth pressure then equals alveolar pressure. This is not necessarily true when RAW is high. The actual figures produced are closer to total lung resistance than airway resistance.

3. *Plethysmograph method.* This is the method of choice for research purposes. The plethysmographic method for total lung capacity has already been mentioned (*see* Chapter 2). Alveolar pressures are obtained from pressure changes in the box, airflow from a pneumotachograph. It requires the patient to pant rapidly and shallowly and that the expiratory flow rate be kept at about 0·5 litres per sec or less.

It can be related to the lung volume (simultaneous) ($SR_{AW} = V_L \times R_{AW}$) at which the measurement is made = specific resistance.

Normal values at flow rates of 0·5 litres per sec range from 0·6 to 2·4 cm per H_2O per litre per min.

Airway Conductance

Some workers favour the use of conductance (G_{AW}) or specific conductance (SG_{AW}) as an alternative to resistance.

Conductance is the reciprocal of resistance, specific conductance is expressed per litre of thoracic gas volumes.

Normal SG_{AW} = 0·13 – 0·35.

Chapter Ten

Blood Gases

The pressure (or tension) of carbon dioxide can be measured in arterial blood ($Pa\text{CO}_2$) or mixed-venous blood ($P\bar{v}\text{CO}_2$); its content may also be measured in arterial ($Ca\text{CO}_2$) or mixed-venous blood ($C\bar{v}\text{CO}_2$). Similar measurements of oxygen can also be made ($Pa\text{O}_2$, $P\bar{v}\text{O}_2$, $Ca\text{O}_2$, $C\bar{v}\text{O}_2$). In addition oxygen saturation ($Sa\text{O}_2$) may be measured.

'Arterialized' capillary blood from the hyperaemic ear lobe is close in composition to true arterial blood. At rest and on exercise arterial and ear lobe $P\text{O}_2$ are not significantly different. At rest arterial $P\text{CO}_2$ is 0·5 mm Hg higher than ear lobe $P\text{CO}_2$: on exercise arterial $P\text{CO}_2$ is 2·5 mm Hg higher than ear lobe $P\text{CO}_2$. At rest and on exercise arterial pH is 0·02 units less than ear lobe pH.

1. $Pa\text{O}_2$ is measured by the use of a Clark type electrode.

$P\bar{v}\text{O}_2$ is usually measured in the same way but an indirect bloodless rebreathing technique is possible with the aid of a sensitive rapid O_2 gas analyser.

2. $Pa\text{CO}_2$ is measured by the use of a Severinghaus type electrode.

Alternatively it may be obtained by the Astrup Interpolation technique. $P\bar{v}\text{CO}_2$ may be obtained in the same ways, or from a bloodless rebreathing method with gas analysis by any of the methods mentioned under $\dot{V}\text{CO}_2$.

3. $Ca\text{CO}_2$ or $C\bar{v}\text{CO}_2$ can be measured with the Van Slyke apparatus.

Alternatively these values may be obtained from McHardy's tables based on $P\text{CO}_2$ and Hb.

4. Ca_{O_2} or $C\bar{v}_{O_2}$ can be measured on the Van Slyke or more convenient automated content or saturation apparatuses, or it can be read from P_{O_2} measurements in the computer-produced physiological tables of Kelman and Nunn (1966).

5. Sa_{O_2} may be obtained by the same apparatuses as for content after tonometry to obtain total O_2 capacity, i.e. Ca_{O_2}/O_2 capacity $\times$ 100 = Sa_{O_2} per cent. Alternatively capacity can be calculated if Hb is known, i.e. O_2 capacity = Hb (in grammes) $\times$ 1·34. Sa_{O_2} may also be obtained from the Severinghaus blood gas nomogram or slide-rule if Pa_{O_2}, Hb and pH are known. (If Sa_{O_2} is obtained in this way Ca_{O_2} can be calculated, i.e. $Ca_{O_2} = Sa_{O_2}/100 \times$ Hb $\times$ 1·34.)

Note: It has been assumed that the subject's Hb has normal properties. In the presence of an abnormal Hb only the direct measurements of oxygen pressure, content and capacity (and hence, saturation) are valid.

Normal Values (at Rest):

Pa_{O_2}	Young		83–100 mm Hg
	Old		75–90 mm Hg
Sa_{O_2}	Young		95–97·5 per cent
	Old		93–96 per cent
Pa_{CO_2}			36–44 mm Hg
$C\bar{v}_{CO_2}$			53–57 volume per cent (ml per 100 ml)
		or	24–34 mmole per litre
Rebreathing Pv_{CO_2}			42–52 mm Hg

Rebreathing Method for $P\bar{v}_{CO_2}$

If a subject rebreathes from a bag containing an O_2/CO_2 mixture approximately that of his mixed venous P_{CO_2}, there will be rapid uptake or evolution of CO_2 to establish equilibrium. At this point mixed venous blood arriving at the alveoli will neither give off nor take up CO_2. This point can be recognized by the plateau on the trace from continuous analysis by rapid CO_2 analyser.

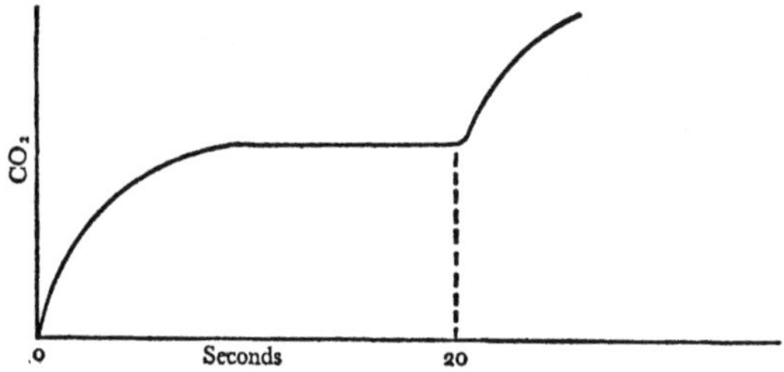

This has been found to be 20 sec (before recirculation occurs which produces further rise in $P\text{CO}_2$).

Instead of using an infra-red CO_2 analyser, therefore, a rebreathing period of 20 sec can be adopted (or 5 breaths, whichever is longer) and the content analysed chemically for CO_2 (Haldane apparatus or one of its modifications: Micro-Scholander).

To avoid the necessity of having a range of O_2/CO_2 mixtures, the patient can prepare his own rebreathing mixture by rebreathing into a 2-litre bag initially containing 1·5 litres of O_2 for 90 sec. After 2 minutes rest breathing air, a 20 sec rebreathing is performed and the bag analysed. The 20 sec procedure can be repeated several times to obtain a 'fine adjustment' of the result. The CO_2 concentration is converted to pressure in the usual way, i.e. $P\text{CO}_2 = F\text{CO}_2 \times (P\text{B} - 47)$.

CO_2 ELECTRODE (SEVERINGHAUS TYPE)

The basic principle is a glass electrode surrounded by buffer covered by a membrane freely permeable to CO_2 (but not electrolytes). The pH of this buffer solution is a simple function of its $P\text{CO}_2$ which by diffusion, is the same as in the blood sample. The pH changes are shown as $P\text{CO}_2$ on the meter.

O_2 ELECTRODE (CLARK TYPE)

The basic principle is a platinum electrode surrounded by a buffer solution and covered by a membrane freely permeable to O_2 (but not electrolytes). If an e.m.f. is applied to the electrode the current which flows is a function of the rate of reduction of O_2 at the tip of the electrode. The meter displays the results as $P\text{O}_2$.

ASTRUP INTERPOLATION TECHNIQUE FOR $P\text{CO}_2$

This depends on the Henderson-Hasselbalch equation:

$$\text{pH} = \text{pK} + \log_{10} \frac{[\text{HCO}_3^-]}{[\text{H}_2\text{CO}_3]}$$

$$= 6{\cdot}1 + \log_{10} \frac{[\text{HCO}_3^-]}{0{\cdot}03 \times P\text{CO}_2}$$

The relationship between pH and $P\text{CO}_2$ can therefore be plotted on semi-log paper.

The procedure consists of (1) measure pH of unknown sample (2) tonometer sample with low $P\text{CO}_2$ gas and measure pH (3) tonometer sample with high $P\text{CO}_2$ gas and measure pH.

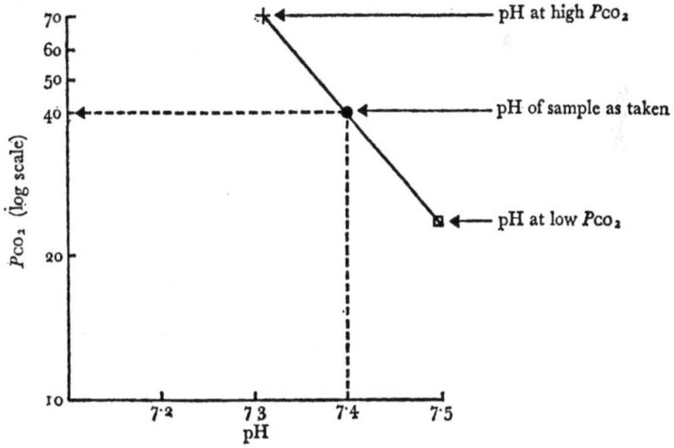

The P_{CO_2} and pH of the tonometered samples are plotted and joined by a straight line. The pH of the original is then plotted on that line and P_{CO_2} read off the scale.

Changes in P_{CO_2} are more or less directly reflected in CO_2 content since their relationship is virtually linear in the physiological range.

CO_2 dissociation curve for whole blood between P_{CO_2} 40 and P_{CO_2} 60

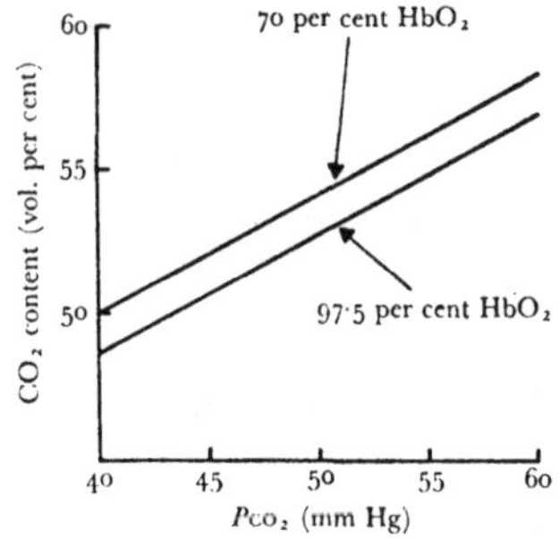

Changes in P_{O_2} however do not bear a simple relationship to O_2 content since the dissociation curve is sigmoid.

HbO_2 dissociation curve (pH 7·4, temp. 37°C)

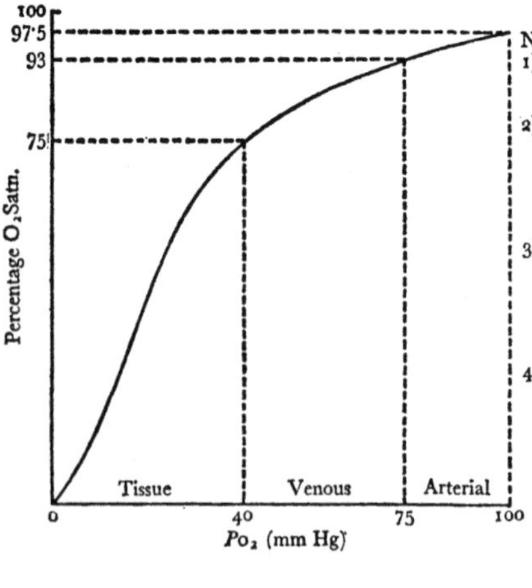

Note:

1) O_2 content can be plotted instead of saturation: the curve would be of the same shape.
2) A fall in pH or a rise in P_{CO_2} shifts the curve to the right. This results in a lower saturation and content at any given P_{O_2} and thus unloading of O_2 to tissues is impaired.
3) The shape of the curves is such that in the lungs increasing P_{O_2} above 75 mm Hg makes little difference to saturation, but in the mixed-venous—arterial range there is rapid resaturation.
4) At tissue level a large quantity of O_2 can be released for a small fall in P_{O_2}.

The blood gas disturbances met with clinically are:

1. Hypoxaemia ($Pao_2\downarrow$) without CO_2 retention
2. Hypercapnia (CO_2 retention, $Paco_2\uparrow$) which is always accompanied by hypoxaemia
3. Hypocapnia ($Paco_2\downarrow$)

Hypoxaemia ($Pao_2\downarrow \rightarrow Sao_2\downarrow \rightarrow Cao_2\downarrow$) may result from:

1. Impaired diffusion
2. Intrapulmonary shunting of blood (R → L)
3. Underventilation
4. Low ventilation – perfusion ratios ($\dot{V}/\dot{Q}\downarrow$)

Hypercapnia with hypoxaemia results from predominant or generalized underventilation or generalized low $\dot{V}/\dot{Q}$ ratios. Hypocapnia is the result of overventilation.

The Inter-relationship between O_2 and CO_2

The alveolar air equation—in a simplified form—states the relationship thus:

$$P\text{AO}_2 = P\text{IO}_2 - P\text{ACO}_2/R$$

and since R is usually about 0·85 and $P\text{IO}_2$ is approximately 150 at sea level and $P\text{B}$ 760:

$$P\text{AO}_2 = 150 - P\text{ACO}_2/0{\cdot}85 \text{ or } 150 - \frac{6}{5}(P\text{ACO}_2)$$

$P\text{AO}_2$ (alveolar Po_2) is usually about 10 mm more than Pao_2 (arterial Po_2). $P\text{ACO}_2$ (alveolar Pco_2) and $Paco_2$ (arterial Pco_2) are usually equal.

Thus with a normal Pco_2 of 40:

$$P\text{AO}_2 = 150 - \frac{6 \times 40}{5} = 102$$

and $Pao_2 = 102 - 10 = 92$

If $Paco_2$ rises to say 60:

$$P\text{AO}_2 = 150 - \frac{6 \times 60}{5} = 78$$

and $Pao_2 = 78 - 10 = 68$

in other words if there is underventilation then alveolar Po_2 (and hence arterial Po_2) falls more than the rise in Pco_2 (CO_2 retention). With generalized underventilation this is reflected in the arterial blood gases as measured clinically—hypercapnia with hypoxaemia.

If, however, underventilation is patchy or localized, compensation may occur in respect of CO_2, e.g.:

a. $\frac{1}{5}$ of lung volume underventilated with $P\text{CO}_2 = 80$
thence $P\text{AO}_2 = 150 - \dfrac{6 \times 80}{5} = 54$, $P\text{aO}_2 = 44$
which gives $S\text{aO}_2$ 75 per cent
and $C\text{aO}_2\ \dfrac{75 \times 20}{100} = 15$ ml/100 ml.

b. $\frac{4}{5}$ of lung volume overventilated with $P\text{CO}_2 = 30$
thence $P\text{AO}_2 = 150 - \dfrac{6 \times 30}{5} = 114$, $P\text{aO}_2 = 104$
which gives $S\text{aO}_2$ 98 per cent
and $C\text{aO}_2\ \dfrac{98 \times 20}{100} = 19{\cdot}6$ ml/100 ml.

c. Combining (a) and (b) for $P\text{CO}_2$ can be direct because of linearity of CO_2 dissociation curve
$\dfrac{80 + 4\,(30)}{5} = 40$ mm Hg.

d. For oxygen (because of S-shaped dissociation curve) (a) + (b) must be combined in terms of O_2 content first:
$\dfrac{15 + 4\,(19{\cdot}6)}{5} = 18{\cdot}7$ ml /100 ml
which gives saturation of
$\dfrac{18{\cdot}7 \times 100}{20} = 93{\cdot}5$ per cent
which would give $P\text{O}_2$ of 75 mm Hg (these O_2 values would be low for a man of 40 years of age).

Thus 20 per cent underventilation can be compensated by overventilation as far as $P\text{aCO}_2$ is concerned but some hypoxaemia persists.

It is clear therefore that Po_2 is the most sensitive measure of underventilation (if diffusion impairment and anatomical shunting are excluded) or low $\mathring{V}/\mathring{Q}$ ratios.

It will also be noted from (b) that overventilation lowers Pco_2, but, even though increasing Po_2, hardly affects either Sao_2 or Cao_2 because of the flat upper part of the O_2 dissociation curve.

Cyanosis is not, as a rule, recognizable unless there is desaturation to 85 per cent saturation which at pH 7·4 would correspond with a Pao_2 of only 50 mm Hg. The older statement that 5 g of circulating reduced Hb was necessary before cyanosis became recognizable amounts to the same effect, i.e. 5 g reduced Hb gives O_2 content of

$$\frac{70}{100} \times 5 \times 1{\cdot}34 = 4{\cdot}7 \text{ ml/100 ml},$$

10 g oxygenated Hb gives O_2 content of

$$\frac{97}{100} \times 10 \times 1{\cdot}34 = 12{\cdot}8 \text{ ml/100 ml}.$$

$$\therefore \text{total } O_2 \text{ content} = 4{\cdot}7 + 12{\cdot}8 = 17{\cdot}5 \text{ ml/100 ml}.$$

$$\therefore O_2 \text{ saturation} = \frac{17{\cdot}5}{20} \times 100 = 87{\cdot}5 \text{ per cent.}$$

It follows therefore that in polycythaemia, cyanosis may be present with a normal oxygen content per 100 ml (or even higher than normal content):

e.g. Hb 21 g per cent, O_2 capacity $= 21 \times 1{\cdot}34 = 28$ ml per 100 ml

$$85 \text{ per cent saturation} = \frac{85}{100} \times 28 = 24 \text{ ml.}$$

It also follows that in anaemia oxygen content can be considerably reduced without cyanosis:

e.g. Hb 9 g per cent, O_2 capacity $= 9 \times 1{\cdot}34 = 12$ ml per 100 ml

$\therefore$ even if all Hb were 100 per cent saturated the content would still be markedly impaired.

The end result of oxygenating Hb is to deliver O_2 to the tissues. This necessitates both adequate content (Cao_2, Sao_2) and pressure (Po_2). Tissue oxygenation is not clinically measured at the present time. Measurements of cardiac output (q.v.) will provide an indication of the overall rate of O_2 delivery (but not to any specific tissue).

In CO_2 retention the respiratory centre may become insensitive to changes in $Paco_2$. As a result hypoxaemia becomes the drive to respiration. If the hypoxaemia is suddenly relieved by administering 100 per cent O_2 the respiratory drive may be abolished leading to cessation of respiration, rapid increase in Pco_2, coma and death! For this reason patients with raised $Paco_2$ must only be given O_2-enriched air via a non-breathing mask (e.g. Ventimask, Edinburgh mask, M-C mask) delivering 24–28 per cent O_2, or by the Hafoe head tent (28·5 per cent or 32 per cent O_2). Blood gases (or at least rebreathing Pco_2) should be monitored.

Chapter Eleven

Acid-base Regulation

The understanding of acid-base regulation and its disturbances has become bogged-down in a morass of confused terminology. It is therefore necessary to start with definitions.

pH

This is the notation for expressing hydrogen ion concentration. The starting point is the Henderson-Hasselbalch equation:

$$pH = pK + \log_{10} \frac{[HCO_3^-]}{[H_2CO_3]}$$

(terms in square brackets represent concentration).

This may be restated in terms of $P\text{CO}_2$ since $H_2CO_3 = 0{\cdot}03 \times P\text{CO}_2$.

The important relationship to remember is:

$$pH \propto \frac{[HCO_3^-]}{P\text{CO}_2}$$

Normal range of pH = 7·40 ± 0·05.

ACIDAEMIA

This is a fall in pH of blood to less than 7·35.

ALKALAEMIA

This is a rise in pH of blood to more than 7·45.

BICARBONATE

A number of 'measures' of bicarbonate as the metabolic

parameter of acid-base regulation have been used in clinical practice. These include the actual plasma bicarbonate, CO_2 combining power, CO_2 content, standard bicarbonate and base excess (the term 'alkali reserve' should apply to CO_2 content, or standard bicarbonate of whole blood equilibrated at 40 mm Hg P_{CO_2}. Many laboratories however use separated plasma. The measure and term are better dropped altogether).

The best of these is the most fundamental, i.e. plasma bicarbonate (measured at the P_{CO_2} as taken). Many laboratories however continue to report standard bicarbonate and base excess, largely because of the ease of reading than from appropriate nomograms when pH and P_{CO_2} have been measured.

ACIDOSIS AND ALKALOSIS

These are terms which are now outmoded (although some authorities would retain them as indicating the processess which would have led to actual pH changes if they had not been corrected), e.g. primary CO_2 retention with compensatory rise in $[HCO_3^-]$ restoring pH to low normal would be called 'respiratory' acidosis. This seems to be an unnecessary and cumbersome addition to terminology.

BASE EXCESS

This is the deviation of buffer base from normal. It was thought to be a more accurate reflection of the 'metabolic component' than other measures. In fact deviation of actual $[HCO_3^-]$ from normal is all that is needed, and can be used in planning therapy to correct acid-base disturbances

i.e. mEq acid or base needed = $0{\cdot}3 \times$ base excess $\times$ body weight = $0{\cdot}3 \times \Delta [HCO_3^-] \times$ body weight.
Normal base excess = 0 ± 2 mEq per litre.

The important chemical reaction relating CO_2 and bicarbonate is:

$$H_2O + CO_2 \rightleftharpoons H_2CO_3 \rightleftharpoons H^+ + HCO_3^-$$

The normal value for actual $[HCO_3^-]$ is 24 ± 2 mEq per litre (standard $[HCO_3^-]$ 23 ± 2, CO_2 combining power 24 ± 3, and plasma CO_2 content 25 ± 2).

Primary CO_2 Retention (Respiratory Acidaemia)

Acute CO_2 retention (from underventilation) produces only a small increase in bicarbonate (5 mm Hg P_{CO_2} ↑ → 1 mEq per litre $[HCO_3^-]$ ↑). Prolonged CO_2 retention leads to a compensatory increase in bicarbonate mediated by the kidneys.

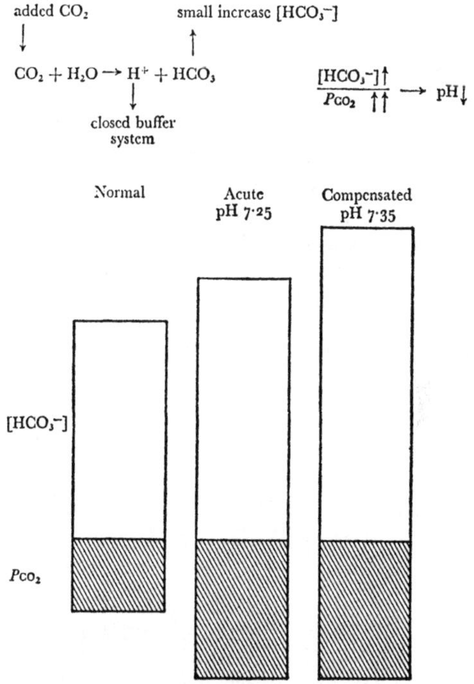

Primary CO_2 Depletion (Respiratory Alkalaemia)

Overventilation causes fall in $P\text{CO}_2$ and rise in pH. If long continued a compensatory reduction in bicarbonate may occur.

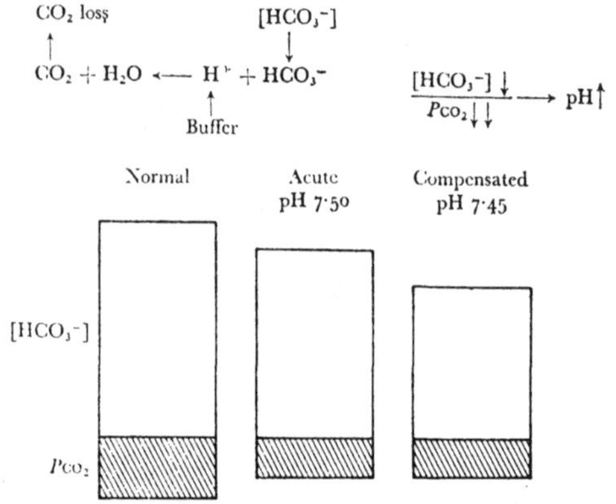

Metabolic Acidaemia

This is a primary addition of fixed acid (e.g. diabetic ketosis) leading to a marked fall in bicarbonate and decrease in pH. Secondary changes from increased ventilation 'blowing off' CO_2 may occur.

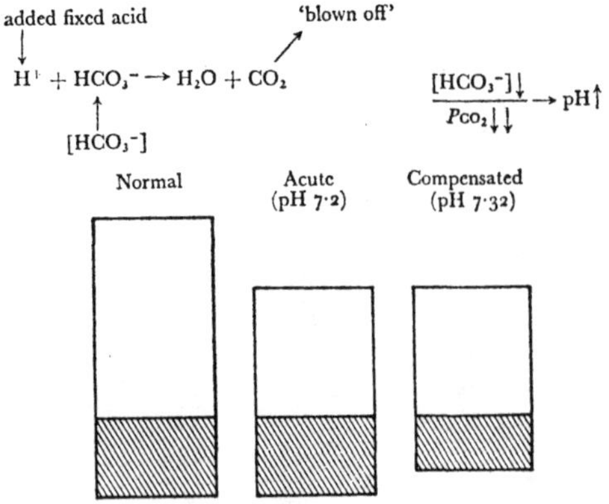

Metabolic Alkalaemia

The primary loss is of fixed acid (e.g. vomiting → loss of HCl). This results in a marked increase in bicarbonate and rise in pH. There may be a decrease in ventilation in the long term producing a secondary rise in $P\text{CO}_2$.

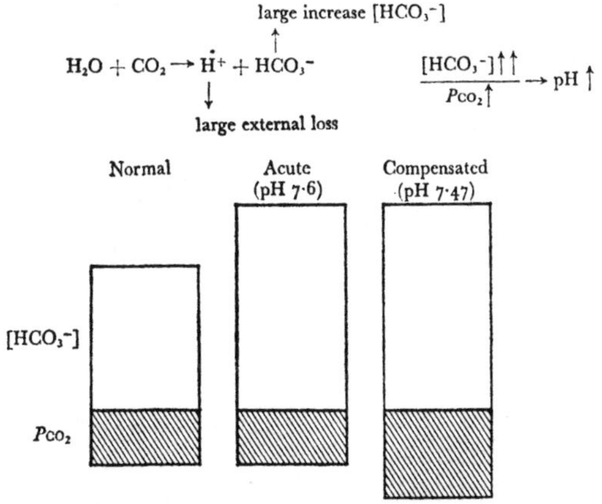

Mixed Disturbances

The primary disturbances are usually clinically evident. The relative contributions of respiratory and metabolic abnormalities in mixed states can be assessed from knowledge of bicarbonate and $P\text{CO}_2$.

CO_2 RETENTION + METABOLIC ALKALAEMIA

This situation could occur for example in acute respiratory failure plus vomiting.

There will be a tendency for pH changes to cancel out, $P\text{CO}_2$ will be raised, plasma bicarbonate will be high.

e.g. $P\text{aCO}_2$ 65, $[HCO_3^-]$ 35, pH 7·4

$\Delta\, P\text{aCO}_2 = 65 - 40 \rightarrow +25 \rightarrow +5$ mEq per litre $[HCO_3^-]$

$\Delta\, [HCO_3^-] = 35 - 24 \rightarrow +11$ mEq per litre

$\therefore$ metabolic component $= +11 - 5 \rightarrow +6$ mEq per litre $[HCO_3^-]$

CO_2 RETENTION + METABOLIC ACIDAEMIA

This situation could arise from an acute respiratory infection in a chronic bronchitic also suffering from diabetes mellitus.

There will be a raised P_{CO_2}, low bicarbonate and low pH.

e.g. Pa_{CO_2} 65, $[HCO_3^-]$ 20, pH 7·2
$\Delta Pa_{CO_2} = +25 \rightarrow +5$ mEq per litre $[HCO_3^-]$
$\Delta HCO_3 = -4$ mEq per litre
$\therefore$ metabolic component $= -4 - 5 = -9$ mEq per litre $[HCO_3^-]$

CO_2 DEPLETION + METABOLIC ACIDAEMIA

This could arise because the fixed acid stimulates respiration as in salicylate poisoning.

There will be a tendency for pH changes to cancel, bicarbonate will be low, P_{CO_2} will be low.

e.g. Pa_{CO_2} 30, $[HCO_3^-]$ 16, pH 7·4
$\Delta Pa_{CO_2} = -10 \rightarrow -2$ mEq per litre $[HCO_3^-]$
$\Delta HCO_3 = -8$ mEq per litre
$\therefore$ metabolic component $= -8 - (-2) = -6$ mEq per litre $[HCO_3^-]$

CO_2 DEPLETION + METABOLIC ALKALAEMIA

This could occur when there is overventilation from say, congestive heart failure accompanied by vomiting.

There will be a low P_{CO_2}, a high pH, and bicarbonate raised.

e.g. Pa_{CO_2} 30, $[HCO_3^-]$ 28, pH 7·6
$\Delta Pa_{CO_2} = -10 \rightarrow -2$ mEq per litre $[HCO_3^-]$
$\Delta HCO_3 = +4$
$\therefore$ metabolic component $= +4 - (-2) = +6$ mEq per litre $[HCO_3^-]$

OTHER FACTORS AFFECTING HCO_3

Potassium

$[K^+]\uparrow \rightarrow [HCO_3^-]\downarrow$

$$\begin{array}{ccc} K^+ \rightarrow \text{Cell} \rightarrow & H^+ + & HCO_3^- \\ \uparrow & & \uparrow \\ \text{retention} & & [HCO_3^-] \end{array}$$

Retained potassium enters cells from which it displaces hydrogen ions. These ions are buffered by bicarbonate thus leading to reduction in plasma bicarbonate concentration.

$[K^+]\downarrow \rightarrow [HCO_3^-]\uparrow$

$$\begin{array}{ccc} K^+ \leftarrow \text{Cell} \leftarrow & H^+ + & HCO_3 \\ \downarrow & & \downarrow \\ \text{external loss} & & [HCO_3^-] \end{array}$$

External loss depletes cellular potassium which is replaced by hydrogen ions. This in turn releases bicarbonate leading to an increase in plasma bicarbonate concentration.

Chloride

$[Cl^-]\downarrow \rightarrow [HCO_3^-]\uparrow$

$[Cl^-]\uparrow \rightarrow [HCO_3^-]\downarrow$

Chloride depletion increases demand for HCO_3^- to accompany Na^+ in renal tubular reabsorptive processes. This stimulates urinary acidification leading to loss of H^+ (and K^+). Bicarbonate 'reabsorption' is thus increased and $[HCO_3^-]$ increases.

Chloride retention lessens demand for HCO_3^- to accompany Na^+ in resorption. HCO_3^- will therefore be lost in urine leading to $[HCO_3^-]$ decrease.

Expansion of Extracellular Fluid

Expansion of extracellular fluid ↑ → Reabsorbed HCO_3^- ↓ → $[HCO_3^-]$ ↓

Thus the alkalaemia of hypokalaemia can be corrected by NaCl infusion both by the Cl effect and the expansion of extracellular fluid effect.

Corticosteroids

Increased circulating corticosteroid (mineralocorticoid) levels produce potassium depletion which, in turn, by the mechanism described above, gives rise to increase in plasma bicarbonate. Conversely, impaired mineralocorticoid secretion causes potassium retention and reduction in plasma bicarbonate.

OHCS ↑ → K^+ ↓ → $[HCO_3^-]$ ↑
OHCS ↓ → K^+ ↑ → $[HCO_3^-]$ ↓

Summary

	Acute			Chronic		
	$[HCO_3^-]$	P_{CO_2}	pH	$[HCO_3^-]$	P_{CO_2}	pH
CO_2 retention	N or S ↑	↑↑	↓↓	↑	↑↑	↓
CO_2 retention	N or S ↑	↓↓	↑↑	↓	↓↓	↑
Metabolic acidaemia	↓↓	N	↓↓	↓↓	↓	↓
Metabolic alkalaemia	↑↑	N	↑↑	↑↑	↑	↑

Note: There may be stages in these processes when pH is within normal range; the terms 'acidosis' or 'alkalosis' with the relevant adjective, i.e. 'respiratory' or 'metabolic', are then used by some authors.
N, Normal. S, Slightly.

Chapter Twelve

Exercise Studies

Many of the variables which are measured at rest can be measured on exercise, and may be more informative under conditions of stress.

Muscular exercise produces a marked increase in ventilation ($\dot{V}_E\uparrow$ $\dot{V}_A\uparrow$) and cardiac output ($\dot{Q}t\uparrow$). If exercise is mild or moderate Pa_{O_2}, Pa_{CO_2} and pH are not changed. If exercise is severe Pa_{O_2} and pH may decrease with rise in Pa_{CO_2}. Mixed venous O_2 content ($C\bar{v}_{O_2}$) decreases (because in tissues P_{O_2} falls, P_{CO_2} rises, pH falls and temperature rises, all of which increase dissociation of HbO_2) and mixed venous P_{CO_2} increases, oxygen uptake ($\dot{V}_{O_2}$) and carbon dioxide output ($\dot{V}_{CO_2}$) increase, and R ($\dot{V}_{CO_2}/\dot{V}_{O_2}$) usually increases.

The normal range of $\dot{V}_E/\dot{V}_{O_2}$ is 25 ± 5 in young adults; in the elderly $27{\cdot}5 \pm 7{\cdot}5$ is more appropriate.

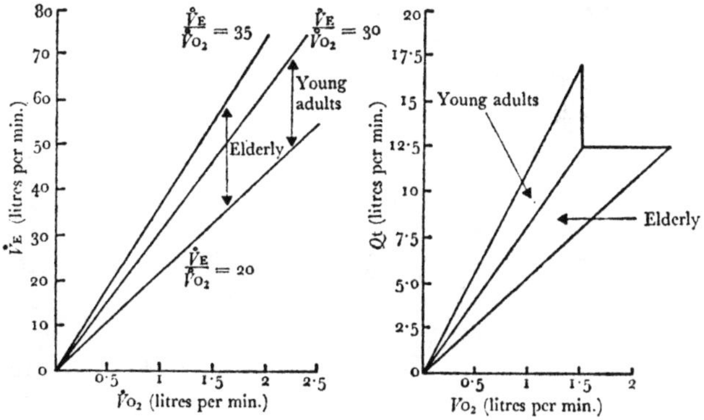

The best tests of cardiorespiratory function during exercise are:

1. Oxygen ventilation equivalent ($\dot{V}_E/\dot{V}_{O_2}$) as this relates ventilation directly to energy expenditure (whereas other indices of excessive ventilation are either unrelated to work done ('excess exercise ventilation', 'Standardized Ventilation') or related to the work load ('ventilatory response to exercise') rather than energy expended and all require measurement of resting $\dot{V}_E$ which can be greatly influenced by such factors as nervousness about procedure, unfamiliarity with mouthpiece and noseclip, etc.

2. Heart rate and ECG monitoring which give an indication of the cardiac factor.

3. Cardiac output ($\dot{Q}t$) for indication whether this is the limiting factor.

4. Blood gases (Pa_{O_2}, Pa_{CO_2}). A rise in Pa_{CO_2} of over 5 mm Hg probably means that the 'breaking point' has been reached (metabolic load too great for ventilation). A fall in Pa_{O_2} may mean the same, but may occur as the result of transfer impairment, maldistribution of impaired air, disproportionate increase in cardiac output, or increased shunting.

The differentiation between limitation of exercise capacity produced by cardiac and respiratory factors is probably best assessed by:

1. Heart rate or cardiac output
2. Blood lactic acid at breaking point
3. Rate of return of $\dot{V}_E$ and $\dot{V}_{O_2}$ to resting levels.

	$\dot{Q}_T$	Heart rate	Lactate	$\dot{V}_E + \dot{V}_{O_2}$ Recovery
Respiratory limitation	Not maximum	<150	<50 mg per cent	Rapid (<5 min)
Cardiac limitation	Maximum	>150	>50 mg per cent	Slow >10 min O_2 debt

Appendix One

Patterns of Disturbed Function

See table on the two following pages.

Pattern	FEV_1	FVC	FEV_1/FVC	TLC	T
Ageing	↓	↓	↓	N	↓
Under-ventilation	often ↓	often ↓	often ↓	N or ↓	I
Asthma	↓↓ †	N or ↓ †	↓↓	N or ↑	I
Chronic bronchitis	↓↓ ‡	↓ ‡	↓↓	N	N c
Emphysema	↓↓	↓	↓↓	↑↑	↓
Pulmonary fibrosis	↓	↓	N	↓↓	↓
Extra-pulmonary restriction	↓	↓	N	N or ↓	I
True R → L shunt	N	N	N	N	I
Pulmonary vascular occlusion	N	N	N	N	I
Pulmonary congestion	↓	↓	N	↓	earl late

Notes: 1. Patterns are typical of established conditions.
2. Mixed patterns are not uncommon.

E	Pao_2	$Paco_2$	*C*	*R*AW	
	↓	N	↑	N	Changes relatively small
↓	↓ ↓	↑ ↑	N or ↓	N or ↑	Often complicates other patterns
	↓	N	↑	↑ ↑	†Increases considerable after bronchodilator
	↓ ↓	↑	N	↑ ↑	‡May show up to 20 per cent increase after bronchodilator
	N or ↓ §	N or ↓	↑ ↑	↑ ↑	§May be further fall on exercise
	N or ↓ ‖	N or ↓	↓ ↓	N	‖Further fall on exercise
r ↑	N	N	↓	N	Usually skeletal deformity
	↓ ↓ *	N or ↓	N	N	*Rises to <600 on 100 per cent O_2
	↓ **	↓	N	N	**a—A gradient for Pco_2 may become measurable
	N	↓	↓	N	Cardiac output subnormal on exercise

Evidence of disturbed $\dot{V}/\dot{Q}$ relationships ($\dot{V}_D/\dot{V}_E$↑, A–aDO₂↑) and abnormal oxygen ventilation equivalent—($\dot{V}_E/\dot{V}_{O_2}$) common to all. All may end with respiratory failure (Pao_2 ↓ ↓ $Paco_2$ ↑ ↑).

Appendix Two

Temperature and Pressure Corrections

By agreed convention:

1. Gas volumes involving uptake or output of gas by the body are converted to standard temperature and pressure, dry (STPD), i.e. 0°C, 760 mm Hg.
2. Other volumes are converted to body temperature and pressure saturated with water vapour (BTPS).

The relationships are:

STPD

$$\text{corrected volume} = \text{measured volume} \times \frac{273}{273 + t} \times \frac{P_B - P_{H_2O}}{760}$$

BTPS

$$\text{corrected volume} = \text{measured volume} \times \frac{310}{273 + t} \times \frac{P_B - P_{H_2O}}{P_B - 47}$$

where t = temperature in °C
P_{H_2O} = water vapour pressure at this temperature
P_B = atmospheric pressure

When calculating a ratio of two variables both must be converted to STPD or BTPS.

STPD to BTPS = STPD volume × 1·136 × $760/P_B - P_{H_2O}$

BTPS to STPD = BTPS volume × 0·88 × $P_B - P_{H_2O}/760$.

(*see* opposite page)

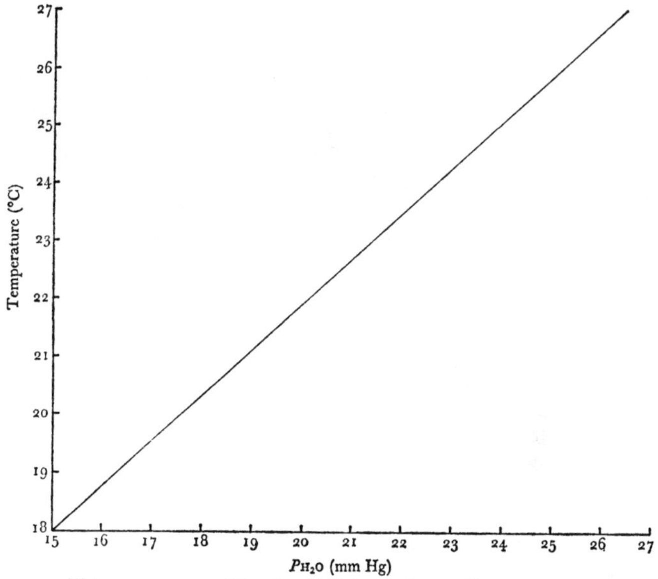

Water vapour pressure (P_{H_2O} (mm Hg)) at normal range of room temperature.

For convenience, when P_B is between 740 and 780 the following factors may be used for conversion of volumes at ambient temperature:

Temperature (°C)	BTPS Ambient X Factor	STPD Ambient X Factor
18	1·113	0·920
19	1·108	0·916
20	1·102	0·911
21	1·096	0·906
22	1·091	0·902
23	1·085	0·897
24	1·080	0·893
25	1·075	0·888
26	1·069	0·883
27	1·063	0·878

BIBLIOGRAPHY

Bates D. V., Macklem D. V. and Christie R. V. (1971) *Respiratory Function in Disease.* 2nd ed. London, W. B. Saunders.

Campbell E. J. M., Dickinson C. J. and Slater J. D. H. (ed.) (1963) *Clinical Physiology.* Oxford, Blackwell Scientific Publications.

Cherniak R. M. and Cherniak L. (1961) *Respiration in Health and Disease.* London, W. B. Saunders.

Comroe J. H., Forster R. E., DuBois A. B., Briscoe W. A. and Calsen E. (1962) *The Lung: Clinical Physiology and Pulmonary Function Tests.* 2nd ed. Chicago, Year Book Medical Publishers Inc.

Cotes J. E. (1965) *Lung Function.* Oxford, Blackwell Scientific Publications.

Fenn W. O. and Rahn F. (ed.) (1965) *Handbook of Physiology: Section 3.* Washington D.C. American Physiological Society.

Filley G. F. (1971) *Acid-Base and Blood Gas Regulation.* Philadelphia, Lea & Febiger.

Kelman G. R. and Nunn J. F. (1966) *Computer Produced Physiological Tables.* London, Butterworths.

McHardy G. J. R. (1967) Paper 939, Tables 32/8–32/13. *Clin. Sci. 32.*

Rossier P. H., Buhlmann A. A. and Wiesinger K. (1960) *Respiration: Physiologic Principles and Clinical Applications.* St. Louis, C. V. Mosby Co.

INDEX

Intersezioni

225.

Carlo M. Cipolla

Le avventure della lira

il Mulino

I lettori che desiderano informarsi sui libri e sull'insieme delle attività della Società editrice il Mulino possono consultare il sito Internet: **www.mulino.it**

ISBN 978-88-15-24089-7

Indice

Prefazione

1. Pochi sanno che la lira nacque, nell'ottavo secolo, come moneta unica europea. «Dalle rive britanniche della Manica – dice Cipolla – alla corte di Aquisgrana, alla pianura padana, alle colline toscane, la lira d'argento fu la comune unità di misura dei valori». Con lo spegnersi dell'autorità unificante di Roma era evaporato anche il segno tangibile di tale autorità: la moneta con l'effigie di Cesare. Per circa cinque secoli, l'Europa era vissuta nell'anarchia monetaria, fino all'estremo rarefarsi della circolazione, al diffondersi dell'economia di baratto. La riforma attuata da Carlo Magno negli ultimi due decenni dell'ottavo secolo fece della lira – libbra d'argento divisa in 240 denari – il segno monetario unico dell'Europa. Seguì, ricorda ancora Cipolla, un secolo di stabilità. I traffici ripresero, il baratto si fece meno frequente, la produzione e il consumo aumentarono in numerose regioni del continente.

A cavallo del ventunesimo secolo, la lira ha concluso la propria avventura, fondendosi nell'euro. Quando Carlo Cipolla – principe degli storici economici italiani – diede alle stampe questo breve libro, non immaginava che la parabola storica della lira stesse volgendo alla fine. Non sappiamo se e in quale modo avrebbe riproposto oggi questo testo. Sappiamo però che l'ironico distacco con il quale talvolta guardava gli oggetti dei propri studi non gli impediva di visitare il passato con gli occhi del presente, i soli disponibili allo storico. Aveva inoltre, fortissimo, il senso delle cesure. Sapeva, come pochi altri, discernere i momenti normali da quelli nei quali la storia, contrariamente alla natura, sembra fare un salto. Credo, dunque, che tutto sommato Carlo Cipolla avrebbe consentito anche oggi alla ristampa di questo suo lavoro.

La storia più che millenaria della lira è poco nota. Questo libretto la ripercorre in modo agile. Aiuta a ricordarne i momenti forti ma anche le debolezze.

2. La moneta riassume in sé, come nessun altro indice sintetico, la vita politica, economica, sociale di un popolo. Rappresentando l'autorità sovrana, è termometro del buon governo. Viene quotidianamente accettata o respinta da milioni di persone. Il suo trasmigrare precede e segue i movimenti transcontinentali delle merci e dei lavoratori. Le sue molteplici forme segnalano l'abbondanza e la scarsità delle risorse. Le avventure della lira sono, pertanto, quelle di un intero popolo.

Come molti altri lavori di Cipolla, *Le avventure della lira* parla soprattutto del primato economico italiano che accompagna quello civile e artistico del Rinascimento e del successivo declino, nella seconda parte del diciassettesimo secolo.

Nel periodo di grande espansione economica fra il tredicesimo e il quindicesimo secolo, il valore intrinseco delle monete italiane diminuì rispetto alla lira, libbra, d'argento più di quanto si svalutarono le monete francesi e inglesi. Questo fenomeno fu allora segno non di debolezza ma di forza economica. L'aumento della domanda di moneta generato dall'aumento della popolazione e del reddito, accanto alla crescente monetizzazione degli scambi, furono le ragioni principali di emissioni a contenuto metallico ridotto. Non si tratta, dunque, avverte Cipolla di cause riducibili, come meccanicamente fanno taluni economisti, «al trito ritornello dei tosatori e dei principi afflitti da manie bellicose e da mogli spenderecce» (p. 68). Né queste circostanze impedirono che il prestigio, la ricchezza, l'affidabilità dei mercanti e dei banchieri veneziani e fiorentini facessero del ducato e del fiorino le monete più ricercate d'Europa. Era questo il periodo in cui il reddito per abitante dell'Italia centro-settentrionale era il più elevato del continente europeo.

L'afflusso dell'oro e dell'argento americani, se fece di Genova la principale piazza bancaria italiana, spostò lentamente dall'Italia all'Europa atlantica il centro della finanza, del commercio e della manifattura. Cipolla data l'«estate di San Martino dell'economia italiana» (p. 74) grosso modo tra il 1550 e il 1620. La lira sarebbe forse allora andata perduta quale moneta italiana se, nel 1562 e nel 1631, le riforme monetarie dei sovrani sabaudi non avessero reintrodotto «definitivamente e con successo in tutto il Piemonte il sistema di computo a lire» (p. 76). La lira restò dunque al centro del sistema monetario dello stato che, due secoli e mezzo dopo, avrebbe dato all'Italia, insieme all'unificazione politica, anche la propria moneta.

3. Nella successiva decadenza economica, sociale e politica dell'Italia i sistemi monetari dei singoli stati si fecero confusi, disorganici, incoerenti gli uni con gli altri. «In ogni stato si trovavano in circolazione, fianco a fianco, pezzi coniati in epoche diverse, con intrinseci i più disparati che sovente era anche difficile appurare. Circolavano parecchie monete straniere» (p. 81). Malgrado i tentativi illuministici di riforma, è sostanzialmente questa la situazione monetaria dell'Italia alla vigilia dell'unificazione politica.

La lira italiana è figlia delle riforme repubblicane e napoleoniche che, mille anni dopo quella di Carlo Magno, ridisegnarono il sistema monetario su base decimale. La lira uscì di scena in Francia, sostituita dal franco, ma mantenne il proprio nome quando nel 1806 Napoleone estese al Regno d'Italia la riforma monetaria francese del 1803. Il franco francese pesava 5 grammi d'argento a 900 millesimi, così come quelli svizzero e belga e come la lira italiana. Dopo la caduta di Napoleone, i sovrani piemontesi non riuscirono a imporre un ritorno al vecchio sistema basato su lira, soldi e denari: la «nuova» lira decimale restò in vigore, con un contenuto d'argento pari a quello del franco francese. Questa stessa moneta fu fatta propria dal nuovo Regno d'Italia il 24 agosto 1862.

Un conto era, tuttavia, l'introduzione di una nuova moneta legale, un altro la sua adozione come principale mezzo di scambio. Le numerosissime monete metalliche degli stati pre-unitari continuarono a circolare accanto alla lira italiana, in un guazzabuglio di tassi di cambio che non facilitava le transazioni e ritardava l'indispensabile creazione di un mercato unico. La sospensione della convertibilità metallica delle banconote, resa necessaria dalla partecipazione dell'Italia alla guerra austro-prussiana del 1866, fu vissuta all'epoca come una tragedia nazionale, ebbe viceversa il benefico effetto di accelerare l'unificazione monetaria del paese. Nel 1883 la convertibilità aurea della lira venne ripristinata ma durò solo un decennio.

Tra il 1893 e il 1895, negli anni che Luzzatto definì i più neri del nuovo regno, il paese visse una delle sue più gravi crisi finanziarie, economiche, politiche. Ne uscì grazie a riforme radicali del sistema bancario, a una politica fiscale e monetaria rigorosa. Grazie al coraggio di una classe dirigente lungimirante, l'Italia del primo Novecento seppe trarre vantaggio da una congiuntura internazionale espansiva, creò la propria base industriale. Saggiamente, la convertibilità metallica non fu ufficialmente ripresa, ma il rigore con il quale furono gestite moneta e finanza pubblica produsse un effetto strabiliante: al cambio ufficiale, la lira faceva sovente «premio sull'oro», come allora si diceva.

Le guerre, come si sa, sono raramente una cosa buona, non lo sono mai per le monete. Nemmeno lo sono le recessioni, in un modo forse più sottile ma ugualmente perverso. La storia della lira tra il 1915 e il 1945 è fatta, salvo brevi periodi, di restrizioni amministrative al suo uso, alla sua convertibilità in monete straniere. Negli anni che seguirono la sconfitta, nel momento più difficile della propria storia unitaria, l'Italia seppe nuovamente agganciare una straordinaria congiuntura internazionale. Dopo la fiammata inflazionistica del 1946 – accettata di buon grado, se non proprio provocata, da Luigi Einaudi per bruciare gran parte del debito pubblico – l'Italia aderì agli accordi di Bretton Woods, partecipò al Piano Marshall e all'Unione Europea dei Pagamenti, fondò, con altri cinque paesi, la Comunità Economica Europea. Contrariamente a quanto avvenne per franco e sterlina, la lira si mantenne straordinariamente stabile durante tutti gli anni Cinquanta e Sessanta (il famoso cambio di 625 lire per dollaro). L'insieme del periodo va ancora oggi sotto il nome di «miracolo italiano», anche per l'eccezionalità della crescita e dell'equilibrio macroeconomico e monetario che caratterizzarono quei decenni. Ma non vi fu nulla di miracoloso: scelte politiche ed economiche coraggiose consentirono all'Italia di partecipare in pieno a quella che fu, in tutta Europa, una vera e propria «età dell'oro».

4. Il lettore vedrà che il libro si conclude con una nota di grande pessimismo. Non poteva essere diversamente, se si considera l'anno di pubblicazione. Nel 1975, Cipolla vedeva la lira come un «fantasma dai piedi di carta» detentore di un «poco invidiabile primato di svalutazione» tra le monete europee. Non si può dargli torto. Nel volgere di pochi anni, la situazione sociale ed economica del paese era radicalmente mutata. Inflazioni belliche a parte, gli anni Settanta furono i meno gloriosi nella storia della lira italiana. Alla fine del 1975, un'ennesima crisi di governo, il basso livello delle riserve e i dubbi americani sulla bontà del debito pubblico italiano esercitarono una pressione sul cambio che si tradusse, nel gennaio successivo, in una lunga sospensione della quotazione della lira al mercato ufficiale. Il provvedimento non aveva precedenti in tempo di pace. Il tasso di sconto, già all'8 per cento, fu portato al 12 per cento. Si aprirono gli anni più tragici della storia italiana postbellica. La moneta registrò puntualmente la situazione, confermando, ancora una volta, la propria endogenità alla società che di essa si serviva. Dopo il primo shock petrolifero, il tentativo di governare la tensione sociale con una perversa indicizzazione dei salari fece salire, nel 1976, l'inflazione al 24 per cento.

Gli anni successivi restano, nella memoria collettiva, come gli anni di piombo. Moro e la sua scorta vennero assassinati. Baffi e Sarcinelli gratuitamente accusati. Per dirla con il Governatore Ciampi, si vollero porre limiti all'impegno di persone in massimo grado dotate di competenza, rigore morale e rispetto delle istituzioni. La Banca d'Italia fu ferita nella propria autonomia nel momento in cui una seconda crisi petrolifera aggravava le tendenze inflative di fondo.

L'inflazione, scesa al 12 per cento nel 1978, superò l'anno dopo il 21 per cento.

Eppure, gli ultimi anni Settanta dimostrarono anche la capacità di reazione del paese. Il 1978, per tanti versi *annus horribilis*, fu quello della coraggiosa adesione al Sistema Monetario Europeo, divenuta operativa nel marzo 1979. La storia successiva è quella di uno sforzo di risanamento della moneta, oltre che della grande impresa. Purtroppo esso riuscì solo a metà. La società italiana, e la classe politica che la rappresenta, riescono quasi sempre a dare il meglio di sé in situazioni di crisi estrema ma, uscite dal pericolo immediato, sovente si accasciano esauste, incapaci di completare l'opera iniziata. Le grandi imprese manifatturiere non furono completamente ristrutturate, gli indispensabili mutamenti nel sistema bancario e finanziario si trascinarono a lungo. In particolare, la tensione riformatrice non si manifestò nell'ambito ove era più necessaria: la finanza pubblica. Sotto questo profilo, gli anni Ottanta costituirono un'enorme occasione mancata, il cui costo l'Italia sta pagando in modo durissimo nella crisi mondiale scoppiata nel 2007 e in quella europea esplosa nella tarda primavera del 2011. La miopia con la quale tra il 1980 e il 1990 si lasciò crescere il debito pubblico dal 50 al 100 per cento del prodotto interno lordo si ripercosse sulla lira. L'inflazione diminuì da circa il 19 per cento (1981) a circa il 6 per cento (1991) ma non fu definitivamente domata. L'aumento dei prezzi restò elevato rispetto a quello dei principali concorrenti internazionali. La vita della lira nel sistema europeo dei cambi rimase precaria: il decennio fu scandito da numerosi «riallineamenti», come erano pudicamente chiamate le periodiche svalutazioni del cambio.

5. Nella seconda metà degli anni Ottanta acquistò nuova linfa la politica di integrazione europea, languente da almeno un decennio. Già nel 1984, il Governatore Ciampi aveva rilevato la crescente domanda di una unità monetaria europea. Negli anni successivi si fece intenso il lavoro diplomatico per realizzare il completamento del mercato unico e la moneta unica europea. Nel 1991, con il trattato di Maastricht, l'Unione Europea varò la propria costituzione monetaria. L'anno successivo, nel mezzo di un difficile passaggio politico che avrebbe portato alla fine dei grandi partiti protagonisti dell'Italia postbellica, la lira attraversò la propria ultima crisi. La prima parte dell'anno era passata in modo relativamente tranquillo, con il cambio stabile entro la cosiddetta «banda stretta» del sistema europeo dei cambi. In maggio, il marco quotava circa 750 lire. In giugno, improvvisamente, il rigetto del trattato di Maastricht da parte del popolo danese fu sufficiente a generare una crisi di sfiducia nel futuro della moneta unica. Esso si tradusse in un attacco speculativo alle due monete percepite come le più deboli nello SME: la sterlina e la lira. All'inizio di settembre il tasso di sconto venne inutilmente portato al 15 per cento. Il 16 settembre la sterlina uscì dal Sistema Monetario Europeo, seguita dalla lira. In ottobre il marco valeva circa 930 lire.

Gli anni che seguirono la crisi valutaria del 1992 fanno parte della recente memoria collettiva: non serve ricostruirli nel dettaglio. La lira, ancora una volta sintesi della vita nazionale, visse la sua ultima avventura. Si trattò, questa volta, di avventura virtuosa, a lieto fine. Come nei momenti migliori della propria storia recente – il periodo a cavallo dei secoli diciannovesimo e ventesimo e l'immediato secondo dopoguerra – l'Italia seppe uscire da una crisi potenzialmente distruttiva agganciando una favorevole congiuntura internazionale, politica piuttosto che economica. Nel difficile autunno 1992, fu abbracciata una rigorosa politica di bilancio. I sindacati accettarono la necessaria moderazione salariale, concordandone le modalità con il governo. La Banca d'Italia mantenne i tassi a breve elevati per tutto il tempo necessario a ridurre e poi definitivamente domare le attese di inflazione. Non furono «lacrime e sangue», ma certamente si trattò di una politica di severità e coerenza quale non si vedeva in Italia da almeno quarant'anni. Il paese comprese l'importanza della posta in gioco, accettò le conseguenze del rigore fiscale e monetario con una tranquillità che probabilmente sorprese taluni uomini politici. L'ultima avventura della lira si concluse, dunque, con la fusione nell'euro grazie alla capacità della classe dirigente di cogliere l'opportunità, forse irrepetibile, offerta dalla storia europea e grazie alla maturità con la quale i cittadini hanno assecondato questa scelta.

6. Nel 1975 Cipolla chiudeva il proprio volume in tono pessimista, in quelli che gli apparivano come gli anni più difficili della storia italiana postbellica. Nel 2001, la ristampa delle *Avventure della lira* apparve, non certo a caso, nel momento in cui la lira concludeva, nell'euro, la propria lunga avventura. Nel decennio successivo terrorismo, guerre, squilibri macroeconomici, incertezze geopolitiche e la lunga «Grande Recessione» hanno creato incertezza, sfiducia e frustrazione per l'apparente incapacità dei governi, delle forze politiche, delle classi dirigenti e intellettuali nel loro complesso di trovare soluzioni adeguate alla gravità del delicato passaggio storico. Al momento di licenziare questa nuova prefazione non sono pochi, in Europa e altrove, quelli che dubitano della tenuta dell'Unione

Monetaria Europea, della sua stessa desiderabilità. Le monete, come sempre, registrano la forza relativa non solo delle economie ma anche delle società di cui sono espressione. Dopo un lungo ristagno della crescita della produttività, a lungo pervicacemente trascurata e addirittura negata, l'Italia è molto indebolita, eppure da essa dipende in grande misura il futuro dell'euro. È grande la tentazione di negare ancora una volta i problemi, di attribuirli tutti all'insipienza altrui e all'improvvida creazione di una moneta unica europea. Eppure, proprio la storia della lira a partire da quando Cipolla consegnò alle stampe *Le avventure della lira* dovrebbe vaccinare contro la tentazione di un ritorno, con la vecchia moneta, alle vecchie pratiche politiche ed economiche, oltre che alla pigrizia intellettuale che essa permetteva. Nella grande incertezza attuale, una cosa si può affermare con buon grado di sicurezza: se oggi la lira fosse ancora la moneta solitaria e marginale di una media potenza economica, sganciata dall'Europa monetaria, essa sarebbe soggetta a tensioni ben maggiori di quelle che costrinsero, nel 1976, le autorità a chiudere per quaranta giorni il mercato dei cambi. E le conseguenze sul reddito, sull'occupazione, sulle speranze degli italiani sarebbero ben più gravi di quelle di allora.

GIANNI TONIOLO

Giugno 2012

Carlo M. Cipolla

Le avventure della lira

Capitolo primo

Un fantasma col piede d'argento

1. La *lira* origina da un peso: un peso che i Romani chiamavano *libbra* e che doveva equivalere all'incirca a 325 dei nostri grammi[1]. Questa libbra aveva già allora legami di parentela con il mondo monetario perché era con riferimento ad essa che si usava determinare il piede delle varie specie monetali. Ma non era una moneta[2].

La trasformazione della libbra in unità del nostro sistema monetale risale alle riforme attuate nella penisola da Carlo Magno tra il 781 e il 794[3]. Prima di Carlo, per tutta la penisola, l'unità monetaria fondamentale era il soldo d'oro con le sue frazioni: non ci fosse stata la conquista carolingica noi forse calcoleremmo ancora i nostri prezzi in termini di *soldi* e *tremissi*[4]. Fu Carlo a rompere la tradizione: sconfitti i Longobardi e occupata parte della penisola, egli estese da noi la riforma monetaria che suo padre e lui stesso avevano

[1] Cfr. in dettaglio qui avanti Appendice II, § 1.

[2] Circa l'uso dell'espressione *libbra* per esprimere un certo ammontare di moneta in certi periodi ed in certe zone nell'antichità cfr. per tutti A. Del Mar, *A History of the Monetary Systems*, cap. III, pp. 94-112. (I riferimenti bibliografici sono fatti in forma abbreviata. I riferimenti completi si trovano nella Bibliografia in fondo al volume.)

[3] Sulla controversa questione della data esatta delle riforme monetarie carolingiche cfr. per tutti P. Grierson, *Cronologia delle riforme monetarie di Carlo Magno*, pp. 65-79. Sulla riforma in genere cfr. P. Grierson, *Money and Coinage under Charlemagne*.

[4] *Tremisse* era la moneta d'oro che rappresentava un terzo del soldo. Per notizie sommarie e riassuntive su questa moneta cfr. E. Martinori, *La moneta*, pp. 534-535.

iniziato nel Regno franco e che re Aethelberto II e poi re Offa avevano attuato nei regni di Mercia e di Kent.

La riforma stabiliva sul piano monetario il monometallismo argenteo e istituiva come unica moneta legale il denaro argenteo di cui le zecche dovevano consegnare 240 pezzi per ogni libbra di argento ricevuta.

In un primo tempo, tra il 768 ed il 793 Carlo coniò denari dal peso di grammi 1,3. A partire dal 789 però Carlo si diede a riformare anche il sistema ponderale e probabilmente in relazione anche a tali riforme, tra la fine del 793 e i primi del 794 elevò il peso del denaro a grammi 1,7[5].

2. In teoria la riforma lasciava alla libbra il carattere che aveva prima – cioè di peso – e non le attribuiva affatto il carattere di moneta. In pratica però le cose andarono diversamente. La nuova unità monetaria, il denaro d'argento, pesando grammi 1,7 d'argento a lega di circa 950 millesimi, aveva un fino di circa grammi 1,6. Dato l'alto potere d'acquisto dell'argento in quel tempo, il valore unitario rappresentato dal denaro era tutt'altro che infimo[6]. È anche vero che i secc. VIII e IX si caratterizzarono come un'epoca di economia primitiva e depressa. Ma insomma potevano capitare anche allora, sia pure non molto frequentemente, transazioni di una certa rilevanza come compravendite di cavalli, di terre, di schiavi, di partite di miglio o di grano in tempi di carestia, di gioie e di oggetti preziosi,

[5] Su quanto precede cfr. P. Grierson, *Money and Coinage under Charlemagne*, pp. 533-534.

[6] Per esempio nel sec. IX in Francia con 4 denari si comperava un intero montone e con un denaro si dava da mangiare a tre poveri per un giorno: cfr. B. Guerard, *Du système monétaire des Francs*, p. 436. Per altri elementi circa il potere d'acquisto della moneta in quei tempi cfr. qui avanti in questo stesso capitolo il § 5.

per le quali il denaro carolingico non riusciva affatto comodo: ce ne volevano centinaia e talvolta migliaia di pezzi per ogni singola transazione. Il guaio era che nella riforma carolingica non s'era prevista la coniazione di un multiplo del denaro d'argento.

Nell'uso del denaro come mezzo di scambio, la difficoltà poteva venir superata sostituendo al denaro stesso altri mezzi di pagamento dal valore unitario più elevato come gioie, metallo in verghe, cavalli, armi o altre merci. Bisogna anche dire che sovente la difficoltà non era neppure avvertita perché per un complesso di svariate ragioni l'economia del tempo s'era avvicinata ad uno stadio «naturale» con larga diffusione del baratto[7]. Per quanto riguarda l'uso delle unità di conto, la soluzione doveva invece per forza essere diversa: bisognava trovare un comune denominatore che rappresentasse un multiplo fisso del denaro[8]. La soluzione trovata fu una soluzione spontanea, nata dall'uso quotidiano e non imposta a quanto ci risulta da nessuna legge e da nessuna autorità. La gente non avendo a disposizione un multiplo effettivo del denaro trovò comodo usare la libbra come multiplo ideale di conto. Siccome da una libbra (peso) di argento la gente otteneva alla zecca 240 denari, invece di dire per esempio «240 denari» la gente preferì dire «1 lira», e invece di dire per esempio «2.163 denari» la gente preferì dire più semplicemente «9 lire e 3 denari».

Con questo espediente la gente evitava di dover fare uso nei suoi conti di cifre troppo grosse. In altri termini: si preferì all'occorrenza esprimere certe somme in «lire» anziché in «denari» per la stessa ragione per cui volendo esprimere le distanze tra una

[7] Cfr. C.M. Cipolla, *Moneta e civiltà mediterranea*, cap. I, e C.M. Cipolla, *Per una nuova storia della moneta*.

[8] Cfr. C.M. Cipolla, *Moneta e civiltà mediterranea*, cap. IV.

città ed un'altra noi preferiamo ricorrere all'unità di «kilometro» anziché far uso dell'unità «metro».

Così cominciò la storia monetaria della lira. Una storia tanto avventurosa quanto strana. E la stranezza era già evidente dall'inizio. La lira moneta nacque come moneta materialmente inesistente, come pura unità ideale di conto. La gente cominciò a parlare di lire, a trattare e vendere in lire, senza che alcuno mai avesse visto o toccato una lira in forma di moneta. La lira venne al mondo come moneta-fantasma. Il curioso è che rimase un fantasma per quasi mille anni[9].

3. Questo strano fantasma rappresentò comunque al suo nascere l'unità di misura dei valori di tutto o quasi l'Occidente cristiano del tempo. Dalle rive britanniche della Manica, alla corte di Acquisgrana, alla pianura padana, alle colline toscane, la lira d'argento fu la comune unità di misura dei valori e dovunque essa significava 240 denari[10]. Le conquiste territoriali dei

[9] Nel suo insieme il sistema monetario uscito dalle riforme carolingiche si esprimeva nel seguente schema di equivalenze:

1 lira = 20 soldi = 240 denari

in cui la lira e il soldo erano monete-fantasma e il denaro era l'unica moneta effettiva (cfr. C.M. Cipolla, *Moneta e civiltà mediterranea*, cap. IV).

Il rapporto 1 lira = 20 soldi = 240 denari rimase in vigore nei vari sistemi monetari dell'Europa occidentale sino alla Rivoluzione Francese quando in Francia prima e poi nei paesi che entrarono nell'orbita francese fu introdotto il sistema decimale. In Gran Bretagna dove l'ondata rivoluzionaria francese non arrivò, il sistema monetario conserva ancor oggi le tre unità raccordate secondo il sistema carolingico ed ancor oggi vi si conteggia sulla base di 1 *pound* (libbra) = 20 *shillings* (soldi) = 240 *pennies* (denari).

[10] La lira inglese, pur essa uguale a 240 denari, era però un poco inferiore alla lira continentale in quanto il denaro inglese sembra fosse lievemente più leggero del confratello carolingico. In effetti il peso unitario dei *pennies* di re Offa sembra si aggirasse in un primo

Carolingi ed i loro rapporti coi re di Mercia e di Kent avevano saputo fare dell'Occidente cristiano un'unica area monetaria che si distingueva da un lato dall'area monetaria bizantina e dall'altro lato dall'area monetaria musulmana[11].

I confini dell'area della lira non abbracciarono però mai tutta l'Italia. Il confine meridionale dell'area tagliava a mezzo la penisola. A sud di Roma o perdurò la tradizione monetaria romano-bizantina o finì col prevalere l'influenza della moneta araba. Roma stessa rappresentò un'area grigia e la lira vi entrò solo sussidiariamente[12] e solo per un certo periodo[13]. Per resistenza bizantina o per espansione musulmana il meridione d'Italia rimase così nettamente tagliato fuori dall'area monetaria occidentale. Anche la lira «si è fermata ad Eboli».

4. Per oltre cento anni dalla nascita del denaro carolingico non vi furono innovazioni di rilievo. Il denaro mantenne inalterati il suo peso e la sua lega e la lira continuò a significare 240 denari. Un secolo di stabilità assoluta è un bel titolo di onore per una moneta: a dire il vero però noi non sappiamo se o quanto quella stabilità fu il frutto della buona amministrazione

tempo attorno ai grammi 1,3 e fosse poi portato a circa grammi 1,5 (cfr. G.C. Brooke, *English Coins*, p. 14 e C. Oman, *The Coinage of England*, pp. 17-18).

[11] Circa il significato qui attribuito al termine «area monetaria» cfr. avanti cap. II, § 2.

[12] Per una buona parte del Medioevo Roma ebbe una doppia monetazione; l'una impiantata sul sistema lira-soldo-denaro (moneta provisina del senato, bolognini papali e moneta paparina), l'altra imitante la monetazione del meridione. Su tutto ciò cfr. C.M. Cipolla, *Studi di storia della moneta*, p. 77.

[13] Dal sec. XVI in poi in Roma e nello Stato Pontificio il sistema di conteggiare a lire, soldi e denari fu definitivamente abbandonato e si conteggiò generalmente in scudi e bajocchi.

carolingica o non piuttosto il sintomo di un secolare ristagno economico.

Col sec. X cominciarono i primi slittamenti. Il conte Maluzzani fece saggiare un denaro del primo Berengario (915-924) e lo trovò al titolo di soli 746 millesimi[14]. Il cav. Brambilla studiando i denari pavesi della prima metà del sec. X, dopo averne passati diversi anche alla prova del crogiolo, rilevò che «anche per quelli di minor modulo il peso ne sia assai volte superiore a grammi 1,4 in esemplari appena discretamente conservati, per il che è da credere fossero emessi quali denari effettivi correnti», ma che «varia ed irregolare» risultava «la mistura del metallo di cui erano formati»[15]. La tradizione tramanda anche che il secondo Berengario, verso il 947, per versare tributi agli Ungari che continuavano a devastare le nostre terre, indebolì la moneta mischiando il rame all'argento con una certa abbondanza[16]. Sembra che queste fossero deviazioni più o meno temporanee. Comunque la situazione non era certo né chiara né sana: e il disordine monetario

[14] G. Mulazzani, *Studi economici*, p. 58, n. 2.

[15] C. Brambilla, *Moneta di Pavia*, p. 139.

[16] Stando al racconto del tempo non riesce comunque chiaro se le monete svilite siano circolate in Italia o se siano state prevalentemente portate fuori confine. Ecco comunque l'interpretazione muratoriana del passo liutprandeo (L.A. Muratori, *Annali d'Italia*, s.a. 947): «anche alla Lombardia circa questi tempi toccò una indiscreta visita degli Ungheri per attestato di Liutprando (1. 5, c. 5) essendo comparso in queste contrade Tassi, re di quei barbari con un copioso esercito. Berengario colla forza non delle armi, ma di gran quantità d'oro li fece ritornare addietro; e non già coll'oro suo, ma con quello che raccolse dalle chiese e dal povero popolo, con avere imposto un testatico di un denaro d'argento per cadauna persona; e lo pagavano infino i fanciulli lattanti dell'uno e dell'altro sesso. Colla somma di tanto argento raccolto, *con cui mischiò del rame*, fece battere dieci moggia di denari, co' quali soddisfece all'accordo stabilito con gli Ungheri e per sé ritenne, da buon economo, tutto quanto egli aveva tolto alle chiese».

rifletteva il disordine politico ed amministrativo. Gli Ottoni riportarono un certo ordine. Ma, come del resto in altri settori, anche nel campo monetario essi furono più i continuatori dei re italici che i restauratori dell'ordinamento carolingico. Essi consacrarono lo slittamento del denaro. L'evidenza numismatica non lascia dubbi sul fatto che i loro denari furono coniati su un nuovo piede monetario. Il peso teorico legale del denaro di Ottone I (961-973) e di Ottone II (973-983) deve essere stato vicino ai grammi 1,4[17], al titolo di

[17] H. Dannenberg, *Die deutschen Münzen*, t. I, pp. 446-448 cita denari ottoniani aggirantisi attorno ai grammi 1,5 al pezzo. C. Desimoni in L.T. Belgrano, *Illustrazione del Registro Arcivescovile*, p. 591, scriveva che i denari di Ottone I «furono anch'essi di buon argento e del peso di grammi 1,46 a 1,37».

C. Brambilla, *Monete di Pavia*, p. 191, ritiene che il peso teorico legale unitario dei denari di Ottone I e di Ottone II dovesse essere di grammi 1,359, ma pesando i pezzi a sua disposizione egli stesso dovette ammettere che ne aveva trovato parecchi pesanti sui grammi 1,4 e oltre.

Q. Perini, *Monete di Verona*, p. 49, trovò che il peso di esemplari di Ottone I della zecca di Verona da lui analizzati variava tra grammi 1,3 e grammi 1,5. Il *Corpus Nummorum Italicorum* cita denari veronesi di Ottone I pesanti grammi 2,21-1,40-1,38. Il dr. O. Murari che in tutta questa materia delle monete ottoniane di Verona ha una profonda conoscenza, da me interpellato, mi scrisse, in data 31 gennaio 1957, che «per il peso di questi denari, considerando i rilievi fatti su esemplari anche a fior di conio, credo non sia fuori dal vero nel considerarlo compreso tra grammi 1,3 e 1,40». Cfr. anche Murari, *I presunti mezzi denari veronesi*, p. 4 e Murari, *La moneta veronese nel periodo comunale*, p. 9, n. 10.

Circa i denari dei primi due Ottoni battuti a Lucca G. Cordero di San Quintino, *Della zecca e delle monete degli antichi marchesi*, pp. 86, 99 e 101 e D. Massagli, *Della zecca e delle monete di Lucca*, pp. 24 e 26, rilevarono che i denari più pesanti tra quelli da essi analizzati si aggiravano attorno ai grammi 1,40. Il *Corpus Nummorum Italicorum* segnala denari lucchesi di Ottone II del peso di grammi 1,63-1,46-1,27.

Tenendo conto di tutte queste rilevazioni, dei dati forniti dal *Corpus Nummorum Italicorum*, della incapacità tecnica del tempo a circa 10/12 cioè di circa 830 millesimi[18]. Il fino del denaro ottoniano deve essersi quindi aggirato al di sotto dei grammi 1,2 di argento puro.

battere pezzi precisamente identici gli uni agli altri, e infine dell'usura nel tempo dei pezzi giunti fino a noi, ritengo di poter concludere per il valore arrotondato che ho indicato qui sopra nel testo.

[18] L'antico testo delle *Honorantie Civitatis Papie* che riferisce appunto circa la situazione amministrativa nel Regnum Italicum all'epoca degli Ottoni, lascia intendere che i denari battuti a quel tempo dovevano essere alla lega di 10/12 («ut nunquam faciant peiores denarios quam semper fecerunt de pondere et *argento de duodecim in decem*»: cfr. A. Solmi, *L'amministrazione finanziaria del Regno Italico*, pp. 22 e 111-127). L'abate Dionisi (*Della zecca in Verona*, ed. Zanetti, p. 306, n. 145) studiando un denaro di Ottone I battuto a Verona lo valutò a bontà di «almeno 10/12». G. Cordero di San Quintino, *Della zecca e delle monete degli antichi marchesi*, p. 101, trattando dei denari lucchesi dei primi due Ottoni rilevava che «il loro titolo per lo più non si allontana gran fatto dalle once 10 di fino argento per libbra: lo ottenni di once 9 e denari 21 in alcuni di essi di conio lucchese che feci assaggiare dalla pubblica coppella di Pisa». G. Brambilla, *Monete di Pavia*, p. 191, scriveva a sua volta che «riguardo al titolo che apparentemente (nei denari pavesi di Ottone I e II) era pressoché in tutti egualmente buono ho procurato di farne operare regolare assaggio con le migliori cautele dell'arte e ne ebbi per risultato per i denari di Ottone I il titolo di 850 millesimi».

La lega di 10/12 corrisponde a 833,33 millesimi; quella di once 9 e denari 21 corrisponde a 822,92 millesimi (cfr. Appendice II). Data la rudimentalità dei metodi di affinazione e amalgama di quei tempi per cui si davano differenze notevoli tra una parte e l'altra della pasta, dire o trovare per quelle monete un titolo di 822 o di 850 è praticamente la stessa cosa. Ritengo quindi che tutte le testimonianze ora citate si confermino fondamentalmente. Il titolo citato qui sopra nel testo è l'arrotondamento in millesimi del tenore stabilito nel testo delle citate *Honorantie*.

Completamente destituita di fondamento è invece l'affermazione di C. Desimoni in L.T. Belgrano, *Illustrazione del Registro arcivescovile*, p. 591, che i denari ottoniani avessero una lega di 958 millesimi. Del pari inattendibile la lega di 973 millesimi attribuita da Q. Perini, *Monete di Verona*, p. 49 a un denaro veronese di Ottone I. Notizie sulle zecche pavese e milanese al tempo degli Ottoni v. anche in Ph. Grierson, *Mint Output in the Tenth Century*, pp. 462-466.

Le vicende del denaro non mancarono di coinvolgere e di travolgere la sua fantomatica compagna: la lira. La gente si era ormai abituata ad usare il termine di lire per intendere «240 denari». E continuò nell'uso ormai secolare anche dopo lo slittamento del denaro. Ma se al tempo dei buoni re carolingi 240 denari (cioè «una lira») pesavano circa 410 grammi (di argento a lega 950 mill.), al tempo degli Ottoni dovevano pesare qualcosa vicino ai 330 grammi (di argento a lega 830 mill.). La lira moneta-fantasma si allontanava così dalla sua unità ponderale da cui aveva tratto la sua origine: la *lira* non era più la *libbra*.

5. Prima di procedere oltre nella nostra storia, si può dire ancora qualcosa sul significato economico della lira in questi inizi della sua carriera. La lira carolingica equivaleva a circa 409 grammi di argento a 950 millesimi. In argento fino quindi la lira carolingica rappresentava quasi 390 grammi. La lira dei primi due Ottoni doveva avvicinarsi ai 330 grammi di peso. La lega era a circa 830 millesimi, quindi il fino doveva avvicinarsi – usando cifre tonde – ai 275 grammi.

Il rapporto di valore tra l'oro e l'argento sembra tendesse a fluttuare intorno a 1:12: cioè a dire sembra che, più su, più giù, in genere occorresse dare circa dodici unità di argento per una unità di oro[19]. In termini di oro fino quindi la lira carolingica doveva equivalere – sempre arrotondando le cifre[20] – a un po' più di 30 grammi, mentre la lira ottoniana doveva equivalere ad un po' meno di 25.

[19] MM GG HH *Legum*, sectio II, *Capit. Regum Francorum* (ed. A. Boretius e V. Krause), p. 320, *Edictum Pistense* (25 giugno 864).

[20] Se si arrotondano continuamente le cifre è per indicare nel modo più immediato al lettore che tutte le conclusioni in tale materia sono e possono essere soltanto largamente approssimative.

Rispetto alle merci bisogna tener conto del fatto che in genere il potere d'acquisto dell'oro e dell'argento era allora molto più alto di quel che non sia oggi. Quindi la lira poteva comperare molti più beni e servizi di quanto le cifre citate prima potrebbero indurre a pensare a prima vista. Ai tempi di Carlo Magno, nell'Italia settentrionale con meno di mezza lira si potevano comperare 18 moggia di miglio in tempo di gravissima carestia; con mezza lira si potevano comperare due campicelli ed un bosco; con una lira si comperava una schiava; con 8 lire capitava di poter comperare cinque belle possessioni con le loro case e tutte le loro terre ed i loro boschi annessi[21].

Ai primi del scc. XI la lira aveva già cominciato a decadere. Ma rappresentava pur sempre un'entità molto rispettabile. E al proposito si può ricordare la lacrimevole storia di *Adalberto infantulo* figlio del conte Ugone al quale il padre morendo lasciò oltre a molti beni immobili un debito di sei lire (*«debitum usque ad argentum denarios bonos libras sex»*). Per questo debito il povero fanciullo dovette penare moltissimo e dopo aver girovagato col suo tutore e bussato a varie porte fu costretto a vendere 18 jugeri di terra nel modenese tra vigneti, arativi, prati e boschi e paludi ricavandone in tutto quelle sei lire con cui finalmente pagò il grosso debito paterno[22].

6. Il periodo corso tra l'età degli Ottoni e la metà del sec. XIII fu un periodo ricco di avvenimenti e profonde innovazioni. Il nostro sistema monetario assunse

[21] Hist. Patriae Monumenta, t. XIII, *Codex diplomaticus Langobardiae*, doc. 81 (col. 154, an. 806), doc. 76 (col. 146, an. 803), doc. 86 (col. 162, an. 810), doc. 84 (col. 158, an. 807).

[22] G. Tiraboschi, *Storia dell'augusta Badia di San Silvestro di Nonantola*, t. II, p. 153 (doc. 117, an. 1021).

durante quel periodo struttura e lineamenti che doveva poi mantenere quasi intatti fino agli inizi dell'età contemporanea. Sotto molti riguardi c'è più diversità tra l'ordinamento monetario ottoniano e l'ordinamento monetario della metà del Duecento che tra questo e quello esistente quasi cinque secoli e mezzo più tardi alla vigilia della Rivoluzione Francese.

Gli accadimenti più rilevanti del periodo fine sec. X-metà sec. XIII si compendiarono nei seguenti tre punti:

a) decadimento del denaro delle zecche tradizionali;

b) comparsa di numerose nuove zecche e formazione di nuove aree monetarie;

c) comparsa di nuovi tipi monetali oltre al denaro.

Ciascuno di questi tre punti merita di essere illustrato e commentato separatamente ed in dettaglio.

7. Le zecche che avevano operato nel periodo 780-1000 a nord di Roma erano state fondamentalmente quelle di Pavia, Milano, Verona, Treviso, Venezia e Lucca[23]. Treviso però aveva cessato di operare già verso la metà del sec. IX quando la Marca Trevigiana fu incorporata in quella Veronese[24]. Verona aveva forse cominciato ad operare in quella precisa epoca, però prove indubbie dell'attività della zecca veronese le abbiamo solo per il sec. X[25]. Venezia, salvo un certo

[23] Solo eccezionalmente altre zecche ebbero temporaneamente qualche attività nel primo periodo carolingico: per esempio Siena (alla cui zecca taluni attribuiscono un noto denaro di Carlo Magno, ma l'attribuzione è in verità molto dubbia), Bergamo, Parma e Pisa che forse batteva ancora al tempo di Ludovico il Pio.

[24] Q. Perini, *Monete di Treviso*, p. 32.

[25] Q. Perini, *Monete di Verona*, p. 34.

periodo nella prima metà del sec. IX, non aveva avuto mai grande importanza. Pavia e Milano avevano operato durante tutto il periodo, e delle due Pavia era stata sempre la più attiva e la più importante. La zecca di Lucca, che aveva avuto un periodo di grande attività al tempo dei Longobardi, aveva vivacchiato nel periodo carolingico riattivandosi un poco nell'età ottoniana[26].

Il fatto fondamentale circa queste zecche è che fino alla fine del sec. X esse avevano operato di conserva e, salvo rare eccezioni, esse avevano battuto i denari suppergiù su un identico piede[27].

Agli albori del sec. XI le zecche principali in attività erano quelle di Pavia, Milano, Verona e Lucca, e il grosso della circolazione monetaria a nord di Roma era rappresentato dai denari di queste quattro zecche. Il nuovo millennio vide tutte e quattro queste zecche entrare in una fase secolare d'intensa attività. Mentre il livello delle emissioni tendeva ad elevarsi, i denari emessi tendevano ad avere peso e lega sempre peggiori. I due fenomeni erano evidentemente collegati. Importa anche rilevare che nella loro generale caduta, i denari delle varie zecche perdettero presto ogni allineamento fra di loro. Tale fatto era certamente in relazione col trionfo del particolarismo politico ed amministrativo. Quali che fossero le cause del fenomeno, comunque, resta il fatto che la linea dei movimenti del denaro e quindi della sua fantomatica compagna non fu più unica. I denari pavesi, milanesi, veronesi e lucchesi si

[26] D. Massagli, *Della zecca e delle monete di Lucca*, pp. 19-24, e D. Promis, *Monete della Repubblica di Siena*, p. 13.

[27] Negli stessi contratti del tempo si trovano espressioni quali «denari de Mediolano et Papia seo de Luca» che evidentemente indicano l'equivalenza delle varie monete. Io comincio a dubitare però che già in periodo ottoniano l'allineamento non fosse più così perfetto.

differenziarono ciascuno seguendo un proprio destino. Di conseguenza i fantasmi si moltiplicarono: una volta staccatisi e differenziatisi tra di loro i denari, comparvero tante lire quanti erano i diversi denari, e cioè la lira di denari pavesi (=240 denari pavesi), la lira di denari milanesi (=240 den. mil.), la lira di denari veronesi (=240 den. veron.) e la lira di denari lucchesi (=240 den. lucch.), ciascuna lira naturalmente con un valore diverso dall'altra. La storia delle avventure della lira si frantuma così, dopo il Mille, nella storia di diverse lire, ciascuna delle quali fedelmente legata al suo proprio denaro.

8. Sul fatto che con la fine del sec. X i vari denari siano entrati in una fase di secolare decadimento e abbiano perso ogni allineamento tra di loro, non esiste dubbio alcuno. I dubbi cominciano quando si voglia precisare la cronologia e l'intensità del fenomeno. I documenti sono troppo scarsi. Le monete superstiti difficilmente databili[28]. Quindi bisogna procedere a tentoni.

Per quanto riguarda il denaro pavese, notizie preziose sono contenute negli annali del genovese Caffaro.

[28] Le monete del tempo non portavano la data della loro coniazione. Per di più esse tendevano all'immobilità del tipo: cioè a dire, per decenni e talvolta per secoli erano battute con gli stessi identici disegni. Quando poi portavano il nome di un imperatore quale «Henricus» non era mai specificato se si trattasse di Enrico I o di Enrico II o di Enrico III, ecc. Di più, in taluni casi, sulla moneta di una data città veniva impresso il nome di un imperatore o re a ringraziamento di particolari benefici ricevuti: e si continuava a imprimerne il nome per lungo tempo dopo la morte dello stesso imperatore o dello stesso re. Così per esempio a Genova, le monete portarono impresso il nome di re Corrado per molti secoli dopo la sua morte. La somma di tutte queste circostanze rende spesso difficile e talvolta impossibile la datazione della moneta medievale.

All'anno 1102 Caffaro annotava che «*moneta denariorum papiensium veterum finem habuit et alia incepta novae monetae brunitorum fuit*». Poi all'anno 1115 annotava che i denari «*bruni prioris novae monetae mense octubris finem habuerunt et... alia moneta minorum brunitorum incepta fuit*». Poiché sino al 1138, anno in cui re Corrado concesse ai Genovesi di battere moneta propria, la moneta prevalente sulla piazza genovese fu sempre la moneta pavese, gli storici sono d'accordo nel ritenere che:

a) *bruni* e *brunetti* erano ancora denari pavesi;

b) l'appellativo di *bruni* e *brunetti* derivava dal peggioramento della lega dei denari che dava loro un aspetto più scuro;

c) poiché posteriormente alle date indicate dal Caffaro si ritrovano ancora citate nei contratti genovesi le vecchie monete, la cronologia del Caffaro non vuole indicare che una moneta sostituì l'altra, ma piuttosto che la zecca pavese cessò di battere un tipo di denaro per passare ad un altro[29].

L'esame numismatico dei pezzi che ci sono conservati conferma indubitabilmente il declino del denaro pavese. La massa dei pezzi pavesi appartenenti al periodo 1000-1150 si differenzia nettamente secondo il Brambilla[30] in quattro gruppi distinti dalle caratteristiche indicate nel Prospetto 1.

I pezzi che cadono nel gruppo *a* sono facilmente riconoscibili come denari di Ottone III (983-1002), Enrico II (1002-1024) e Corrado II (1024-1039).

[29] Per tutto quanto precede cfr. P.F. Casaretto, *La moneta genovese*, pp. 8-14.

[30] Cfr. C. Brambilla, *Monete di Pavia*, pp. 224-235. Talune delle attribuzioni specifiche del Brambilla vanno corrette tenendo conto del *Corpus Nummorum Italicorum*: ma questi elementi di dettaglio non toccano le distinzioni fondamentali citate nel testo.

Ma difficile è l'attribuzione dei denari dei gruppi *b*, *c*, *d*. I pezzi di questi tre gruppi sono immobili nel tipo e se pur portano tutti l'indicazione di *Henricus* non indicano mai se si tratti di Enrico III (1039-1056), di Enrico IV (1056-1106) o di Enrico V (1106-1125). Cercando di mettere d'accordo i risultati d'indagine numismatica con le indicazioni di Caffaro, il Brambilla ed il Desimoni avanzarono l'ipotesi che i pezzi del gruppo *c* fossero i *bruni* (quindi posteriori al 1102) e i pezzi del gruppo *d* fossero i *brunetti* (quindi posteriori al 1115). Ma si tratta sempre di ipotesi. La confusione poi è aumentata dal fatto che i documenti dell'epoca indicano l'esistenza di pezzi da mezzo denaro e fanno nascere quindi il sospetto che qualcuno dei gruppi *a*, *b*, *c*, *d* rappresenti non *danari* ma *medaglie* (mezzi denari)[31].

L'aria di mistero che circonda la storia del denaro pavese si dipana poco dopo la metà del sec. XII quando due diversi documenti, l'uno del 1162 e l'altro del 1164, permettono di calcolare che il denaro pavese doveva contenere in quegli anni circa 0,2 grammi di argento fino[32]. Così, se possono sussistere numerosi

[31] Così per esempio Desimoni ritiene che lo slittamento effettivo del denaro pavese si sia compiuto in tre tempi segnati dal passaggio dal gruppo *a* al gruppo *b* e al gruppo *c*. Ma ritiene che i pezzi del gruppo *d* non rappresentino denari ulteriormente sviliti bensì frazioni dei pezzi del gruppo *c*. Brambilla ritiene invece che lo slittamento del denaro fosse contenuto nel passaggio dal gruppo *a* al gruppo *b* e che i pezzi del gruppo *c* altro non fossero che gli spezzati («*medaglie*» o «*oboli*») dei denari del gruppo *a*, ed i pezzi del gruppo *d* gli spezzati dei denari del gruppo *b*. Per tutto questo cfr. C. Brambilla, *Monete di Pavia*, pp. 230-238.

[32] In una convenzione tra Federico I ed i Piacentini dell'11 maggio 1162 un marco di argento fino figura equivalere a 960 denari pavesi. C. Brambilla, *Monete di Pavia*, pp. 276-278, con buoni argomenti, ritiene che il marco di cui si tratta fosse il marco di Colonia. Questo marco equivaleva allora a circa 215 dei nostri grammi. Da ciò si deduce che il denaro pavese doveva equivalere a grammi 0,224 di argento fino.

PROSPETTO 1. *Caratteristiche dei denari pavesi del periodo 1000-1150*

Gruppo	Peso massimo (grammi)	Lega (mill.)	Fino (grammi)
a	1,3-1,4	800	1-1,1
b	1,3-1,4	600	0,8
c	1,1	500	0,5
d	1	430	0,4

I dati contenuti in questo prospetto sono tratti da C. Brambilla, *Monete di Pavia*, pp. 224-235.

dubbi sui tempi ed i gradi del decadimento del denaro pavese, non vi sono dubbi né sull'esistenza del fenomeno né sulla sua intensità complessiva: ai primi del sec. XI il denaro pavese conteneva ancora circa un grammo di argento fino; poco dopo la metà del sec. XII s'era ridotto a poco più di grammi 0,2. È impor-

In una convenzione del 1164 fra lo stesso Federico I, i Genovesi e Barisone giudice di Arborea si dichiara l'eguaglianza di un marco d'argento con 1032 denari pavesi. Poiché anche in questo caso sembra si trattasse del marco di Colonia, risulterebbe che il denaro pavese doveva equivalere a grammi 0,21 di argento fino.

È evidente che la differenza tra i due documenti citati è del tutto insignificante. Circa il testo e la datazione esatta della convenzione tra Federico I, i Genovesi e Barisone cfr. P.F. Casaretto, *La moneta genovese*, p. 165, n. 1. Va peraltro notato che le parità calcolate in base alle due convenzioni federiciane ora citate, rappresentano quel che qui avanti nell'Appendice I si è definita la parità ß. Questa parità, come si dice nell'appendice stessa, tende a dare risultati più alti della parità metallica calcolata sulla base dell'intrinseco del denaro. Per questa ragione, dato che finora si era calcolata la parità metallica del denaro sulla base del suo intrinseco, nel testo si è arrotondata per difetto la parità, portandola a grammi 0,2. È da rilevare che riferendosi tutti questi calcoli al sec. XII si è adottata l'equivalenza di 215 grammi per un marco di Colonia. Il Brambilla ed il Casaretto assunsero l'equivalenza di gr. 233,86 ma questa equivalenza vale solo per i secoli seguenti. Cfr. A. Luschin von Ebengreuth, *Allgemeine Münzkunde*, pp. 163, 164 e 167.

PROSPETTO 2. *Caratteristiche dei denari veronesi del periodo 1050-1150*

Gruppo	Peso massimo (grammi)	Lega (mill.)	Fino (grammi)
a	0,6	510	0,3
b	0,6	260	0,16
c	0,6	260	0,16
d	0,45	229	0,1

I dati contenuti in questo prospetto sono tratti da O. Murari, *Denari veronesi di un ripostiglio del sec. XII*, pp. 19-27.

tante rilevare che il denaro milanese aveva subito più o meno la stessa sorte[33].

Le difficoltà che si incontrano nello studio dei movimenti del denaro pavese ricompaiono quando si cerca di seguire i contemporanei movimenti del denaro veronese. Un'analisi condotta dal Murari sui pezzi di un tesoro del sec. XII e su altri pezzi già noti nello stesso periodo fornisce però anche in questo caso elementi che permettono almeno qualche generica valutazione. Secondo l'analisi del Murari i denari veronesi del periodo 1050-1150 si differenziano secondo quattro gruppi, ciascuno dei quali s'individua per le caratteristiche indicate nel Prospetto 2.

I denari del gruppo *a* vengono attribuiti al periodo di Enrico IV (1056-1106) ed Enrico V (1106-1125); i denari del gruppo *b* al periodo tra il 1125 e il 1152; ed i denari del gruppo *d* al periodo di Federico I (1152-1183). Incerta rimane l'attribuzione dei denari del gruppo *c* che peraltro si differenziano da quelli del gruppo *b* praticamente solo per certe caratteristiche estrinseche di tipo.

[33] Un esame al crogiolo e alla bilancia effettuato da B. Biondelli, *La zecca e le monete di Milano*, p. 64, su 240 denari milanesi di Enrico IV provò che ciascuno di quei denari conteneva in media grammi 0,22 di argento fino.

Come si vede le notizie e le attribuzioni sono troppo vaghe per permettere confronti precisi fra i movimenti della moneta pavese e i movimenti della moneta veronese. Però anche nel caso della moneta veronese come nel caso della moneta pavese, il senso generale dei movimenti non lascia ombra di dubbi. La moneta veronese tra la metà del sec. XI e la metà del sec. XII decadde progressivamente: il denaro che alla metà del sec. XI conteneva approssimativamente grammi 0,3 di argento fino, dopo la metà del sec. XII non doveva contenere approssimativamente più di grammi 0,1[34].

Circa i movimenti della moneta lucchese purtroppo si sa ancora meno che per i movimenti della pavese e della veronese. Però nel 1164 un documento fornisce taluni elementi – indirettamente confermati da altre fonti – in base ai quali si riesce a calcolare che attorno a quell'anno il denaro lucchese doveva contenere circa 0,35 grammi di argento fino[35].

[34] Se l'intrinseco del denaro veronese era di 0,1 grammi di fino, la parità della lira veronese era di circa 24 grammi. Nel 1154 come ancora nel 1203 la lira di denari veneziani (*libra denariorum venetialium*) equivaleva a poco meno di 24 grammi di argento. Documenti degli anni corsi tra il 1172 ed il 1194 dimostrano che la lira veneziana era considerata equivalente alla lira veronese. Cfr. L. Buenger Robbert, *The Venetian Money Market*, pp. 34 e 58.

[35] Nella convenzione stipulata nel 1164 tra Federico I, i Genovesi e Barisone (convenzione già citata qui addietro alla nota 32) si dichiara che un marco d'argento equivaleva a 48 soldi (=576 denari «lucenses de Pisa vel Luca»: G. Cordero di San Quintino, *Cenni intorno al commercio dei Lucchesi*, p. 97). Gli studiosi sono in genere d'accordo nel ritenere che il marco sia quello di Colonia, equivalente a circa 215 dei nostri grammi (cfr. P.F. Casaretto, *La moneta genovese*, pp. 169-172 e C. Desimoni, *La décroissance graduelle du denier*, p. 72; il Desimoni cade però nell'errore di attribuire la convenzione al 1172 anziché al 1164 e sia il Desimoni che il Casaretto cadono nell'errore di attribuire al marco di Colonia del sec. XII un peso di

Nell'insieme non si può certo dire che l'analisi dei movimenti monetari dell'Italia centro-settentrionale nei secc. XI e XII quale ce la permettono i pochi, magri, reticenti dati superstiti sia molto soddisfacente. Non occorre un grande sforzo di fantasia per immaginare l'espressione di stupito disgusto che la lettura di queste note deve provocare sul volto della maggior parte degli economisti abituati a maneggiare il materiale statistico disponibile per l'età contemporanea. Purtuttavia, qualcosa si può dire: e cioè che in base al contenuto di argento fino dei denari, poco dopo la metà del sec. XII, la lira lucchese avrebbe dovuto equivalere a un po' meno di 85 grammi di argento fino, la lira pavese a un po' meno di 50 grammi e la lira veronese a un po' meno di 25 grammi. A quel tempo però il denaro era sceso a leghe tanto basse (cioè: era talmente cresciuta la proporzione del rame mischiato all'argento) che un computo esatto dovrebbe cercare di tener conto anche del valore del rame contenuto nel denaro[36]. Purtroppo non si hanno dati soddisfacenti sul valore del

gr. 233,86 invece che di circa 215 come indicato qui addietro nella nota 32). Se ne deriva che il denaro lucchese doveva equivalere a grammi 0,373 di argento fino. Per le ragioni già addotte qui addietro nella nota 32 circa i metodi di calcolazione delle parità metalliche, la parità citata qui sopra nel testo è stata arrotondata per difetto.

Altri documenti del 1200 testimoniano che tra il 1160 ed il 1200 il denaro lucchese aveva avuto il proprio intrinseco di fino diminuito ulteriormente per circa il 50 per cento (cfr. D. Herlihy, *Pisan Coinage*, p. 149). Questo dato porterebbe a calcolare una parità metallica del denaro pisano tra la fine del Millecento ed i primi del Duecento di poco meno di 0,2 grammi. Altri documenti ancora testimoniano che tra la fine del sec. XII e gli inizi del XIII un marco di Colonia equivaleva a 1.200 denari pisani, il che darebbe una parità del denaro di circa 0,19 grammi (A. Castellani, *Nuovi testi fiorentini*, pp. 869-870). Come si vede tutte le varie testimonianze concordano e portano, per vie diverse, ai medesimi risultati.

[36] Cfr. qui avanti, *Appendice I*.

rame a quel tempo. In via ipotetica si può peraltro ritenere che le parità argentee citate dovrebbero venir aumentate al massimo di qualche grammo. Nel complesso credo che non si vada molto discosti dal vero se, senz'altra pretesa che quella di una larga approssimazione, si afferma che, rispetto alla lira ottoniana di due secoli prima equivalente a circa 275 grammi di argento fino, alla metà del sec. XII le lire lucchese, pavese e veronese accusavano un deterioramento nell'intrinseco dell'ordine del 70-80 per cento.

9. Le cause di questo generale decadimento erano fondamentalmente insite nei movimenti generali dell'economia dell'Italia centro-settentrionale del tempo. Tra gli inizi del sec. XI e la fine del sec. XII la popolazione aumentò e si verificò contemporaneamente un deciso processo di sviluppo economico. La divisione del lavoro si accentuò ed il paese fu spinto da forme e strutture di economia quasi naturale verso forme e strutture di economia sempre più decisamente monetaria. La moneta metallica tese a divenire, soprattutto nei centri cittadini, il mezzo usuale di scambio e di pagamento. Conseguenza di questi movimenti di fondo fu una decisa tendenza espansiva della domanda di moneta. Di contro l'offerta di metalli preziosi si dimostrò anelastica ed incapace di tener dietro all'incremento della domanda di argento a scopo monetario. Per quanto in quei secoli ci si desse a frugare nelle viscere della terra e ad attivare nuove miniere, l'incremento della produzione argentifera si suppone sia rimasto entro limiti modesti. In tali condizioni, tre erano le soluzioni possibili: *a*) trovare sostituti alla moneta metallica nelle tradizionali forme della «moneta primitiva»; *b*) trovare sistemi e metodi di pagamento evoluti che facessero risparmiare

i rari mezzi di scambio esistenti ed aumentassero l'efficienza del sistema monetario; *c*) svilire l'intrinseco della moneta metallica aumentando il numero dei pezzi in circolazione.

Praticamente tutte e tre le soluzioni furono tentate. Per quanto riguarda le soluzioni di tipo *a*, sappiamo che in quei secoli, soprattutto nei centri mercantili maggiori, si usò del pepe o di altre merci del genere come sostituti della moneta metallica. Per quanto riguarda le soluzioni di tipo *b*, bisogna ammettere che devono risalire a quell'epoca i primi, rudimentalissimi anonimi sviluppi di pratiche che si trasformeranno poi in istituti ed organizzazioni bancari e creditizi. Ma nell'insieme i metodi escogitati di tipo *a* si dimostrarono inadatti e contro la tendenza dei tempi, e quelli di tipo *b* insufficienti. La società italiana dovette ripiegare sulla soluzione *c*. Il denaro e la sua inseparabile compagna – la lira – furono progressivamente sacrificati.

Quale fosse in pratica il meccanismo attraverso cui la pressione dell'aumentata domanda di moneta fece progressivamente svilire il denaro, con precisione non lo sappiamo. Però lo si può arguire per via indiretta, sulla base di quel che sappiamo per i secoli immediatamente successivi. Per quanto la gente del tempo non avesse concetti precisi e raffinati in materia di domanda di moneta, massa di circolante, velocità di circolazione e cose del genere, tuttavia arrivava a capire quel che veniva chiamato allora «*penuria argenti*» o «*carestia monetae*». E una volta che le autorità avvertivano questa «*carestia*», autorizzavano la zecca a coniare, da uno stesso peso di argento, un maggior numero di pezzi. Non va trascurato poi il fatto che ogni decisione in senso inflazionistico era facilmente sollecitata e caldeggiata dalle zecche. Quegli istituti – per lo più appaltati – operarono per tutto il Medioevo come vere e proprie imprese private, col criterio del profitto aziendale. Più pezzi coniavano e più guadagnavano. Svilendo l'intrinseco del denaro, si dava a chi portava argento alla zecca un maggior numero di denari. E l'«illusione monetaria» doveva avere l'effetto di accelerare l'afflusso alla zecca di metallo tesoreggiato.

10. In effetti il decadimento intrinseco del denaro – lo si è già accennato – si accompagnò ad una forte espansione delle emissioni. Bisogna ammettere che purtroppo su questo altro fenomeno non abbiamo alcun dato quantitativo, né c'è da illudersi di poterne mai rintracciare. A quei tempi non c'erano uffici di statistica che si occupassero di queste cose. Ma che il fenomeno si sia verificato e per di più in proporzioni ragguardevoli, questo è fuori di ogni dubbio e ne abbiamo prova palpabile nello straordinario numero di denari «enriciani» di Pavia, Verona e Lucca che sono pervenuti sino a noi. Chi ha una pur minima dimestichezza con la numismatica sa che gli «enriciani» sono pezzi di scarso pregio non solo perché sono minuscoli, malformi e vili di metallo, ma anche perché sono straordinariamente comuni. L'inflazione dei secc. XI e XII fa sentire così attraverso i secoli le sue ultime ripercussioni sui listini dei prezzi dei numismatici moderni.

L'espansione della massa monetaria non si limitò del resto alla sola espansione delle coniazioni delle zecche di Pavia, Milano, Verona e Lucca. Un po' in conseguenza del trionfo politico ed amministrativo, ma soprattutto in conseguenza della generale «fame di moneta», una dopo l'altra, numerose città dell'Italia centro-settentrionale cominciarono ad aprire zecche ed a battere moneta. Ascoli, Parma e Susa già nel sec. XI. Genova dopo il 1138. Asti e Piacenza verso il 1140. Pisa prima del 1151. Cremona verso il 1155. Volterra verso la stessa epoca. Ancona prima del 1170. Siena verso il 1180[37]. Brescia verso il 1184. Bologna dopo il 1191. Arezzo prima del 1196. Ferrara e Mantova prima della fine del sec. XII. Firenze ed Acqui tra la fine del sec. XII e gli inizi del XIII. Fermo nel 1220. Reggio Emilia nel 1233. Bergamo forse verso la stessa epoca[38]. Modena nel 1242. Vercelli nel 1255. Ciamberì prima del 1263. Torino nel 1297[39].

11. La caduta del denaro fu a mio avviso più un bene che un male. Sostanzialmente permise alla società italiana del tempo di evitare che la anelasticità

[37] D. Herlihy, *Pisan Coinage*, p. 155, scrive che «in 1193 for the first time the money of Siena herself is mentioned». Ma poi, con lettera personale del 16 novembre 1955, lo stesso autore gentilmente mi comunicava che «there is a reference to Sienese coinage about ten years before the earliest reference I found at the time. The reference is in Schneider, Regestum Senense».

Nello stesso articolo (p. 159) l'affermazione dello Herlihy che la moneta di Volterra fu coniata per la prima volta nel 1165 non è esatta: ciò che sappiamo è che a quella data la moneta di Volterra correva già. Ma non sappiamo esattamente in che anno cominciò a correre: cfr. A. Lisini, *Le monete e le zecche di Volterra*, pp. 259-261.

[38] Federico I concedette al Vescovo di Bergamo, Gherardo, il diritto di battere moneta nel 1156. Ma sembra che tale concessione rimanesse per qualche tempo senza effetto e che a Bergamo si cominciasse effettivamente a battere moneta solo nella prima metà del sec. XIII, forse verso il 1236-38 (cfr. A. Mazzi, *La convenzione monetaria del 1254*, introduz. e p. 63; O. Murari, *Le monete di Bergamo*, p. 26, n. 5).

[39] In diversi casi una città non cominciò a battere moneta proprio subito nell'anno stesso in cui le fu concesso dall'autorità imperiale il diritto di zecca. Così per esempio Modena ebbe nel 1226 il diploma imperiale che le concedeva il diritto di batter moneta: ma in pratica l'apertura della zecca modenese non si ebbe sino al 1242 (A. Crespellani, *Zecca di Modena*, pp. 3-4). Per Bergamo vedi qui addietro nota 38. Sopra nel testo, quando mi è stato possibile, ho citato la data dell'effettiva apertura della zecca cittadina anziché la data del riconoscimento giuridico del diritto di zecca.

dell'offerta dei metalli preziosi e la mancanza di una efficiente organizzazione creditizia esercitassero una pressione deflazionistica che avrebbe strozzato il processo di sviluppo economico. Tuttavia essa non fu una soluzione ragionata di una politica monetaria ben chiara e logicamente pensata. Rappresentò piuttosto il risultato spontaneo e incontrollato di forze varie e di reazioni empiriche. Ed è possibile che, alla lunga, il decadimento del denaro cominciasse a destare in diversi circoli preoccupazioni e riflessioni amare. D'altra parte è certo che dopo la metà del sec. XII, il denaro, di qualsiasi zecca esso fosse, s'era ridotto a proporzioni quanto mai minuscole. Credo che chiunque oggi veda in un museo un denaro della seconda metà del Millecento si chieda come mai quella gente potesse fare continuamente uso di pezzi tanto scomodi perché tanto piccoli e tanto fragili. Quel che io credo si chieda oggi la gente che visita i musei deve esserselo chiesto anche la gente del tempo, perché alla metà del sec. XII si assiste a tentativi di riforma che mirano evidentemente a reintrodurre in circolazione moneta più forte. L'esigenza era tanto più avvertita quanto più, in conseguenza del processo stesso di sviluppo economico, si facevano ogni giorno più frequenti transazioni di importanza sempre più elevata. Per i grossi affari il minuscolo e fragile denaro doveva dimostrarsi sempre più inadeguato. S'aggiunga che città come Genova, Venezia e Pisa avevano preso parte attiva nel commercio internazionale assumendovi un ruolo di deciso predominio. Per i loro mercanti, nei traffici in porti e con paesi stranieri, il minuscolo denaro di cattivo argento doveva essere un ben poco adatto mezzo di scambio[40].

[40] Per esempio in una accurata indagine sul mercato monetario veneziano nel sec. XII L. Buenger ha appurato che gli operatori

Questi i presupposti delle riforme monetarie che cominciarono poco dopo il 1150 e che culminarono nel 1252.

12. Si cominciò in Lombardia, dove la riforma ebbe colore politico e si inserì nella lotta tra Federico I e i comuni lombardi. Forse Federico vedeva nella restaurazione della moneta un simbolo della vagheggiata restaurazione dell'autorità imperiale. Sta di fatto che tra il 1155 e il 1161, dopo aver intimato a Milano di non battere più moneta, fece coniare – forse nella sua zecca di Noceto sotto la sorveglianza di un *Radulphus theutonicus* – i *denarios imperatoris* – detti quindi volgarmente *denari imperiali* – che dovevano contenere poco meno di grammi 0,5 di argento fino al pezzo[41]. Rispetto al denaro pavese e milanese del

veneziani dovevano ricorrere costantemente agli iperperi d'oro bizantini come usuale mezzo di scambio e pagamento nelle transazioni internazionali e all'ingrosso. Analoghe osservazioni possono venir fatte scorrendo le imbreviature dei notai genovesi.

C'è anche da rilevare che il denaro argenteo, scaduto com'era nel proprio intrinseco, finiva con l'essere un cattivo ambasciatore della nuova potenza economica delle città italiane. Cfr. al proposito la storiella che circolava tra i toscani nel Trecento e riportata da R.S. Lopez, *Back to Gold*, pp. 237-238.

[41] Circa il peso del denaro cfr. B. Biondelli, *La zecca e le monete di Milano*, p. 64 e P.F. Casaretto, *La moneta genovese*, p. 173.

Circa la data in cui comparve per la prima volta il denaro imperiale, c'è una tale complicata storia di opinioni corse al proposito che è necessario chiarire un po' le cose per evitare la ripetizione di inesatti luoghi comuni.

Alla metà del sec. XVIII, il padre A. Fumagalli, *Le vicende di Milano* (p. 220 della ristampa del 1854), attirò l'attenzione degli eruditi su un passo dello storico fredericiano Acerbo Morena in cui si dice che nel Borgo di Noceto, dove già si coniava *monetam imperatoris* «Radulphus Theutonicus» soprastante alla zecca fece costruire nell'estate del 1163 una grossa torre per conservarvi il tesoro imperiale (cfr. MGH. SS. XVIII, ed. G.H. Pertz, p. 641). Il tempo, il denaro imperiale conteneva circa il doppio di argento fino. La nuova moneta inizialmente non riuscì

Fumagalli avanzò l'ipotesi – del resto non documentata – che questa zecca di Noceto cui faceva cenno il Morena fosse sorta «non prima dell'eccidio di Milano cagionato dalle armi di Federico l'anno 1162»: in quell'anno – sempre secondo il Fumagalli – si sarebbe data così «esecuzione alla sentenza decretata da lui (Federico) sette anni prima contro i milanesi» (cioè la perdita del diritto di zecca).

Le osservazioni dell'erudito padre cistercense colpirono G.A. Zanetti il quale nel 1783 (nota 11 apposta alla storia «Della zecca di Guastalla» del padre I. Affò in *Delle monete d'Italia*, III, p. 8) le collegò con la comparsa del denaro imperiale ed avanzò l'ipotesi (basata in fondo sul solo fatto che allo Zanetti non risultavano accenni o citazioni di denari imperiali avanti il 1163) che il denaro imperiale fosse stato coniato per la prima volta a Noceto nel 1163. Continua lo Zanetti: il Barbarossa aveva aperto la zecca imperiale in antitesi alla zecca della devastata Milano. Così dicendo però lo Zanetti formulava una seconda ipotesi del tutto gratuita: che cioè la zecca di Noceto fosse stata aperta nel 1163. Il testo del Morena – ripeto – riferisce soltanto che nel 1163 fu costruita a Noceto una grossa torre per la custodia del tesoro imperiale; lascia intendere che a Noceto esisteva una zecca; ma non dice affatto che la zecca fu aperta nel 1163, anzi lascia chiaramente intendere che quando la torre fu costruita la zecca esisteva già.

Le ipotesi dello Zanetti sedussero G.R. Carli (che non fu quindi il primo a sostenere questa tesi come erroneamente scrisse il Biondelli, *La zecca e le monete di Milano*, p. 58). Carli ancora nell'ediz. mantovana del 1754, I, pp. 350-351 non aveva saputo dire altro al proposito se non che «nel duodecimo secolo monete vi (a Milano) si stamparono col nome di imperiali». Ma nella ristampa delle sue *Opere* (Milano, 1784, t. V, pp. 9-12) dopo aver osservato che «Acerbo Morena fu se non erro il primo che nominasse denari imperiali» concluse che «i denari detti furono imperiali perché coniati in nome e in proprietà dell'Imperadore Federigo nella propria di lui zecca eretta in Noceto vicino a Milano dopo la distruzione di detta città».

In seguito a questa presa di posizione del Carli, G.A. Zanetti, rieditando due anni dopo (1786) nel tomo IV della sua raccolta *Delle monete d'Italia* il lavoro di C. Doneda (*Della zecca e delle monete di Brescia*), alla nota 287 di p. 417 scrisse più decisamente che mai che «già fu da noi accennata l'epoca di questa moneta (denaro imperiale) e attribuita al 1163 quando il suddetto imperatore (Federico I) aperse una zecca nel borgo di Noceto. Noi ora ci confermiamo in questo a rimpiazzare completamente l'antica: denari pavesi e denari milanesi continuarono a circolare a fianco de-

sentimento leggendo che il signor conte Carli nella ristampa delle sue opere concorse di buon grado nella nostra opinione».

Col crisma dello Zanetti e del Carli, la tesi che il denaro imperiale fosse nato nel 1163 a Noceto dilagò. La accettò nel 1789 il padre I. Affò, «Della zecca e moneta parmigiana» in G.A. Zanetti, *Dalle monete d'Italia*, V, p. 27; la ripeté incondizionatamente B. Biondelli, *La zecca e le monete di Milano*, p. 58; la seguì P.F. Casaretto, *La moneta genovese*, p. 173 e il Repossi, *Milano e la sua zecca*, p. 142, definendo il denaro imperiale scrisse che «da Acerbo Morena per la prima volta venne accennato tale nome di moneta».

Alla fine del secolo scorso C. Brambilla, *Monete di Pavia*, p. 272, deve aver cominciato a nutrire qualche sospetto sulla faccenda, perché, pur esprimendosi in maniera molto cauta e dubitativa, sembrò propendere per il 1161 come data della nascita del denaro imperiale. G.B. Salvioni, *La moneta bolognese*, pp. 157-158, andò molto più in là e sulla base di taluni diplomi federiciani ritenne di poter anticipare la prima coniazione del denaro imperiale al 1155. Va rilevato però al proposito che anche le affermazioni del Salvioni sono un po' pericolose: è vero che ci sono i diplomi, ma non sappiamo quando le disposizioni contenute nei diplomi siano state mandate in effetto. Comunque qualche decennio più tardi P. Falconi, *Le monete piacentine*, I, p. 33, accennava a documenti piacentini del 1162 in cui si parlava esplicitamente già di denari imperiali.

Facciamo il punto: non c'è nessun motivo di dubitare che esistesse una zecca imperiale a Noceto; è molto verosimile che – data la breve distanza – tale zecca di Noceto fosse stata aperta da Federico I in antitesi polemica alla zecca comunale di Milano; è altamente probabile che a Noceto si battessero i cosiddetti denari imperiali; non è provato che i denari imperiali venissero battuti solo a Noceto; è certo che i denari imperiali furono coniati prima del 1163. La nascita del denaro imperiale va quindi retrodatata: ma a quando?

L.C. Bollea, *Documenti degli archivi di Pavia*, p. 28, doc. 18, pubblicò agli inizi di questo secolo un documento pavese datato 22 febbr. 1153 con il seguente testo: «... argenti denariorum bonorum papiensium solidos vigintiquattuor imperialium...». I denari imperiali vanno quindi considerati come nati già prima del 1153? Tenendo conto del fatto che Federico I fu incoronato re dei Romani e di Germania il 9 marzo 1152 e venne in Italia solo nel 1154 (la prima dieta di Roncaglia è del 5 dicembre 1154), mi pareva però un po' strano che egli avesse fatto battere i denari imperiali in Italia in angli imperiali al cambio di due pavesi o milanesi per ogni imperiale. Ma ebbe in ogni modo un notevole successo. Le stesse zecche di Milano, di Pavia e di altre città lombarde, alleate o nemiche del Barbarossa, si misero a battere denari di tipo imperiale. Un cronista del tempo dice che già nel 1175 «*imperiales mediolanenses currebant per totam Ytaliam*»[42]. E in prosieguo di tempo l'imperiale prevalse poi di gran lunga su ogni altro denaro divenendo nel corso del sec. XIII il mezzo di scambio e l'unità di conto più usata nella regione lombarda e nelle zone finitime.

Qualche decennio dopo la riforma monetaria imperiale, una riforma analoga era tentata con successo a Venezia e a Genova. A una data imprecisabile tra la

titesi a quelli dei comuni a soli pochi mesi dalla sua incoronazione e prima ancora di venire nella penisola, a meno di ammettere che a battere per primo gli imperiali fosse stato qualche altro imperatore. Ho allora pregato il dr. G. Aleati di Pavia di controllare sul documento originale (tuttora conservato in Biblioteca Universitaria Pavia, pergamene diverse, n. 5) se la lezione data dal Bollea era esatta. Il dr. Aleati mi informò gentilmente che nel documento in questione non si parla affatto di imperiali: il Bollea interpretò erroneamente per «*imperialium*» l'abbreviazione paleografica di «ideo pro».

In conclusione: in attesa che qualche scoperta archivistica chiarisca meglio la questione, mi pare che alla luce dei documenti conosciuti e della logica della storia politica di quegli anni, si può soltanto dire che i denari imperiali devono essere stati battuti per la prima volta in Lombardia (a Noceto, forse) da Federico I in qualche anno tra il 1152 ed il 1162.

Del tutto destituita di fondamento ed inesatta l'informazione riportata da E. Martinori, *La moneta*, p. 102, che «l'appellativo imperiale è aggiunto al denaro... dopo che Federico I nella pace di Costanza del 1183 e col Trattato di Reggio ebbe dato ai Milanesi e confermato tutte le regalie dell'Impero e con esse il privilegio di zecca».

[42] RR II SS t. IX (ed. G. Bonazzi) (Città di Castello, 1902), *Chronicon Parmense*, p. 6, lin. 14. La vecchia edizione muratoriana (col. 762) dava erroneamente la data 1165 invece che 1175 e B. Biondelli, *La zecca e le monete di Milano*, p. 58, n. 3, traendo dalla edizione muratoriana, cita appunto la data 1165.

fine del sec. XII e gli inizi del XIII[43] la zecca di Venezia cominciò a battere un pezzo di buon argento a 965 millesimi al peso di circa grammi 2,2 (contro i 250 mill. di lega e i grammi 0,36 di peso del denaro allora corrente). Tale nuovo pezzo, chiamato *grosso* o anche *ducato d'argento* o anche *matapan*, corse allora per 26 denari locali (detti poi per contrapposizione *piccoli*)[44]. Suppergiù nello stesso torno di tempo[45] la zecca genovese iniziava a coniare un pezzo di buon argento a circa 960 millesimi (contro i 300 mill. circa del denaro del tempo) e dal peso di poco meno di un grammo e mezzo. Tale pezzo – chiamato *grosso* – equivale a 4 denari genovesi del tempo. A differenza della riforma imperiale la riforma veneziana e genovese non mirava a introdurre polemicamente un denaro rivalutato in sostituzione o in concorrenza del denaro corrente. Non

[43] La prima coniazione del grosso veneziano è ricordata dai cronisti Martino da Canale, Andrea Dandolo e Marin Sanudo, ma le testimonianze non sono concordi circa la data dell'avvenimento. Variamente interpretando le testimonianze del tempo, taluni studiosi moderni hanno suggerito il 1193, altri il 1194, altri ancora il 1202. R. Cessi, *Problemi monetari*, p. XVIII, n. 2 e P. Grierson, *La moneta veneziana*, p. 79, favoriscono la data del 1202. L. Buenger Robbert, *The Venetian Money Market*, p. 44, favorisce invece la data del 1194.

[44] Cfr. per tutti N. Papadopoli, *Le monete di Venezia*, parte I, pp. 84-86, e R. Cessi, *Problemi monetari veneziani*, pp. XVIII-XXI. La lega del grosso veneziano e forse anche quella del grosso genovese tendevano a imitare la buona lega del denaro *sterlino inglese* che per essersi mantenuto stabile nei secoli (cfr. cap. II, par. 7) era giunto a fama internazionale.

[45] C. Desimoni, *Tavole dei valori*, p. 514 e *Tavole descrittive*, p. XXXV, fissa attorno al 1172 la data d'apparizione del grosso genovese. Ma l'unico sostegno della sua tesi sono alcune calcolazioni (*Le prime monete d'argento*, pp. 181-182) decisamente infondate perché il peso del marco di Colonia che il Desimoni adotta non è quello che il marco di Colonia aveva a quel tempo (cfr. qui addietro note 32 e 35). Inoltre il documento su cui si fonda il Desimoni è del 1167 e non del 1172. Prove indubbie dell'esistenza di grossi genovesi le abbiamo per ora solo per i primi decenni del sec. XIII.

annebbiati da preoccupazioni politiche, i Veneziani e i Genovesi avevano capito che ciò di cui l'economia abbisognava non era una rivalutazione del denaro, ma piuttosto la creazione di un multiplo del denaro che non doveva sostituire ma affiancarsi a quest'ultimo: non la deflazione ma un più razionale sistema di mezzi di pagamento. L'aver capito che la nuova unità non doveva sostituire il denaro rese possibile ai Veneziani e ai Genovesi di fare in maniera che il loro nuovo pezzo rappresentasse un valore unitario proporzionatamente più alto rispetto al denaro locale di quanto fosse l'imperiale rispetto al denaro pavese o milanese.

In Toscana, in un primo tempo, si cercò la soluzione di tipo federiciano. Verso il 1192 Pisa, Volterra e Siena coniarono un nuovo denaro che doveva rappresentare una rivalutazione del denaro allora corrente nelle città toscane perché ne imitava il peso (circa 0,8 grammi) ma ne migliorava sensibilmente la lega (800 millesimi invece di 200)[46]. Ma i fatti devono aver dimostrato ai toscani che quella non era la via buona da seguire. Nei primi decenni del secolo successivo il generale orientamento è nella direzione dell'esempio genovese e veneziano. Siena coniò un grosso verso il 1220. Pisa la imitò qualche anno più tardi. Poi, dopo il 1230 più o meno tutte le zecche toscane cominciarono a battere grossi[47]. Documenti del 1245 e del 1249 indicano che il grosso delle zecche toscane doveva contenere circa 2,3 grammi di argento fino e valeva 12 denari pisani o lucchesi del tempo[48].

[46] Cfr. D. Herlihy, *Pisan Coinage*, p. 156, il quale però scrive di un peso di grammi 0,7 al pezzo. In seguito ad ulteriori rilievi e tenendo conto dell'usura dei pezzi io sono invece propenso a ritenere un peso di grammi 0,8.

[47] D. Herlihy, *Pisan Coinage*, p. 165.

[48] A. Castellani, *Nuovi testi fiorentini*, pp. 869-870.

L'ultimo, rivoluzionario atto di tutto questo secolare processo di riforme ed innovazioni si compì nel 1252. Ormai tutti avevano preso la strada di coniare multipli del denaro che adempissero alla funzione di mezzi di scambio nelle transazioni internazionali e all'ingrosso e nelle faccende dell'alta finanza. Poi intervennero probabilmente anche motivi di prestigio. Infine una spinta decisiva dovette venire da un generale ribasso del valore dell'oro rispetto all'argento: ribasso che si avvertì sul mercato italiano e mediterraneo verso la metà del sec. XIII. Nel 1252 il grande passo fu compiuto: Genova e Firenze coniarono una moneta d'oro purissimo del peso di grammi 3,5, che prese il nome di *genovino d'oro* a Genova e di *fiorino d'oro* a Firenze[49]. Venezia seguirà l'esempio nel 1284 e conierà il *ducato d'oro* (detto poi *zecchino*) con le stesse caratteristiche d'intrinseco del *fiorino* e del *genovino*[50]. Il monometallismo argenteo stabilito da Carlo Magno e rispettato durante quasi cinque secoli, era finito.

[49] Per tutti cfr. R.S. Lopez, *Back to Gold*, pp. 219-240.

[50] N. Papadopoli, *Le monete di Venezia*, I, pp. 62-122; F.C. Lane, *Monete di conto veneziane*, pp. 58 ss.; P. Grierson, *La moneta veneziana*.

Capitolo secondo

Medioevo e Rinascimento

1. Il processo di sviluppo economico in atto nell'Italia centro-settentrionale durante i secc. XI, XII e XIII aveva modificato profondamente antichi equilibri e tradizionali rapporti di forza e di ricchezza. Città come Pavia che avevano brillato nei secoli dell'alto Medioevo erano inesorabilmente risospinte in secondo piano. A nuove età, nuovi ricchi. Altre città ed altre regioni si fecero avanti. Ed il settore monetario, al solito sensibilissimo, registrò fedelmente le nuove situazioni.

Nel Veneto, per buona parte ancora del sec. XI fu sempre la moneta veronese a tenere il campo. Nella stessa Venezia, sin oltre il 1180 il mezzo di scambio più usato nella pratica quotidiana del commercio al minuto continuò ad essere il denaro veronese. La pace di Costanza fu l'elemento occasionale (e fornì l'appiglio giuridico) che fece precipitare una situazione matura. Dopo il 1183 la moneta veneziana si sostituì a quella veronese sulla piazza di Venezia e poi, in prosieguo di tempo, si impose via via praticamente in tutta la regione veneta[1].

[1] Nel periodo 1150-1183, il 56 per cento dei documenti relativi a transazioni sul mercato veneziano esprime i valori in moneta veronese. Nel periodo 1184-1205 la percentuale crolla a circa l'11 per cento. Tra il 1150 e il 1183 la moneta di Venezia appare soltanto nel 4 per cento delle transazioni di cui ci è rimasta memoria. Nel periodo 1184-1205 la percentuale sale al 42 per cento: cfr. L. Buenger Robbert, *The Venetian Money Market*, pp. 17-18. Nel Trentino e in Tirolo venne invece a prevalere dalla fine del sec. XIII la moneta meranese: cfr. A. Stella, *Politica ed economia*, cap. I.

In Lombardia per tutto l'alto Medioevo la moneta dominante era stata quella di Pavia. Dall'XI sec. e più decisamente col sec. XII fu invece la moneta milanese che prese progressivamente il sopravvento. A Cremona la moneta milanese si sostituì alla pavese già durante il sec. XI[2]. A Vigevano – una grossa borgata sita proprio tra Milano e Pavia – la moneta pavese tenne il campo sino alla metà del sec. XII. Da allora, nei documenti vigevanaschi, l'usuale misura di valori fu la moneta milanese[3]. A Parma, nell'ultimo quarto del sec. XII i prezzi venivano correntemente espressi in *imperiali milanesi*[4].

Quel che in Lombardia fece alla moneta pavese la moneta milanese lo fecero, dopo la metà del sec. XII, la moneta genovese in Liguria e l'astigiana, la secusina e la viennese in Piemonte e Savoia.

In Toscana il predominio monetario di Lucca fu infranto verso la metà del sec. XII da Pisa. La moneta pisana fu la moneta dominante fino ai primi decenni del sec. XIII. Verso la metà del Duecento finalmente la *leadership* monetaria della Toscana passò a Firenze[5].

2. Alla metà del Duecento appariva ormai definitivamente chiaro che cinque erano le monete fondamentali dell'Italia a nord di Roma, e cioè le monete di Venezia, di Milano, di Asti e dei duchi di Savoia[6],

[2] U. Gualazzini, *Rapporti fra capitale e lavoro*, p. 14, n. 1.

[3] A. Colombo, *Cartario di Vigevano*, pp. 57, 83, 97, 103, 123, 128, 146, 159, 171, 256, 268.

[4] *Chronicon Parmense*, cit., p. 6.

[5] D. Herlihy, *Pisan Coinage*, pp. 143-166. Cfr. anche la nuova edizione dello stesso articolo in AA.VV., *Le zecche minori*, p. 175.

[6] In Asti, Savigliano, Cuneo, Mondovì l'unità di conto e di scambio più comunemente usata fu la moneta di Asti. Nelle altre zone del Piemonte e della Savoia si usò prevalentemente – ma non esclusivamente – la moneta viennese e secusina. In talune zone vicine alla Lombardia come Novara, Ivrea, Biella si usava invece l'imperiale di Milano. Cfr. D. Promis, *Monete dei Reali di Savoia*, t. I, pp. 48-49.

di Genova e di Firenze. Per quanto riguarda i tipi ed i conii, le monete delle altre città cercarono talvolta di confondersi e talvolta cercarono di distinguersi dai pezzi delle cinque monetazioni fondamentali. Ma per quanto riguarda i movimenti economici non c'è dubbio che quelle furono sempre trascinate da queste. I movimenti economici della moneta di una qualsiasi zecca dell'Italia a nord di Roma sono, dalla metà del sec. XIII in poi, quasi sempre riconducibili ai movimenti delle monete di uno dei cinque centri citati e naturalmente in genere di quello geograficamente più vicino o più influente per ragioni economiche o politiche.

Si potrebbe così dire che dalla metà del sec. XIII e più decisamente col sec. XIV l'Italia centro-settentrionale va considerata divisa in cinque aree monetarie: l'area della lira veneziana, l'area della lira imperiale di Milano, l'area della lira astigiana (poi della sabauda), l'area della lira genovese e l'area della lira fiorentina. Naturalmente usato per quei secoli il termine «area monetaria» va inteso in un significato del tutto diverso da quello che ha nel linguaggio tecnico moderno. All'interno di ogni «area» non c'erano quei controlli sui cambi che caratterizzano ed individuano le «aree» monetarie moderne, né la circolazione monetaria era monopolizzata da un solo tipo di moneta. Gli stati facenti parte più o meno volontariamente di una data «area» non godevano di completa «sovranità monetaria». All'interno di ogni «area» – così come all'interno di ogni singolo stato – circolava liberamente ed in piena legalità una massa notevole di monete di altri stati o di altre aree. Il fatto fondamentale che caratterizzava ed individuava quel che si è chiamato qui un'«area monetaria» era, a mio avviso, il fatto che le monete dei vari stati o città facenti parte di una data «area» seguivano tutte abbastanza fedelmente, sia pure con diversa intensità, i movimenti di una data moneta dominante.

Naturalmente i confini delle cinque «aree» a nord di Roma variarono nel corso del tempo. E d'altra parte ci furono anche ampie zone grigie in cui aree diverse si sovrapponevano e zone scoperte che non rientravano in alcuna delle cinque aree citate.

3. Nell'ordinamento monetario quale s'era ormai precisato alla metà del sec. XIII e quale rimase nei secoli successivi, la massa metallica circolante veniva a distinguersi nettamente in due gruppi. Da una parte il solito denaro che, ridotto nell'intrinseco, si confinò esclusivamente nell'area delle transazioni locali come usuale mezzo di scambio e di pagamento nelle compravendite al minuto, nella liquidazione dei salari e nelle piccole e medie operazioni di credito locale. Dall'altra parte i grossi e i fiorini d'oro (e sotto tale termine si intendono e si intenderanno in seguito anche i genovini e i ducati d'oro) che per l'alto valore unitario rappresentato si isolarono ben presto nell'area delle transazioni internazionali, delle operazioni all'ingrosso e di quelle dell'alta finanza. Il linguaggio corrente del tempo sottolineò questa netta distinzione indicando come «*moneta piccola*» l'un gruppo monetario e come «*moneta grossa*» l'altro gruppo. Non c'è dubbio che tale terminologia originò dal diverso diametro dei pezzi appartenenti ai due gruppi, ma in prosieguo di tempo essa assunse un significato puramente economico. Praticamente le due «monete», cioè la piccola e la grossa, anziché formare insieme gli elementi vari ma raccordati di un unico ed organico sistema monetario, subito formarono due ben distinti sistemi monetari, ciascuno con una sua propria e distinta area di circolazione sia geografica, che sociale e di affari. Le conseguenze di

tale fatto si fecero vedere ben presto e rappresentarono per secoli il grosso ed insoluto problema della politica monetaria[7].

Le forze inflazionistiche che continuarono ad operare si concentrarono sulla «*moneta piccola*» che rimaneva – come si è detto – la moneta predominante nella circolazione interna e che costituiva l'unità di base del sistema dei prezzi interni. Bisogna anzi aggiungere che nella nuova situazione la pressione inflazionistica fu sollecitata ed accentuata tra l'altro anche dal carattere esclusivamente «interno» assunto dalla «*moneta piccola*» e dal nuovo meccanismo del sistema e del mercato monetario[8].

Mentre la «*moneta piccola*» veniva travolta da convergenti forze inflazionistiche, la «*moneta grossa*» – si è detto – si ritirava nella rarefatta atmosfera delle transazioni internazionali e dell'alta finanza dove motivi economici e ragioni di prestigio concordemente la sostenevano in una privilegiata posizione di stabilità intrinseca.

Continuando l'una moneta a slittare e l'altra rimanendo stabile o quasi nel corso dei secoli, necessariamente i rapporti di scambio tra le due monete andarono continuamente e progressivamente crescendo. Per esempio il ducato d'oro che a Venezia nel 1284 valeva 576 denari veneziani, nel 1500 ne valeva 1.488, e nel 1750 ne valeva 5.280. Quel che accadde a Venezia si ripeté, sia pure con intensità maggiore o minore, su ogni altra piazza d'Italia.

[7] Cfr. C.M. Cipolla, *Moneta e civiltà mediterranea*, cap. III.

[8] Il meccanismo che traduceva un rialzo dei «cambi» in una gonfiatura dei profitti e perciò interessava il ceto imprenditoriale in una politica di deprezzamento della moneta piccola è analizzato dettagliatamente in C.M. Cipolla, *Mouvements monétaires*, pp. 25-27.

In queste condizioni la «*moneta grossa*» non aveva e non poteva assumere le funzioni ed il ruolo di multiplo della «*moneta piccola*»: mancava l'elemento essenziale, cioè la stabilità del rapporto. Restava così insoluto il problema per cui la lira era nata. In altre parole: se per esempio a Venezia il ducato d'oro fosse rimasto sempre e stabilmente ancorato al rapporto fisso di, diciamo, 576 denari per ducato, la lira sarebbe divenuta un'unità di conto superflua: il ducato avrebbe adempiuto alla funzione di multiplo del denaro nella contabilità quotidiana col vantaggio di essere oltre che un comodo multiplo di conto anche una moneta effettiva. Il fatto che il rapporto tra ducato e denaro fosse invece incerto e mutevole rese impossibile questa soluzione[9]. La mobilità del rapporto dimostrava quotidianamente che «*moneta piccola*» e «*moneta grossa*» non appartenevano ad un unico sistema monetario ma formavano invece due sistemi distinti. Perciò la gente non ebbe altra scelta che continuare con l'antico espediente della fantomatica unità tramandata dalla notte dei tempi.

4. Le vicende e le circostanze ora descritte meritano di essere osservate anche da un altro punto di vista. Quando per esempio a Firenze si coniò per la prima volta il fiorino d'oro, si cercò praticamente di dar corpo a quel fantasma che era stato fino ad allora la lira. A Firenze difatti il fiorino fu coniato con tali caratteristiche intrinseche da valere esattamente 240 dei denari correnti nel 1252. Ma, come si è detto nel paragrafo precedente, il fiorino rimase intrinsecamente stabile, mentre il denaro continuò a slittare con la naturale conseguenza che il rapporto tra le due monete

[9] Cfr. più dettagliatamente C.M. Cipolla, *Moneta e civiltà mediterranea*, pp. 43-51.

fu continuamente spinto al rialzo. Dopo venticinque anni dalla sua coniazione il fiorino a Firenze era già passato a valere dai 240 denari fiorentini originari a 396 denari[10]. In altre parole, il pezzo che doveva materialmente rappresentare la lira, dopo un certo numero di anni dalla sua coniazione non corrispose più ad una lira (=240 denari) ma ad un valore più alto ed in prosieguo di tempo continuò a valere sempre di più. Gli uomini avevano cercato di dar corpo al fantasma ma non vi erano riusciti. Tentarono altre volte. A Venezia, il 27 maggio 1472, sotto il dogado di Nicolò Tron, fu battuto un pezzo di buon argento a lega 948 millesimi ed al peso di grammi 6,5 di maniera che doveva valere esattamente 240 denari veneziani del tempo: tale pezzo fu appunto chiamato «*lira tron*»[11]. A Milano nel 1474, sotto il ducato di Galeazzo Maria Sforza, si fecero battere dei pezzi di buon argento a lega 962 millesimi ed al peso di grammi 9,8 che rappresentassero appunto 240 denari imperiali milanesi del tempo[12]. In Piemonte e in Savoia nel 1562, Emanuele Filiberto, riformando e riordinando il sistema monetario, fece coniare un pezzo al titolo di 895,83 millesimi ed al peso di circa 12,72 grammi che doveva appunto rappresentare la lira («*lira instar omnium*») e formare il cardine di tutto il nuovo sistema[13]. Ma in tutti i casi si ripeté la storia che era occorsa al fiorino. Dopo un certo numero di

[10] C.M. Cipolla, *Studi di storia della moneta*, pp. 41 e 57. Cfr. anche A. Castellani, *Nuovi testi fiorentini*, pp. 941-942.

[11] N. Papadopoli, *Monete di Venezia*, parte II, pp. 4, 5, 10 e 11.

[12] Cfr. il capo IV dell'ordine ducale di battitura del 4 giugno 1474 in *De Monetis Italiae*, ed. F. Argelati, parte III, p. 49. Questi pezzi che dovevano rappresentare la lira sono chiamati, nell'ordine di battitura, *grossi* o *grossoni*. Più tardi presero il nome di *testoni*.

[13] M. Chiaudano, *La riforma monetaria di Emanuele Filiberto*, pp. 289-310.

anni dalla loro prima coniazione, i pezzi che dovevano rappresentare la lira cominciarono a crescere e ad assumere valori progressivamente sempre più alti rispetto alla lira stessa. Fintantoché esistevano sul mercato monetario due monete – la grossa e la piccola – distinte fra di loro e soggette a pressioni diverse e fintantoché la lira di conto rimaneva ancorata ad un sottomultiplo appartenente al gruppo della moneta piccola mentre rappresentava ancora un valore unitario tale da spingere automaticamente il pezzo che la doveva rappresentare nel gruppo della moneta grossa, ogni tentativo di materializzare la lira doveva fatalmente fallire. Per queste ragioni, durante tutto il Medioevo e parte dell'età moderna la lira rimase un fantasma: l'ombra duecentoquaranta volte ingrandita di una monetina che continuava a svilire.

5. Nel corso dei secoli peraltro il denaro nelle varie parti della penisola si ridusse talmente che ad un certo punto, in un'area dopo l'altra, non fu più possibile coniarlo. A Milano e a Venezia, per esempio, gli ultimi denari si batterono nella prima metà del sec. XVI. Si era dato frattanto inizio, in una zecca dopo l'altra, alla coniazione di pezzi da tre denari («*terlini*»), quattro denari («*quattrini*»), cinque denari («*cinquini*»), sei denari («*sesini*»), otto denari («*ottini*»). Eventualmente si coniarono anche i pezzi da dodici denari («*soldini*»). Ogni lira comunque continuò a significare 240 denari, mentre il suo valore venne ad appoggiare sulla moneta metallica che rappresentava il multiplo immediato del denaro scomparso. Cioè: fino a quando fu coniato il pezzo da un denaro la lira fu materialmente rappresentata (e il suo valore fu determinato) da 240 di questi pezzi. Quando il denaro non fu più coniato ed al suo posto furono coniati per esempio i pezzi da 4 denari

(«*quattrini*»), la lira continuò a significare 240 denari ma fu materialmente rappresentata (ed il suo valore fu determinato) da 60 (=240/4) quattrini.

D'altra parte già dalla metà del sec. XII – abbiamo visto – i denari vennero coniati in una lega molto bassa di argento e progressivamente più vile. Dalla fine del sec. XV, in una zecca dopo l'altra, i più immediati sottomultipli cominciarono a venir coniati addirittura di puro rame. Vi sono anche motivi per ritenere che già nel sec. XV, e forse anche da prima, queste piccole monetine tendessero a circolare – almeno per certi periodi – ad un valore nominale superiore al loro valore intrinseco: cioè, usando un'espressione tecnica, tendessero a circolare come moneta-segno[14]. In tali circostanze non avrebbe molto senso calcolare l'equivalente metallico della lira fondandosi sull'intrinseco delle sue piccole monetine di base. Nell'Appendice sono spiegate in maggior dettaglio le ragioni – del resto evidenti – che sconsigliano di seguire tale procedimento. D'altra parte poiché dal 1252 si posseggono per la maggior parte delle città italiane serie continuative dei cambi correnti tra la lira ed i più importanti tipi di monete auree (che circolavano come «monete piene»), nelle pagine che seguono, per il periodo 1252-1700 si seguirà il metodo di calcolare l'equivalente metallico della lira sulla base di detti cambi. Per una valutazione ed una esposizione più dettagliata di questo metodo, rinvio ancora il lettore all'Appendice. Qui è ormai tempo di riprendere il filo dei movimenti della lira.

6. Nel 1252, l'anno fatidico della ricomparsa della moneta aurea, in base al cambio col fiorino, la lira ge-

[14] Cfr. le osservazioni di C.M. Cipolla, *Mouvements monétaires*, p. 16.

novese e la lira imperiale di Milano dovevano equivalere ciascuna a circa 7 grammi di oro e la lira fiorentina doveva equivalere a circa 3,5. A quel tempo il rapporto di scambio tra oro e argento doveva essere approssimativamente come da 1 a 10: in tal caso la lira genovese e l'imperiale di Milano dovevano equivalere ciascuna a circa 70 grammi di argento e la lira fiorentina a circa 35 grammi[15]. Per la lira veneziana non conosciamo cambi con il fiorino anteriori al 1284, anno in cui la Serenissima abbandonò il monometallismo argenteo, ma per altre vie possiamo arrivare a concludere che la lira veneziana attorno al 1252 doveva equivalere a poco meno di 2 grammi di oro fino ovvero a circa 20 grammi di argento puro[16].

[15] Per le parità auree cfr. Appendice III, Tab. A1. Per il rapporto AU/AR cfr. C.M. Cipolla, *Studi di storia della moneta*, pp. 129-130.

[16] Sulla base del cambio tra moneta piccola ed il grosso d'argento, si può asserire che tra il 1220 ed il 1265 la parità argentea della lira veneziana rimase stabile alla quota di grammi 19,5 di fino. Tra il 1265 ed il 1282 invece passò prima a grammi 18,7 e quindi a grammi 16,3 (N. Papadopoli, *Monete di Venezia*, parte I, app. I, tav. I, pp. 382-383 e, per l'andamento dei cambi tra *piccolo* e *grosso*, sui quali è calcolata la parità argentea, cfr. R. Cessi, *Problemi monetari veneziani*, p. XXIX e G. Luzzatto, *L'oro e l'argento nella politica monetaria veneziana*, pp. 259-270).

Per quanto riguarda la parità aurea sappiamo con una certa precisione che nel 1226 una lira veneziana poteva acquistare quasi 2 grammi di oro puro non coniato (B. Cecchetti, *Saggio sui prezzi*, p. 1473 e più dettagliatamente le ricerche di L. Buenger). Nel 1284 il cambio col ducato d'oro fornisce una parità aurea della lira di grammi 1,5 (N. Papadopoli, *Monete di Venezia*, parte I, app. I, tav. II, p. 384). La differenza tra il dato del 1226 ed il dato del 1284 origina da due fatti: anzitutto il decadimento della moneta piccola dopo il 1265 denunciato dai movimenti della parità argentea; in secondo luogo il fatto che la parità del 1226 è calcolata in base al prezzo del metallo in pasta (parità β, cfr. Appendice I) mentre la parità del 1284 è calcolata in base al cambio con una moneta coniata (parità γ, cfr. Appendice I).

Prima di vedere quanto accadde alle varie lire dopo il 1252, cerchiamo di dare un ultimo sguardo al periodo precedente. Quasi un secolo prima, dopo la metà del Millecento, se le nostre calcolazioni sono esatte, la lira imperiale di Milano doveva equivalere a circa 103 grammi di argento[17], la lira genovese a circa 75[18], e la veneziana a poco più di 20[19]. Firenze, alla metà del sec. XII, non aveva ancora moneta propria ed usava la moneta di Lucca e Pisa, la cui lira doveva equivalere allora a poco meno di 85 grammi di argento fino[20]. Sulla base di questi dati e sacrificando molto alla

[17] B. Biondelli, *La zecca e le monete di Milano*, p. 64.

[18] Quando nel 1141 iniziò la monetazione genovese, il denaro di Genova conteneva grammi 0,366 di argento fino e la lira genovese doveva quindi equivalere a circa grammi 88 (cfr. C. Desimoni, *Tavole descrittive*, p. XXXIV; C. Desimoni, *Sui denari minuti*, p. 224; P.F. Casaretto, *La moneta genovese*, pp. 45-46; M. Chiaudano, *La moneta di Genova*, § 3). Nel 1164 invece, stando alla «convenzione» già citata qui addietro alle note 32 e 35 del cap. I, la lira genovese era scesa – arrotondando per difetto – a circa 75 grammi di argento fino. Nel testo si è adottata la parità del 1164 anziché quella del 1141 perché anche la parità citata per la moneta lucchese è derivata dalla «convenzione» del 1164 e la parità citata per la moneta imperiale milanese è presso a poco della stessa epoca.

Va peraltro osservato che C. Desimoni (sia in *Le prime monete*, pp. 181-182 che in L.T. Belgrano, *Illustrazione del Registro Arcivescovile*, p. 597) attribuendo erroneamente alla convenzione del 1164 la data del 1172 ed attribuendo erroneamente al marco di Colonia del XII sec. il peso di grammi 233,862 invece di quello di circa grammi 215 (cfr. qui addietro nota 32 al cap. I: il peso di grammi 233,862 fu di epoca più tarda) concluse che nel 1172 il soldo genovese doveva equivalere a grammi 4,176 e la lira quindi a circa grammi 83,5. M. Chiaudano, *La moneta di Genova*, § 3, riportò poi che nel 1162 un'oncia d'oro valeva 430 denari genovesi: evidentemente però si tratta di una oncia di lega e non di oro fino.

[19] Cfr. qui addietro cap. I, nota 34.

[20] Cfr. qui addietro cap. I, § 8. La lira fiorentina ai primi del Duecento doveva equivalere a circa grammi 46,8 di argento fino (cfr. A. Castellani, *Nuovi testi fiorentini*, t. II, pp. 869-870).

precisione statistica[21], in via di grossolana approssimazione si potrebbe dire che tra la metà del sec. XII e la metà del sec. XIII la lira genovese accusò un deterioramento intrinseco dell'ordine del 5 per cento, la lira veneziana circa lo stesso[22], la lira imperiale di Milano dell'ordine del 30 per cento e la lira toscana dell'ordine del 60 per cento[23]. Rispetto ai due secoli precedenti e al secolo seguente, il secondo corso tra la metà del Millecento e la metà del Duecento rappresentò quindi – eccezion fatta per la Toscana – un periodo di relativa stabilità monetaria.

7. Tentando paragoni sul piano internazionale, è facile vedere che le lire delle città italiane erano il gruppo di testa tra le monete occidentali nel fenomeno di secolare deterioramento intrinseco.

Nel 1266, quando Luigi XI riordinò il sistema monetario francese e diede alla Francia «*la bonne monnaie de Monsieur Sainct Loys*», la *lira tornese* di Francia equivaleva a poco più di 80 grammi di argento fino[24].

[21] L'imprecisione deriva dal fatto che le parità della metà del sec. XII rappresentano α e quelle della metà del sec. XIII rappresentano γ. Per le ragioni spiegate qui avanti nell'Appendice I, le differenze tra parità calcolate con metodi diversi sono per una parte sia pur modesta imputabili alla diversità dei metodi di calcolazione anziché all'effettivo decadimento della moneta.

[22] Il decadimento della lira veneziana fu fatto anteriore al sec. XIII, perché dal 1200 al 1270 la parità argentea della lira stessa risulta stabilizzata (cfr. qui addietro nota 16). Tale stabilità può forse venire attribuita alle importanti riforme monetarie attuate da Enrico Dandolo e continuate dai suoi successori. Ma non si può escludere la possibilità di influenza della nuova posizione politica di Venezia in Oriente (Impero Latino di Costantinopoli 1204-1261) e di eventuali maggiori facilità di rifornimento di metalli preziosi.

[23] Le percentuali citate sono tutte arrotondate per le ragioni più volte accennate.

[24] A. Dieudonné, *Monnaies royales françaises*, p. 225 e R. Sedillot, *Le franc*, p. 63.

In Inghilterra il *penny* (denaro) non era mai stato toccato dal 1066: alla metà del sec. XIII aveva dunque ancora un peso teorico di grammi 1,45 circa e la sua lega era regolarmente quella dello «*ancient right standard of England*», cioè argento «*sterling*» pari a 925 millesimi[25]. Di conseguenza il *pound* (lira) inglese – equivalente come le sue sorelle italiana e francese a 240 denari – attorno alla metà del sec. XIII aveva ancora una parità teorica di poco più di 320 grammi di argento fino.

8. I movimenti delle varie lire tra il 1252 ed il 1500 sono indicati dai dati raccolti nella Tab. A1 dell'Appendice III. Le date che ho scelto per indicare le tappe dei movimenti delle lire all'interno del periodo 1252-1500 non sono state scelte a caso. Il punto 1315-25 è stato scelto perché in esso finì un lungo periodo di svalutazione dell'argento rispetto all'oro e il rapporto di cambio AU/AR toccò allora il limite più alto mai raggiunto nell'età medievale[26]. Il punto 1390-1400 è stato scelto perché in esso il rapporto AU/AR era tornato normale (per quei tempi), e soprattutto perché con esso terminò quella fase lunga di stabilità della parità argentea delle varie lire cui accennerò in seguito[27].

Nell'insieme, tra la metà del sec. XIII e la fine del XV, la lira milanese subì un deterioramento intrinseco di quasi il 90 per cento, la genovese di oltre l'80 per cento, la fiorentina di circa l'85 per cento, la veneziana di circa il 70 per cento. Non abbiamo dati sicuri sulla

[25] R. Ruding, *Annals of the Coinage of Great Britain*, t. I, pp. 12 e 201; A.E. Feaveryear, *The Pound Sterling*, pp. 7-9 e 350.

[26] Sui movimenti del rapporto AU/AR cfr. per tutti C. Desimoni, *La moneta e il rapporto dell'oro all'argento*, pp. 3-56; e C.M. Cipolla, *Studi di storia della moneta*, pp. 129-130.

[27] Cfr. qui avanti § 9.

parità della lira astese alla metà del sec. XIII, ma sappiamo che tra gli inizi del Trecento e la fine del Quattrocento la lira astese subì un deterioramento dell'ordine del 90 per cento. Tenendo conto del fatto che esistono indizi di un sensibile slittamento della moneta astese anche durante la seconda metà del Duecento[28], si può affermare con sicurezza che il deterioramento intrinseco della lira astese sia stato, tra il 1252 ed il 1500, superiore al 90 per cento.

Alla fine del Quattrocento, la lira di maggior valore era quella genovese che aveva una parità argentea di poco meno di 13 grammi di fino. La lira imperiale equivaleva a grammi 8,6. La lira veneziana a grammi 6,2. La lira fiorentina a grammi 5,7. E la lira astigiana a grammi 2,4 (sulle parità auree cfr. i dati raccolti nella Tab. A1 dell'Appendice III). Circa il potere d'acquisto delle varie lire, per una prima vaga approssimazione si può ricordare che, appunto alla fine del Quattrocento, la giornata di un «*maestro*» muratore (cioè un operaio qualificato) era pagata a Genova tra lire 0,45 e lire 0,50; a Milano tra lire 0,50 e lire 0,60; a Firenze tra lire 0,80 e 0,90; a Venezia tra lire 1,10 e lire 1,30[29].

Sul piano internazionale, si può rilevare che sulla fine del Quattrocento la lira tornese di Francia equivaleva a circa 22 grammi di argento fino[30] e la inglese

[28] Cfr. C.M. Cipolla, *Studi di storia della moneta*, p. 26.

[29] Per Genova cfr. Archivio di Stato di Genova, *Archivio Segreto, n. 733*, «Ufficii monetae», *Diversorum 1431-1500*; per Firenze cfr. Archivio di Stato di Firenze, *Signori e Collegi, Delib.* 108, c. 160; per Venezia cfr. Archivio di Stato di Venezia, *San Giorgio Maggiore*, b. 76 (polizze). Per Milano cfr. C.M. Cipolla, *L'economia milanese*, p. 368. I pochi dati citati nel testo sembrerebbero confermare quanto viaggiatori e mercanti del tempo riferiscono a più riprese: e cioè che Venezia era la città dove il vivere era più caro.

[30] A. Dieudonné, *Monnaies royales françaises*, p. 308; R. Sedillot, *Le franc*, p. 74.

TAV. 1. *Denaro di Carlo Magno*, zecca di Milano 774-814 [cfr. cap. I, §§ 1 e 2].

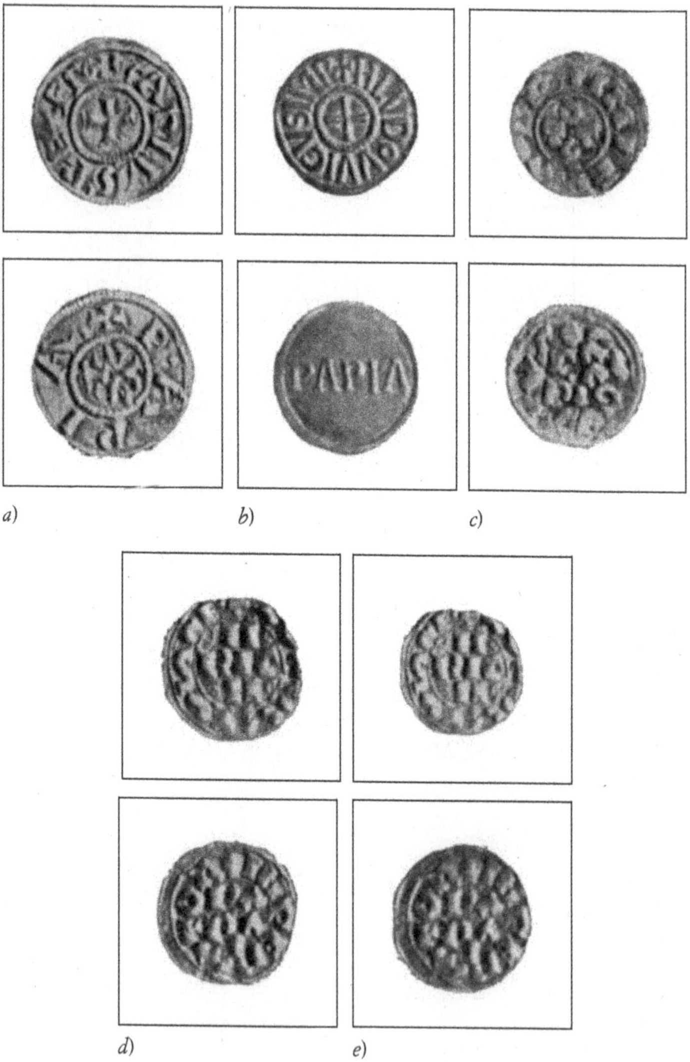

TAV. 2. Decadimento del *denaro pavese*: (*a*) denaro di Carlo Magno, (*b*) denaro di Ludovico il Pio, (*c*) denaro di Ottone I, (*d*) denaro di Enrico III di Franconia, (*e*) denaro di Federico II. La riduzione del diametro del denaro è solo parzialmente indicativa dell'effettivo decadimento del denaro. In realtà oltre che nel diametro il denaro si ridusse anche di spessore e soprattutto venne composto di lega sempre peggiore [cfr. cap. I, § 8].

a) *b*)

TAV. 3. Denaro *piccolo* (*a*) e denaro *grosso* (*b*) veneziani di Enrico Dandolo (1192-1205). Il semplice raffronto fotografico sottovaluta la differenza tra l'una e l'altra moneta, in quanto tale differenza non era soltanto di diametro ma anche di spessore e di lega [cfr. cap. I, § 12].

a) *b*) *c*)

TAV. 4. Il *genovino* d'oro (*a*) del tipo più antico, il *fiorino* d'oro (*b*) del tipo più antico (1252-1260) e il *ducato* d'oro veneziano (*c*) di Giovanni Dandolo (1284-1289) [cfr. cap. I, § 12].

a) *b)* *c)*

TAV. 5. Lira Tron del doge Nicolò Tron (*a*) e *grossone*, o *testone*, di Galeazzo Maria Sforza (*b*). Benché di diametro quasi uguale, il pezzo milanese è di spessore, e quindi anche di peso, maggiore del pezzo veneziano [cfr. cap. III, § 4].

«Lira italiana» di Napoleone I (*c*). Questo pezzo pesava grammi 5 ed era di argento a 900 mill. di lega [cfr. cap. III, § 4].

TAV. 6. Pezzi metallici da 1 lira dall'unificazione alla prima guerra mondiale.

TAV. 7. Pezzi metallici da 1 lira dalla prima alla seconda guerra mondiale.

TAV. 8. Pezzi metallici da 1 lira post-seconda guerra mondiale.

ancora a circa 172 grammi[31]. Anche tra la metà del Duecento e la fine del Quattrocento, la lira che era capitombolata di più era stata la lira delle città italiane.

9. Lo slittamento delle varie lire tra il 1252 ed il 1500 non rappresentò un movimento continuo. Quando noi possiamo diagrammare in base a serie continue il movimento stesso, noi possiamo facilmente rilevare che si manifestarono alternativamente periodi di slittamento e periodi di stabilità. Ciascuna di queste fasi di stabilità aveva una durata media variante in genere tra i 10 ed i 25 anni[32]. Ma ve ne fu poi una che, per eccezionali circostanze, si protrasse per più decenni ed è visibile anche nei movimenti di lungo periodo delineati nella Tab. A1 (App. III): questa fase coprì grosso modo i tre quarti di secolo corsi tra il 1325 ed il 1400[33]. In un primo tempo, e cioè tra il 1325 ed il 1348, la parità argentea continuò a scemare, ma poiché nel frattempo il rapporto AU/AR passò da 1:13 a 1:10, la parità aurea rimase stabile. Poi nel 1348 scoppiò quell'apocalittica sciagura che fu la peste nera. Gli storici hanno appurato che qualcosa come un quarto o forse addirittura un terzo della popolazione fu allora falciato dalla spaventosa epidemia. Un tale collasso nei totali di popolazione deve aver necessariamente comportato una drastica contrazione della domanda di moneta, ed è tutt'altro che improbabile che intimi rapporti siano esistiti tra questi avvenimenti e la stabilità delle parità metalliche nella seconda metà del Trecento.

[31] A.E. Feaveryear, *The Pound Sterling*, p. 350.

[32] C.M. Cipolla, *Studi di storia della moneta*, p. 103.

[33] Cfr. C.M. Cipolla, *Studi di storia della moneta*, i grafici 1-2 a pp. 83 e 84.

10. Se si volesse riassumere schematizzando quelle che dovettero essere fondamentalmente le ragioni ultime dello slittamento intrinseco delle lire italiane tra il 1252 ed il 1500, io credo che si dovrebbe fissare l'attenzione sui seguenti sette fattori inflazionistici:

a) aumento della domanda di moneta in relazione ad un aumento della popolazione, del reddito e del grado di monetarizzazione dell'economia;

b) aumento della spesa e del deficit statale;

c) pressione di determinati gruppi sociali;

d) squilibri nella bilancia dei pagamenti;

e) regime delle zecche e tecnica delle emissioni monetarie;

f) erosione e tosatura dei pezzi in circolazione;

g) fluttuazioni nel rapporto di mercato AU/AR.

Della pressione dei gruppi mercantili-imprenditoriali, pei quali il deterioramento della moneta piccola significava, soprattutto attraverso il complicato sistema dei cambi con la moneta grossa, un aumento dei profitti, si è già detto in dettaglio in altro libro cui sono costretto a rinviare[34]. Della pressione dell'aumento della domanda di moneta di fronte ad una offerta di metalli preziosi che restò ostinatamente anelastica, si è già accennato qui addietro nel paragr. 9 del cap. I: si sa con precisione di casi in cui le autorità avvertendo che il mercato soffriva per «*magna penuria monetae*» diedero ordine alla zecca di battere da uno stesso peso di metallo un maggior numero di pezzi monetali. Ho anche accennato nel paragrafo precedente all'allentamento che tale pressione manifestò forse dopo la peste nera. Circa il regime delle zecche, si è già detto che

[34] Cfr. C.M. Cipolla, *Mouvements monétaires*, pp. 25-26; C.M. Cipolla, *Moneta e civiltà*, pp. 47-50.

esse – sia che fossero appaltate sia che fossero gestite direttamente dalle autorità statali – operavano sulla base del profitto. Questo fatto le interessava ad una inflazione delle emissioni cui esse tendevano in modi numerosi e diversi. Criteri sani e chiari per regolamentare le emissioni, del resto, mancavano completamente; le autorità al proposito brancicavano nel buio; e tutto questo aumentava la pericolosità del particolare regime operativo delle zecche. Difficoltà della bilancia dei pagamenti e conseguente rarefazione di *moneta grossa* sul mercato furono sovente l'origine di svalutazioni della *moneta piccola* effettuate allo scopo di favorire le esportazioni[35]. Quanto al bilancio statale c'è da ricordare che la pericolosità per la moneta di un deficit budgetario era allora accentuata dal fatto che la maggior parte dei governi cittadini era controllata da classi le quali sostenevano che fosse più «*honestum*» manipolare la moneta che aumentare le tasse[36].

Tutti questi vari elementi, che si sono potuti qui accennare solo di sfuggita, dovrebbero almeno servire a dare una idea di quanto complesso fosse il viluppo delle cause del decadimento secolare della moneta e

[35] Sul meccanismo in base al quale una svalutazione della *moneta piccola* favoriva le esportazioni, cfr. per tutti C.M. Cipolla, *Mouvements monétaires*, pp. 23-25.

[36] Tra i numerosissimi esempi che si potrebbero citare al proposito cfr. il documento veneziano del 22 febbr. 1441 in cui è detto: «cum faciat pro nostro dominio hoc tempore penurie pecuniarum recuperare pecunias *per omnem modum et viam honestam*, et in zecha nostra argenti alias fierent parvuli sive bagatini pro Brixia, Pergamo, Verona et Vicentia sub diversis stampis secundum cursum locorum qui quidem bagatini tenebant marchas 8 raminis et 1 argenti... et si fierent de dictis bagatinis qui teneant marchas 8½ raminis et ½ argenti, comune nostrum maximam utilitatem et lucrum reciperet» (il doc. è riportato per intero in V. Padovan, *Monete dei Veneziani*, p. 265).

di quanto sempliciotte siano quelle «spiegazioni» che pretendono risolvere il grosso problema soltanto con il trito ritornello dei tosatori e dei principi afflitti da manie bellicose o da mogli spenderecce.

Noi non abbiamo elementi per misurare il peso relativo di ciascuna delle sette sorgenti di pressione inflazionistica che abbiamo elencato prima. È chiaro che nei vari centri esse devono essersi combinate in maniera diversa e con peso diverso: il che solo può spiegare perché le varie lire abbiano accusato tassi diversi di slittamento. D'altra parte sarebbe completamente errato ritenere che l'importanza relativa di ciascuna di quelle sorgenti sia rimasta costante nel tempo. Per esempio io sono convinto che nell'epoca comunale e fino alla metà del Trecento, quando il governo della maggior parte delle nostre città era nelle mani delle consorterie mercantili e quando la spesa statale era ancora misera cosa, il deterioramento della moneta avvenne soprattutto sotto la pressione dei punti *a*, *b*, *d*. In prosieguo di tempo, quando apparvero le Signorie, il bilancio statale si ingrossò, le guerre si fecero sempre più costose e cominciò ad apparire una larva di burocrazia statale, allora si fecero via via relativamente sempre più attive e più importanti nella storia dell'inflazione secolare le forze di cui ai punti *e* e *d*.

Dalla fine del Trecento non c'è dubbio che la storia del decadimento della moneta fu un po' la storia del graduale progresso dell'importanza della spesa statale. Ma noi dobbiamo stare attenti a non sopravvalutare l'importanza di questo elemento nei secoli del più lontano passato trasferendo a quei secoli una realtà che è solo recente ed è frutto di una plurisecolare – fortunata o sfortunata a seconda dei punti di vista – evoluzione.

A questo punto è necessario fare anche un'altra considerazione. Quelli che all'inizio di questo paragrafo sono stati elencati come i sette «fattori inflazionistici» possono essere considerati come «cause» del deterioramento della moneta solo dal punto di vista *ex post*. Come ebbi a scrivere altrove[37], dal punto di vista *ex ante* essi rappresentano soltanto vari e possibili problemi che una data società si può trovare a dover risolvere – problemi pei quali comunque il deterioramento della moneta non rappresenta certo l'unica e necessaria soluzione. Se per esempio aumenta la domanda di moneta si può ricorrere ad altre forme di moneta o sviluppare il credito o lasciar cadere i prezzi. Se aumenta il disavanzo statale, si possono aumentare le tasse o comprimere la spesa pubblica. Se si crea uno squilibrio nella bilancia dei pagamenti, si può cercare di frenare le importazioni o stimolare le esportazioni. Per ognuno dei problemi messi in lista esistevano ed esistono soluzioni alternative allo svilimento della moneta. Ma lo svilimento della moneta è la soluzione comune a tutta una gamma di problemi ed è anche la soluzione più facile: quella che, come avrebbe detto Pantaleoni, «ogni imbecille saprebbe immaginare». Per questo da che mondo è mondo, ogni moneta nel corso del tempo prima o poi, più o meno, ha finito sempre con lo svalutarsi.

11. Qualunque ne siano state le «cause», resta da chiedersi se il deterioramento della moneta che abbiamo rilevato e misurato per i secoli scorsi fra la metà del X e la fine del XV sec. abbia rappresentato o no o in che misura un fenomeno di «inflazione secolare».

[37] C.M. Cipolla, *Currency depreciation*, pp. 414-415.

Per inflazione secolare io intendo un movimento tendenziale al rialzo dei prezzi e dei salari i quali per un protratto periodo di tempo accusino un aumento di un tanto percentuale medio all'anno, astrazion fatta dai movimenti di breve periodo. Nel nostro caso specifico il problema è quello di sapere se verso la fine del sec. XV i prezzi ed i salari si trovassero su livelli medi sensibilmente più alti di quelli dei secc. XI e XII ed eventualmente quale fu il rapporto tra tale aumento ed il deterioramento della parità metallica della moneta. Purtroppo noi manchiamo di indagini dirette e di conoscenze precise circa i prezzi ed i salari dei secc. XI-XV. Quindi si è costretti ad avanzare per ipotesi indiziarie e per vie indirette.

Si è accennato qui addietro che tra l'XI e la fine del XIII sec. diversi elementi inducono a sospettare una espansione secolare della domanda di metalli preziosi per scopi monetari. Sulla base del lusso rinascimentale e dello sviluppo economico nel settore agricolo, non sarebbe difficile immaginare un'altra ondata espansiva secolare tra la fine del Trecento e la fine del Quattrocento nella domanda di oro e di argento per scopi monetari ed industriali. D'altra parte, sulla scorta di quel poco che si conosce, gli storici tendono in genere ad affermare che l'offerta di oro e di argento sia sempre rimasta, fin verso la metà del sec. XV, relativamente anelastica. Il guaio è che nessuno è in grado di quantitativizzare le asserite tendenze. Se comunque le affermazioni degli storici fossero esatte tra l'XI ed il XIII sec. e poi ancora tra la fine del sec. XIV e la fine del sec. XV si sarebbe dovuto verificare un tendenziale rincarimento dell'argento in termini degli altri beni e dei servizi, cioè a dire un tendenziale ribasso dei prezzi dei beni e dei servizi in termini di argento. In tali condizioni, è vero che noi abbiamo osservato e misurato tra l'XI ed il XV sec. un progressivo deterioramento della parità metallica della moneta, ma rimane da sapere se tale deterioramento intrinseco venne compensato o no o in che misura da una rivalutazione secolare dell'argento in termini di beni e servizi. Se riflettiamo alla fine fatta da molti canoni feudali ed enfiteutici che in quei secoli vennero abbuonati o dimenticati perché svuotati nel loro significato reale, siamo fortemente indotti a ritenere che si sia sviluppato un fenomeno di «inflazione secolare» (nel caso si voglia tener per buona l'ipotesi della maggioranza degli storici di una rivalutazione secolare dell'argento, bisogna ammettere che il tasso di rivalutazione dell'argento fu inferiore al reciproco del tasso di deterioramento intrinseco della moneta). Ma queste sono tutte ipotesi. E la risposta al problema è ancora nascosta tra le vecchie carte degli archivi.

12. Su un terreno decisamente più solido si comincia a camminare dagli ultimi decenni del Quattrocento. Il primo fatto indubbio in cui ci si imbatte è che le condizioni dell'offerta dei metalli preziosi migliorarono in maniera decisiva. I portoghesi, spingendosi lungo le coste occidentali dell'Africa, riuscirono a giungere alle zone aurifere della Guinea e della Costa d'oro e contribuirono ad aumentare il flusso di oro all'Europa. La prima coniazione del *cruzado* aureo portoghese, fatto con oro della Guinea, è del 1457. Ma il miglioramento più sensibile si verificò per l'argento, a seguito dell'attivazione delle ricche miniere della regione sassone-boema e del Tirolo. Buona parte di quell'argento colò in Italia in cambio delle molte merci che l'Italia forniva allora al mercato tedesco. I centri che se ne avvantaggiarono di più furono naturalmente quelli che più stretti legami avevano con l'Alta Germania: e cioè Milano e

Venezia. È documentato che, negli ultimi decenni del Quattrocento, Milano e Venezia furono i due più importanti mercati per l'argento in Italia. È documentato che se zecche italiane volevano allora rifornirsi di argento facevano capo a Milano o Venezia[38]. Nel campo numismatico vero e proprio la maggior disponibilità di argento sul mercato italiano negli ultimi decenni del Quattrocento è documentata dalla comparsa di quelle magnifiche monete grosse e pesanti di ottimo argento che prenderanno il nome di «*testoni*». Non è un caso se i primi «*testoni*» furono battuti a Venezia e a Milano: e la stessa cronologia degli avvenimenti è indicativa dei legami che unirono gli avvenimenti stessi: la produzione argentifera delle miniere di Scwaz (Tirolo) triplicò tra il 1470 e il 1490; quella delle miniere dello Schneeberg (Sassonia) passò da poche centinaia di marchi attorno al 1450 a parecchie migliaia dopo il 1470[39]. La coniazione della *lira Tron* a Venezia è del 1472; la coniazione della *lira di Galeazzo Maria* è del 1474[40].

13. La scoperta dei ricchi giacimenti auriferi ed argentiferi dell'America spagnola e portoghese aprì improvvisamente nuove ed importanti fonti di metallo prezioso. Per tutti i secc. XVI e XVII le fantastiche «flotas de Indias» riversarono in Europa tesori immensi ed inusitati di oro e di argento[41]. Tra le varie conseguenze di quell'eccezionale afflusso, è opportuno qui segnalarne subito due:

[38] Per Milano cfr. C.M. Cipolla, *Argento tedesco e monete genovesi*, p. 101. Per Venezia cfr. K.O. Mueller, *Welthandelsbräuche*, p. 27.

[39] Cfr. J.U. Nef, *Silver Production in Central Europe*, p. 586.

[40] Cfr. qui addietro cap. II, § 4.

[41] Cfr. A. Soetbeer, *Edelmetall-Production*, pp. 47-92; E.J. Hamilton, *American Treasure*, pp. 11-45.

a) l'importanza della produzione americana e il rapporto che vi si manifestò tra produzione aurifera e produzione argentifera furono tali da modificare sensibilmente il rapporto di scambio tra oro ed argento sul mercato europeo. L'argento che fu prodotto in quantità più elevate – proporzionalmente al tradizionale rapporto di scambio – tese a svilirsi rispetto all'oro. Il rapporto di scambio tra i due metalli, che nell'Europa occidentale dai tempi romani aveva sempre teso a fluttuare – salvo rare e temporanee eccezioni – tra 1:10 e 1:13, tese progressivamente e inesorabilmente ad elevarsi raggiungendo nella seconda metà del sec. XVII la quota di 1:15;

b) per quanto in particolare riguarda la penisola italiana, la nuova localizzazione geografica delle maggiori fonti di rifornimento dei metalli preziosi spostò il mercato principale dell'oro e dell'argento da Milano e Venezia a Genova.

Francesco Marchiori, maestro della zecca veneta, ai primi del sec. XVIII riassumeva la situazione generale così: «le sorgenti dell'oro che inaffiano l'Europa sono le due Americhe, spagnola e portoghese. Ognuna di esse con le rispettive loro flotte ne tramandano di tempo in tempo. E suole essere di due raggione: una si dice il tesoro per conto di due rispetivi Re, l'altra il tesoro per conto del commercio. L'America spagnola al presente non è più sì feconda di questo prodotto in Europa come lo fu ne passati tempi, anzi dalla qualità di quel suo oro si può arguire che quelle miniere siano divenute alquanto aride. All'incontro la portoghese pare molto più feconda e per la qualità e per la quantità che ne tramanda. Quest'oro dell'una e dell'altra Americha solea venire per la maggior parte in bare o verghe, in grane, polvere et in specie effettive... Le flotte che trasportano questi tesori sogliono respetto la spagnola dar fondo a Cadice e respetto la portoghese a Lisbona. Si che queste due piazze sono quelle che inaffiano di un tal prezioso genere l'Europpa. Il comercio dunque con dette due piazze non si può negare essere solo quello che attrae l'oro all'altre nazioni... Si sono rese patrone di tale commercio le quattro nazioni: inglese, olandese, francese et genovese»[42].

14. I due secoli corsi tra il 1500 ed il 1700 possono venir suddivisi, da un punto di vista economico, in tre distinti periodi: 1) dal 1500 al 1550 circa, il periodo delle guerre spagnole, di devastazioni, carestie, pestilenze e miserie a non finire; 2) dal 1550 al 1620 circa, l'estate di San Martino dell'economia italiana con espansione economica di lungo periodo e ricostruzione economica generale del paese; 3) dal 1620 al 1700 circa, il tragico periodo del declino economico dell'Italia, della fine definitiva della supremazia economica degli italiani, del passaggio dell'Italia dal gruppo privilegiato dei paesi sviluppati alla gran massa grigia e miseranda dei paesi sottosviluppati.

Nella Tab. A2 dell'Appendice III ho cercato di fornire la parità metallica delle varie lire ai *turning points* di queste varie fasi: cioè attorno al 1550, attorno al 1620 e alla fine del sec. XVII. La cosa mi è stata possibile per Genova, Milano e Venezia. Per Firenze e per Torino mi sono dovuto limitare a fornire la parità solo per la metà del Cinquecento e per gli inizi del Settecento; per Firenze a causa della mancanza di dati[43],

[42] Archivio di Stato di Venezia, *Provveditori in zecca 18*, Memorie di Fr. Marchiori maestro di zecca, pp. 14 ss.

[43] Con il che non voglio dire che negli archivi fiorentini non esistano dati in proposito: voglio dire soltanto che non è mai stata fatta una seria indagine sui corsi monetari in Toscana nei secc. XVI e XVII e io non ho avuto l'opportunità di colmare tale lacuna.

per Torino a causa di un complesso di circostanze sulle quali è opportuno soffermarsi.

Anzitutto devo far rilevare che se nella Tab. A1, per i secoli medievali, mi ero riferito per il Piemonte alla moneta astigiana, nella Tab. A2, per i secc. XVI e XVII mi sono riferito alla moneta sabauda: ciò perché tra l'autunno del Medioevo e gli albori dell'età moderna nell'area sabaudo-piemontese la moneta ducale si impose a fronte delle monete comunali. Circa poi la parità della lira sabauda, va osservato che nel corso dell'ultimo secolo del Medioevo si era introdotto in Savoia ed in Piemonte dalla Francia meridionale l'uso di contare a denari, quarti, grossi e fiorini invece che a denari, soldi e lire[44]. Questo uso si diffuse presto e a tal punto da soppiantare completamente il sistema tradizionale.

Nel 1562 Emanuele Filiberto, attuando una generale riforma monetaria[45], tentò di reintrodurre nel suo stato il sistema di conto a lire, soldi e denari. Si illuse anche di dar corpo alla lira di conto coniando un pezzo argenteo che doveva rappresentarla: la cosiddetta «*lira instar omnium*» dal titolo di 895,83 millesimi e dal peso di grammi 12,72[46]. Ma la riforma non era destinata ad avere effetti duraturi. Il pezzo che doveva rappresentare la lira presto cominciò a valere più di una lira. Di più. La lira non entrò nelle abitudini del popolo. Emanuele Filiberto fece il possibile per tenerla in vita e fino alla sua morte nella contabilità di stato si contò sempre a lire, soldi e denari. Ma la gente continuò a computare a grossi e fiorini. E dopo

44 D. Promis, *Monete dei Reali di Savoia*, t. I, pp. 48-50.

45 Su questa riforma cfr. M. Chiaudano, *La riforma monetaria di Emanuele Filiberto*, specialmente pp. 283-308.

46 Conteneva quindi esattamente grammi 11,395 di fino.

la morte di Emanuele Filiberto, la lira scomparve anche dai registri statali[47]. Quel che non era riuscito ad Emanuele Filiberto riuscì però a Vittorio Amedeo I. La riforma monetaria di questo duca attuata nel 1631 reintrodusse definitivamente e con successo in tutto il Piemonte il sistema di computo a lire, soldi e denari in sostituzione del sistema a grossi e fiorini[48]. A causa di tutte queste complicate vicende, nella Tab. A2 io non ho potuto dare la parità metallica della lira sabauda né per gli anni attorno al 1550 né per gli anni attorno al 1620 per la semplice ma decisiva ragione che in quegli anni in Piemonte la lira non esisteva. Mi sono pertanto limitato a dare la parità metallica della lira per il 1562 – l'epoca della riforma di Emanuele Filiberto – e per la fine del sec. XVII.

15. In base ai dati contenuti nella Tab. A2 dell'Appendice III si può osservare che le principali lire italiane accusarono tra il 1550 ed il 1700 un deterioramento nella parità argentea dell'ordine del 40-50 per cento e nella parità aurea dell'ordine del 50-60 per cento (la differenza nel tasso tra l'una parità e l'altra essendo determinata dall'aumento del rapporto di scambio tra l'oro e l'argento). Unica eccezione la lira fiorentina il cui tasso globale di deterioramento tra il 1542 ed il 1711 fu decisamente inferiore a quello delle altre lire (15 per cento per la parità argentea e 37 per cento per la parità aurea).

[47] M. Chiaudano, *La riforma monetaria di Emanuele Filiberto*, p. 298.

[48] Sulle circostanze che resero possibile il successo della riforma di Vittorio Amedeo I, cfr. le osservazioni di G. Praj, *La moneta piemontese*, p. 234.

Geminiano Montanari, rilevando la relativa stabilità della moneta granducale, ne attribuiva il merito alle «ottime regole che v'hanno apposto» e soprattutto al fatto che la zecca fiorentina «non s'è mai curata di farci guadagno» sulla moneta piccola limitandone drasticamente le emissioni[49]. E a Geminiano Montanari faceva eco una relazione piacentina che additava ad esempio «le monete di Firenze quali non hanno mai ricevuto alcuna alterazione, essendo tutte sorte di monete ridotte ad un'istessa bontà»[50].

16. Dalla metà del sec. XVI noi possiamo disporre anche di alcune serie di prezzi e di salari. Non si tratta né di materiale abbondante né di materiale qualitativamente molto adatto per accurate analisi statistico-economiche. Comunque ce n'è abbastanza per capire almeno grosso modo in che senso siano andate le cose.

Nel periodo 1550-1620 vi fu una normale correlazione inversa tra il movimento lungo della parità metallica delle varie lire e il movimento lungo dei prezzi e dei salari: cioè a dire, mentre le monete svilirono in termini di argento e di oro, i prezzi dei beni e dei servizi – in termini di moneta – tesero ad aumentare. Il rialzo medio dei prezzi e dei salari però sembra essere stato generalmente superiore all'inverso del deterioramento delle parità metalliche della moneta. A Firenze tra il 1500 ed il 1620 la lira fiorentina accusò un deterioramento nella parità aurea dell'ordine del 40 per cento e nella parità argentea dell'ordine del 20 per cento. Il livello medio dei prezzi e dei salari nello stesso periodo manifestò un rialzo del 120 per cento[51].

[49] G. Montanari, *Zecca in consulta di Stato*, pp. 356-357.

[50] Cfr. U. Meroni, *Cremona fedelissima*, p. 258.

[51] Cfr. G. Parenti, *Prime ricerche sulla rivoluzione dei prezzi*. A p. 144 il Parenti calcola un indice che dovrebbe rappresentare il

Vi sono motivi sufficienti per ritenere che anche sugli altri mercati si verificò un fenomeno del genere[52]. È già stato indicato in altra sede che non esiste nessuna ragione logica per cui il rialzo dei prezzi *debba* risultare *esattamente* (inversamente) proporzionale al deterioramento metallico della moneta[53]. In ogni modo non vi è dubbio che nel caso italiano tra la metà del sec. XVI e gli inizi del XVII l'esistenza del fenomeno va spiegata sia con la generale svalutazione dell'oro e dell'argento a seguito dell'aumento della produzione mondiale di tali metalli[54], sia con i movimenti generali dell'economia italiana del tempo[55].

Nel periodo 1620-1700 la correlazione tra i movimenti lunghi delle parità metalliche e i movimenti lunghi dei prezzi fu invece positiva: in altre parole, mentre le monete continuarono a svilire in termini di oro e di argento, i prezzi dei beni in termini di moneta invece di aumentare, diminuirono essi pure. Il caso sul quale siamo meglio informati è quello di Milano. La lira imperiale milanese tra il 1620 ed il 1700 vide la sua parità aurea deteriorata per un 30 per cento e la sua parità argentea per un 20 per cento. Contemporaneamente

livello dei prezzi quali espressi in termini di grammi di puro argento. L'indice qui sopra citato nel testo si riferisce invece a prezzi espressi nella corrente unità monetaria ed è stato da me calcolato sulla base dei dati forniti dallo stesso Parenti a p. 59 e nelle appendici.

[52] L'esistenza del fenomeno è provata dal fatto che tutti gli studiosi che per gli altri mercati si sono occupati dell'argomento hanno riscontrato un rialzo anche nell'indice dei prezzi delle merci e dei servizi espressi in grammi di metallo puro.

[53] Per tutti cfr. C.M. Cipolla, *Moneta e civiltà mediterranea*, appendice.

[54] Per tutti cfr. G. Parenti, *Prime ricerche sulla rivoluzione dei prezzi*, pp. 159-166 e A. Fanfani, *Indagini sulla rivoluzione dei prezzi*, passim.

[55] C.M. Cipolla, *La pretendue révolution des prix*, pp. 513-516.

i prezzi accusarono un ribasso medio dell'ordine del 40 per cento[56]. A spiegare questo paradosso concorrono due ordini di cause: la flessione della curva storica della produzione mondiale dei metalli preziosi e soprattutto il crollo della domanda globale effettiva (di beni e di servizi) che accompagnò il tragico «declino economico» dell'Italia durante il sec. XVII[57]. Questi due fattori deflazionistici furono evidentemente più forti della pressione inflazionistica rappresentata dalla svalutazione della moneta in termini di oro e di argento.

17. Alla fine del sec. XVII, la lira sabauda equivaleva a grammi 5,8 di argento fino, la lira genovese a grammi 4,9, la lira imperiale di Milano e la lira fiorentina a grammi 3,9 e la lira veneziana a grammi 3 (per queste parità e le relative parità auree cfr. Appendice III).

Per quanto riguarda il potere d'acquisto delle stesse lire, in via di prima e vaga approssimazione, sappiamo che alla fine del sec. XVII la giornata di un «maestro» muratore era pagata in media a Milano lire imperiali 1,75, a Genova lire 1,80 genovesi, a Firenze lire 1,90 fiorentine.

[56] A. De Maddalena, *Prezzi e aspetti di mercato in Milano*, p. 178.

[57] C.M. Cipolla, *The Decline of Italy*, pp. 178-187.

Capitolo terzo

Illuminismo e Risorgimento

1. Anche in campo monetario il Settecento fu il secolo delle riforme. Allo spirito limpido e sistematico dell'Illuminismo, il sistema monetario ereditato dal Medioevo sembrava retaggio non meno barbaro dei fidecommessi o dei vincoli corporativi. E ci si diede quindi a cercar di riordinare le cose in quel che appariva come «il gran guazzabuglio della moneta».

In effetti di riforme ce n'era bisogno. I sistemi monetari dei singoli stati così come li ereditava il Settecento erano una confusa mistura in cui s'erano incrostati insieme elementi di età differenti, reliquati vari di situazioni e provvedimenti diversissimi.

In ogni stato si trovavano in circolazione, fianco a fianco, pezzi coniati in epoche diverse, con intrinseci i più disparati che sovente era anche difficile appurare. Poi circolavano parecchie monete straniere. E il tutto in un modo disordinato, irrazionale e casuale. Per esempio nello Stato di Milano all'epoca del Beccaria sembra circolassero – senza contare i pezzi di rame e di biglione – 22 monete d'oro e 29 d'argento: di questi 51 tipi «otto facevano doppio con le altre e tre avevano corso identico; eppure solo quelle di L. 15, L. 14 s. 15, L. 6 s. 16, s. 15 erano il doppio esatto di quelle da L. 7 s. 10, L. 7 s. 7 d. 6, L. 3 s. 8, s. 7 d. 6 ed avrebbero potuto formare con esse un sistema di multipli e sottomultipli se essendo tutte forestiere e di corso irregolare non fosse stato assai difficile possederle contemporaneamente»[1].

Di più, continuava quella distinzione tra «*moneta grossa*» e «*moneta piccola*» che pure era un anacronistico reliquato medievale. Nel Medioevo, come s'è già detto qui addietro, «*moneta grossa*» e «*moneta piccola*» componevano all'interno di ogni stato due ben distinti sistemi monetali con aree di circolazione geografiche d'affari e sociali nettamente distinte. Ma nel corso dei secoli questa netta distinzione era andata scomparendo. La diminuzione del potere d'acquisto dell'argento in termini di lavoro portò la «*moneta grossa*» nelle mani di tutti e ne fece mezzo di scambio usuale nelle contrattazioni locali e quotidiane. La «*moneta piccola*» d'altra parte a seguito dell'erosione plurisecolare fu sempre più decisamente confinata al mero ruolo di moneta divisionaria. Così «*moneta grossa*» e «*moneta piccola*» non rappresentarono più due sistemi monetari distinti ma vennero a formare un sistema unico in cui una moneta (la «*piccola*») assumeva il ruolo di sussidiaria e frazionaria dell'altra. Il guaio era che la fusione s'era andata realizzando casualmente: e spettava ora agli uomini di raccordare i due gruppi con rapporti semplici e soprattutto stabili. Il problema s'era in fondo già posto agli economisti del Seicento. Ma non era stato risolto.

E c'era infine la questione della «*moneta immaginaria*», anch'essa un reliquato dell'età medievale. Nel più lontano Medioevo la lira-fantasma era nata – si ricorderà – perché non circolavano multipli del denaro; ed era poi rimasta perché «*moneta grossa*» e «*moneta piccola*» avevano rappresentato due sistemi monetari distinti, perché i rapporti di scambio tra i tipi d'un

[1] L. Einaudi, *Teoria della moneta immaginaria*, p. 14.

gruppo e i tipi dell'altro gruppo non erano mai stati stabilizzati, perché infine la lira rappresentava a quei tempi ancora un tale valore che, se coniata, entrava subito a far parte della «*moneta grossa*» mentre per definizione era un multiplo della «*moneta piccola*». Nel corso dei secoli tutte queste circostanze erano andate scomparendo. Nel Settecento non esistevano più: «*moneta grossa*» e «*moneta piccola*» componevano un unico sistema monetario, e la lira era dovunque scesa ad un valore che, se coniata, avrebbe circolato per le mani di tutti.

Semplificare e riordinare la circolazione, raccordare e mantenere stabili rapporti di scambio tra le unità monetarie fondamentali e le unità frazionarie, dare stabilmente corpo alla fantomatica «*moneta immaginaria*»: questi erano sostanzialmente i problemi che si ponevano in campo monetario agli economisti e agli statisti del Settecento, e questi furono i problemi che essi cercarono di risolvere con tutta la buona volontà e l'ottimismo del loro spirito «illuminato».

2. In ogni stato, i memoriali, le discussioni, i progetti di riforma monetaria si ripeterono a non finire. Se si volesse analizzare in accurato dettaglio la storia di tutte le proposte, i progetti, le legislazioni relative alle varie riforme monetarie ideate o attuate nel corso del Settecento occorrerebbe un'intera biblioteca. Qui basti accennare ad alcuni dei fatti più salienti: la decisione di Vittorio Amedeo nel 1717 di non appaltare più la zecca sabauda e farne invece assumere la gestione direttamente dallo stato[2]; la riforma della moneta argentea attuata a Venezia nel maggio del 1722 e

[2] D. Promis, *Monete dei Reali di Savoia*, t. I, p. 307.

la stabilizzazione della quota del 1733[3]; la coniazione della «*madonnina*» a Genova nel 1745 che diede finalmente corpo alla «*lira corrente*» genovese; il parziale riordinamento del sistema monetario genovese nel 1759[4]; la generale riforma monetaria attuata negli stati sabaudi tra il 1754 ed il 1755[5]; la riforma monetaria in Lombardia resa esecutiva, dopo tante discussioni, con l'editto dell'ottobre 1778[6]; la riforma monetaria genovese del 1792[7].

Ciascuna di queste riforme ebbe i suoi caratteri peculiari e i suoi tratti distintivi. Non ce n'è una che sia identica ad un'altra. Ma prese nel loro insieme, si vede facilmente che sono tutte sorelle, che hanno tutte un denominatore comune: la teoria monetaria dei «filosofi» illuministi. I principi di base che le informano sono sempre gli stessi: *a*) che bisognava stabilizzare una volta per sempre la parità metallica della moneta; *b*) che bisognava limitare e controllare la quantità in circolazione della «*moneta piccola*» (detta anche «*moneta erosa*» o «*moneta eroso-mista*» o «*moneta bassa*»); *c*) che bisognava razionalizzare il sistema dei multipli e dei sottomultipli della moneta unitaria di base in relazione alle effettive necessità di conto e di pagamento; *d*) che le monete di vario taglio dovevano essere in

[3] N. Papadopoli, *Le monete di Venezia*, parte III, pp. 586-587 e 641-642.

[4] R. Sensi, *Moneta e mercato monetario a Genova durante il sec. XVIII* (tesi di laurea discussa alla Facoltà di Economia e Commercio della Università di Genova, anno accademico 1951-52), pp. 62 s. e 78 s.

[5] D. Promis, *Monete dei Reali di Savoia*, t. I, pp. 326-329.

[6] *La riforma monetaria in Lombardia*, ed. C.A. Vianello, è una raccolta di documenti sulla riforma; è consigliabile però utilizzarlo con molta cautela perché il Vianello non fu un accurato editore di testi.

[7] R. Sensi, *Moneta e mercato monetario*, pp. 83-87.

esatto rapporto di intrinseco metallico relativamente al rapporto di scambio nominale esistente tra di esse e sulla base di un dato rapporto di cambio tra oro, argento e rame; *e*) che pertanto in ogni stato un determinato numero di lire, in qualsiasi tipo o taglio di moneta nazionale venisse pagato, doveva rappresentare sempre la stessa ed identica quantità di metallo fino.

Tutti principi sanissimi e di cui c'era veramente bisogno. Peraltro come le varie riforme erano fondamentalmente informate agli stessi basilari principi, così in esse si ripeterono sempre anche gli stessi errori tecnici. Così per esempio anche quando si «nazionalizzarono» le zecche, si mantenne alle stesse il carattere di imprese operanti sulla base del profitto. Poi organizzando i sistemi monetari su base strettamente bimetallica si ipotizzò sempre un rigido ed immutabile rapporto di scambio tra oro ed argento. Ed infine benché si insistesse tanto sulla necessità di controllare la quantità in circolazione della «*moneta bassa*» per adeguarla strettamente «ai bisogni del minuto commercio», non si riuscì a scoprire la formula per attuare un simile continuo adeguamento[8].

Non c'è dubbio che queste lacune e questi errori minarono sensibilmente l'efficienza delle varie riforme settecentesche. Però non si può negare che le riforme stesse portarono nel mercato un innegabile miglioramento. Fosse poi effetto delle riforme o fosse anche effetto di molti altri fattori concomitanti, sta di fatto che il sec. XVIII, ed in particolare la seconda metà, rappresentò un periodo di relativa stabilità monetaria. Alla vigilia della Rivoluzione Francese le parità metalliche erano: per la lira sabauda grammi 0,35 d'oro o grammi 5,4 d'argento; per la lira genovese grammi

[8] Cfr. C.M. Cipolla, *Moneta e civiltà*, pp. 40-50.

0,22 d'oro o grammi 3,5 d'argento; per la lira milanese grammi 0,24 d'oro o grammi 3,5 d'argento; per la lira veneziana grammi 0,16 d'oro o grammi 2,4 d'argento; per la lira fiorentina grammi 0,26 d'oro o grammi 3,8 d'argento[9].

3. A questo punto della nostra storia[10], per ragioni che si vedranno in seguito, è opportuno abbandonare il filo della storia della moneta italiana e rendersi conto di quel che stava capitando in Francia.

Alla vigilia della Rivoluzione Francese, l'unità monetaria francese era sempre la lira tornese, divisa in 20 soldi e 240 denari; la sua parità metallica nel 1789 era di grammi 0,29 di oro o grammi 4,5 di argento fino.

Nel pieno dell'ondata rivoluzionaria, una legge del 7 ottobre 1793 (16 vendemmiaio anno II) aveva cercato di introdurre una nuova unità monetaria – chiamata *Repubblicana* – equivalente a 9 grammi di argento fino e che doveva essere la base di un sistema di tagli diversi in rapporto decimale. Ma era rimasta lettera morta. Due mesi più tardi, però, una nuova legge meno ambiziosa lasciava in vita la vecchia lira ma stabiliva che «i conti delle spese pubbliche, invece d'essere tenuti come nel passato in lire, soldi e denari, saranno tenuti in lire, decimi e centesimi». La legge questa volta si dimostrò efficace: il sistema decimale penetrò il sistema monetario ed aprì la prima breccia nell'ordinamento ormai millenario creato dai buoni re carolingi.

[9] I vari stati non adottarono un identico rapporto legale AU/AR; ciò spiega perché non esista sempre lo stesso rapporto tra parità aurea e parità argentea delle varie lire.

[10] Sui sistemi monetari degli stati italiani alla fine del sec. XVIII utilissimo è il J.M. Benaven, *Le caissier italien*, Lyon, 1787.

Meno di due anni più tardi, il 7 aprile 1795 (18 germinale anno III), una nuova legge stabilì che «l'unità monetaria prenderà il nome di franco al posto di quello di lira usato fino ad oggi». Poi, il 15 agosto 1795 (28 termidoro anno III) venne ulteriormente stabilito che: *a*) l'unità monetaria porterà il nome di franco; *b*) il franco si dividerà in 10 decimi ed il decimo in 10 centesimi; *c*) il titolo della moneta d'argento sarà di 9 parti di argento puro e di una parte di lega; *d*) il pezzo da un franco peserà grammi 5.

I ponti col passato erano definitivamente rotti. La nuova Francia aveva un nuovo sistema monetario. E questo nuovo sistema monetario venne definitivamente consacrato e regolamentato con la legge fondamentale del 7 aprile 1803 (17 germinale anno XI) in cui si stabiliva che: *a*) l'unità monetaria franco doveva pesare 5 grammi d'argento al titolo di 900 millesimi; *b*) sarebbero stati battuti anche pezzi d'oro da 20 e da 40 franchi al titolo di 900 millesimi ed al peso unitario rispettivamente di grammi 6,451612 e di grammi 12,903224 (per cui un franco veniva ad equivalere in oro fino a grammi 0,2903225); *c*) la coniazione era libera e coloro che avrebbero portato oro e argento alla zecca non avrebbero avuto da pagare altro che le pure spese di coniazione.

La Francia veniva così a porsi in regime di bimetallismo al rapporto AU/AR di 1:15,5. «Senza dubbio i due metalli non erano rigorosamente su un piede di parità. I 5 grammi di argento (a titolo 900 mill.) erano l'unità monetaria e l'oro sembrava relegato in secondo piano. Ma sia pure con questa riserva, la legge del germinale consacrava il bimetallismo»[11].

[11] Per tutto quanto precede cfr. R. Sedillot, *Le franc*, pp. 79 e 167-173.

4. Il predominio politico, militare, economico e culturale francese in Italia durante il periodo rivoluzionario e napoleonico lasciò fortemente la sua impronta anche nel settore monetario. L'occupazione militare francese prima e l'annessione politica alla Francia poi imposero il nuovo sistema monetario francese al Piemonte[12]. Lo stesso accadde a Genova e alla Liguria con l'annessione alla Francia del giugno 1805[13]. In Toscana l'influenza francese si manifestò più blanda e si limitò alla parziale riforma del 1803 che portò il sistema monetario su base decimale[14]; l'unità monetaria fondamentale rimase la tradizionale lira e anche dopo l'annessione della Toscana alla Francia, Napoleone con decreto del 3 marzo 1809 permise che «la zecca fosse mantenuta sull'antico piede continuandovi fino a nuovo ordine la fabbricazione delle tre specie solite a battersi cioè rusponi, dieci paoli e biglione in doppi soldi e quattrinelli»[15].

L'istituzione del Regno napoleonico d'Italia del 1805 provocava intanto interessanti sviluppi anche in Lombardia e nel Veneto. Con decreto del 21 marzo 1806 Napoleone ordinava che la moneta del Regno d'Italia dovesse essere «uniforme alla moneta legale già in corso nel nostro Impero di Francia». Il decreto contemplava tre gruppi di moneta: di rame, d'argento e d'oro. Il pezzo da 1 lira doveva pesare 5 grammi di argento al titolo di 900 millesimi (=4,5 grammi di fino): benché conservasse il nome di lira era quindi so-

[12] D. Promis, *Monete dei Reali di Savoia*, t. I, p. 347; G. Carboneri, *La circolazione monetaria*, pp. 82-97.

[13] C. Desimoni, *Tavole descrittive*, pp. 248-249; G. Carboneri, *La circolazione monetaria*, pp. 100-101.

[14] A. Galeotti, *Monete del Granducato di Toscana*, pp. 440-441.

[15] A. Galeotti, *Monete del Granducato di Toscana*, p. 453.

stanzialmente la replica del franco francese. Sul diritto, la nuova lira doveva recare la leggenda «Napoleone imperatore e re» e l'anno di emissione; al rovescio lo stemma del Regno e l'indicazione del valore nominale[16]. Questa fu la prima moneta coniata che portò il nome di «lira italiana».

5. La Restaurazione portò naturalmente col nuovo riassetto politico anche un riassetto dei sistemi monetari. La storia di questo riassetto è abbastanza complicata.

Nel Lombardo-Veneto tra il 1815 ed il 1866 si possono distinguere tre tempi. In un primo tempo il nuovo governo lasciò in circolazione le monete del periodo napoleonico e si limitò ad introdurre le monete austriache d'oro e d'argento coniate secondo il cosiddetto *sistema di convenzione*. Il *sistema di convenzione* derivava direttamente dalla convenzione del «20 *Gulden Münzfuss*» stipulata il 21 settembre 1753 tra l'imperatrice Maria Teresa e la Baviera ed era un sistema a base bimetallica con un rapporto legale AU/AR che al tempo della convenzione era stato stabilito a 1:14,155 ma che nel 1786 era stato portato a 1:15,290. Così fino al 1823. Il 1° novembre di quell'anno una Sovrana Patente di Francesco I introduceva nel Lombardo-Veneto un nuovo ordinamento monetario, fondamentalmente raccordato ai sistemi monetari delle altre parti dell'Impero: il nuovo sistema era ancora su base bimetallica al rapporto AU/AR di 1:15,290 (ed era perciò ancora detto *di convenzione*), ma la nuova unità monetaria fondamentale era la *lira austriaca* del peso di grammi

[16] Per tutto quanto precede cfr. M. Roberti, *Milano capitale napoleonica*, t. III, pp. 212-213.

4,331 di argento al titolo 900 millesimi (fino grammi 3,898)[17]: nei propositi del legislatore questa nuova *lira austriaca* doveva sostituire definitivamente le vecchie lire milanese e italiana e il sistema monetario del Lombardo-Veneto doveva pertanto più strettamente inserirsi nel sistema monetario dell'Impero[18]. Tale ordinamento restò in vigore dal 1823 sino al 1858. Dal 1° novembre 1858, terzo tempo: per tutti i territori dell'Impero Austro-Ungarico e quindi anche per il Lombardo-Veneto veniva stabilito un nuovo ordinamento monetario in accordo al trattato stipulato a Vienna il 24 gennaio 1857 tra l'Impero e gli stati dello Zollverein tedesco. Il nuovo sistema era su base monometallica argentea e la nuova unità monetaria fondamentale era il *fiorino valuta austriaca* (da non confondere col vecchio *fiorino di convenzione*) del peso di grammi 12,345 d'argento al titolo di 900 millesimi (fino grammi 11,11)[19]. Questo sistema rimase in vigore sino all'arrivo dei Piemontesi, in Lombardia nel 1859 e nel Veneto nel 1866.

[17] Per tutto quanto precede cfr. U. Tucci, *Le monete del Regno Lombardo-Veneto*, pp. 1-7. «Nelle province venete, però, si conservò l'uso di esprimere le contrattazioni correnti in *lire venete*. Per ridurre le *lire austriache* in *lire venete* si costumava moltiplicarne l'importo per sette e dividere il prodotto per quattro, realizzando così un rapporto di 1 a 1,75 mentre l'articolo 20 della Sovrana Patente del 1823 l'aveva stabilito in 1:1,69, 59/64». La lira italiana napoleonica fu valutata pari a lire austriache 1,148.

[18] Un documento dell'epoca dichiarava che «lo scopo del cambiamento fu di introdurre nel Lombardo-Veneto il sistema di convenzione in vigore nelle altre province dell'Impero austriaco, conservando tuttavia la divisione decimale dell'unità fondamentale. Nello stesso tempo si cercò di eliminare gli inconvenienti derivanti dalla circolazione di monete effettive appartenenti a sistemi diversi» (*Un'inchiesta inglese del 1857*, ed. G. Felloni, in *Archivio Economico dell'Unificazione Italiana*).

[19] U. Tucci, *Le monete del Regno Lombardo-Veneto*, pp. 7-10. Il rapporto tra la precedente unità monetaria e la nuova fu stabilito così: una *lira austriaca*=0,35 *fiorino valuta austriaca*.

In Toscana, durante i primi anni della Restaurazione l'unità fondamentale di conto e di pagamento fu la lira del peso di grammi 3,929 d'argento a 917 millesimi (fino grammi 3,603). In taluni tipi di contratto e pagamento si usava però di preferenza far uso del *paolo*, in altri dello *zecchino*, in altri del *ruspone*, in altri ancora addirittura del *franco francese*. Cercando di portare maggiore ordine e maggiore uniformità in questa materia, il governo granducale con notificazione del 10 luglio 1826 autorizzò la zecca ad emettere una moneta d'argento chiamata *fiorino*, che nelle intenzioni del legislatore doveva divenire la «sola ed unica base della monetazione toscana». Questo fiorino doveva suddividersi in 100 quattrini e doveva pesare grammi 6,875 di argento a 917 millesimi (fino grammi 6,304)[20]. Sia prima con la lira che poi con il fiorino, il sistema monetario toscano fu sempre a base monometallica argentea e le monete d'oro in circolazione non avevano valuta legale ma venivano negoziate al loro valore commerciale[21].

Negli stati sabaudi, in un primo momento, nel clima fazioso della Restaurazione, si cercò di ripristinare l'antico sistema prerivoluzionario basato sulla tradizionale *lira* di venti soldi da dodici denari ciascuno. Ma in prosieguo di tempo, poiché l'uso di contare in franchi da cento centesimi si era radicato nel popolo ed il vecchio sistema stentava a venir reintrodotto, si decise di adottare un sistema monetario ricalcato su quello napoleonico. Con le Regie Patenti del 6 agosto 1816 Vittorio Emanuele I ordinò che d'allora innanzi

[20] Cfr. G. Parenti, *Monete e cambi nel Granducato di Toscana*, pp. 2-5. Il rapporto tra lira toscana e fiorino fu stabilito a L. 1, s. 13, d. 4 per un fiorino.

[21] G. Parenti, *Monete e cambi nel Granducato di Toscana*, p. 3.

l'unità monetaria legale fosse la *lira nuova di Piemonte* (per distinguerla dall'antica di venti soldi) suddivisa in centesimi di lira. La parità metallica fu fissata dalla legge in grammi 4,5 d'argento fino o grammi 0,290322 di oro fino per lira con un rapporto legale AU/AR pari a 1:15,5[22].

6. Bisogna peraltro stare attenti a non dare a tutti i mutamenti cui si è accennato lo stesso significato che daremmo oggi ad un «cambio di moneta». Oggi, se la moneta viene «cambiata», *tutta* la massa del vecchio tipo viene in un tempo più o meno lungo tolta di circolazione e sostituita *completamente* con i mezzi di nuovo tipo. Allora le cose – salvo casi del tutto eccezionali – procedevano in maniera molto meno drastica. Dopo che s'era deciso di «cambiare» la moneta ci si accorgeva in genere che l'operazione veniva a costare troppo e allora ci si accontentava di emettere un certo numero di pezzi nuovi limitandosi di conseguenza a ritirare solo una parte dei pezzi vecchi in circolazione. La massa del circolante risultava così, dopo ogni «cambiamento», un ibrido miscuglio di moneta nuova e di reliquati più o meno archeologici di monetazioni passate. In Toscana, dopo il tentativo del governo granducale di introdurre nel 1826 il nuovo fiorino d'argento, un osservatore contemporaneo commentava «che l'inconveniente monetario è aumentato e non diminuito con l'introduzione del fiorino; infatti esistono ed hanno corso legale in Toscana fra plateali d'argento e d'oro 24 specie di moneta diversa»[23]. E un

[22] Per tutto quanto precede cfr. G. Felloni, *Monete e zecche negli stati sabaudi*, pp. 1-5. Il prezzo da una *lira nuova* non venne coniato. Se ne coniarono soltanto multipli e sottomultipli.

[23] A. Zobi, *Manuale storico*, pp. 392-393.

economista moderno, studiando quelle stesse vicende, osservava recentemente che «la nuova moneta stentò molto ad introdursi nell'uso e perché venne a mancare la serie delle monete effettive che ci si proponeva di emettere e perché il ragguaglio in fiorini di alcune monete in circolazione presentava qualche difficoltà»[24]. A Venezia ancora nel 1866 circolavano insieme *fiorini vecchi, fiorini nuovi, carantani antichi, carantani antichi di convenzione* e persino *lirazze, scudi della croce* e *giustine* di coniazione anteriore al 1797[25]. A Milano ad onta di tutte le innovazioni napoleoniche ed austriache si continuò per certi mercati e certi tipi di contrattazione a riferirsi ancora sino al 1860 alla vecchia *lira milanese*[26]. In Liguria, nonostante le Regie Patenti sabaude del 1816 e il Regio Editto del 1826 che imponevano la *lira nuova di Piemonte*, «la consuetudine di contare in lire (genovesi) fuori banco di tariffa ed abusive sopravisse ancora per molti anni; ciò fu dovuto soprattutto alla grande quantità circolante di monete genovesi d'antico conio che le Finanze non ritirarono al tempo del riordinamento monetario del 1826, data l'ingente perdita in cui sarebbero incorse»[27].

7. Considerata nel suo insieme, la situazione monetaria della penisola prima dell'unificazione appariva piuttosto confusa. Uno studioso ne tracciava recentemente questo quadro:

[24] G. Parenti, *Monete e cambi nel Granducato di Toscana*, p. 2.

[25] G. Carboneri, *La circolazione monetaria*, p. 188.

[26] Il Nelkenbrecher nel suo *Manuale di monete, pesi e misure*, p. 366 dell'ed. italiana, osservava che «le antiche monete della Lombardia son messe fuori di corso... Però la lira da 20 soldi da 12 denari di Milano serve ancora nelle comuni contrattazioni; tanto è ciò vero che nei listini si pongono i corsi delle monete in valuta austriaca ed in valuta milanese e quelli della seta nella sola milanese».

[27] G. Felloni, *Monete e zecche negli stati sabaudi*, pp. 2-3.

... Può affermarsi che, tanto nel 1859, allorché ebbe inizio il movimento di unificazione territoriale, quanto nel 1862 allorché fu decretata l'unificazione monetaria, il tipo monometallico argenteo predominava nettamente nella circolazione metallica del paese, rispetto al tipo bimetallico, e predominavano nettamente anche i sistemi non decimali sui sistemi decimali.

Delle sei unità monetarie legali vigenti nel 1859, due (la lira nuova di Piemonte e la lira nuova di Parma) erano identiche nel contenuto e nelle altre caratteristiche alla istituenda lira italiana e, mediatamente, al franco francese; una (la lira toscana) aveva un valore intrinseco leggermente inferiore, ma non era coniata e quindi non era usata nello scambio monetario; le altre tre (lo scudo domano, il fiorino di nuova valuta austriaca e il ducato del Regno delle Due Sicilie) si elevavano, come valore intrinseco, molto al di sopra della unità monetaria italiana (fra 2 e mezza e 5 volte).

... Un ulteriore significativo elemento di differenziazione sia per quanto attiene alla situazione comparativa pre-unitaria sia per quanto concerne il passaggio al nuovo sistema del 1862, si ritrova nell'ampiezza di ciascun sistema di monetazione effettiva in termini di quantità dei multipli e sottomultipli dell'unità monetaria legale immessi nella circolazione, di quantità e qualità delle specie difformi dal sistema legale, aventi corso come circolazione sussidiaria, e infine, di proporzioni fra le specie coniate di ciascuna categoria di metallo.

Prendendo anzitutto in considerazione il numero delle specie effettive, appartenenti al sistema legale, si osserva che l'estensione di ciascuna serie di valuta coniata varia da un minimo di otto pezzi per le province toscane, di cui cinque multipli e tre sottomultipli (non essendo l'unità monetaria coniata, fungeva da moneta-tipo un multiplo di valore molto superiore alla lira, paragonabile allo scudo), a un massimo di ventitré pezzi per le province meridionali di cui otto multipli e dieci sottomultipli (anche in questo caso, non essendo l'unità monetaria usata nello scambio, fungeva da moneta-tipo un sottomultiplo di valore tuttavia superiore alla lira e paragonabile allo scudo).

... In quattro dei sei sistemi vigenti nel 1859 si avevano valute auree coniate; in realtà, tuttavia, esse presentavano un'effettiva diffusione tra il pubblico soltanto nei due stati ancorati al sistema bimetallico decimale: Piemonte (8 pezzi) e Parma (2 pezzi). Le valute coniate più largamente usate erano quelle argentee, il cui numero (da 5 a 7 in tutti i gruppi monetari) risulta pressoché eguale in tutti gli stati, indipendentemente dalle altre caratteristiche del sistema legale. Esse rappresentavano, verosimilmente, la moneta corrente avente più ampia utilizzazione nelle contrattazioni quotidiane nascenti nella sfera dei consumi[28].

Tutto ciò per quel che riguarda la circolazione metallica. Il settore bancario contava poco allora. Vedremo in seguito che il grosso dello stock monetario del paese consisteva di specie metalliche. Comunque, pur nel suo piccolo, il sistema bancario cooperava a complicare ulteriormente le cose. Gli Istituti di emissione – in cui si identificava allora sostanzialmente l'intero sistema bancario – erano la *Banca Nazionale Sarda* (sorta nel 1844 e divenuta poi Banca Nazionale nel Regno d'Italia) e la *Banca Nazionale Toscana* (sorta nel 1857 dalla fusione delle Banche di sconto di Firenze e di Livorno) oltre a Istituti minori quali la *Banca degli Stati Parmensi* (sorta nel 1858 e chiusa nel 1861), lo *Stabilimento mercantile di Venezia* (sorto nel 1853 e assorbito dalla Banca Nazionale nel 1866), la *Banca Pontificia per le Quattro Legazioni* a Bologna (che aveva sostituito nel 1855 la succursale bolognese della Banca per gli Stati Pontifici e cessò nel 1860) e la *Banca degli Stati Pontifici* (sorta nel 1850-51 e divenuta poi Banca Romana)[29].

[28] R. De Mattia, «L'unificazione monetaria italiana», in *Archivio Economico dell'Unificazione Italiana*.

[29] Oltre agli stabilimenti di emissione citati nel testo esistevano poi il Banco di Napoli, il Banco di Sicilia e la Banca Toscana di

Nessun accordo legò mai tali Istituti: le loro emissioni si caratterizzarono di una assoluta indipendenza di tipo e di taglio per cui il paese vide circolare una gamma straordinariamente larga – relativamente all'importo rappresentato – di biglietti. Le continue emissioni di nuovi tipi, per evitare le contraffazioni ed il logorio dovuto all'imperfezione della tecnica dei biglietti, concorsero ad accentuare la confusione. Di più, dato che anche la regolamentazione riguardante l'attività di emissione era fondamentalmente diversa da Istituto a Istituto, ne risultava che anche sotto l'aspetto sostanziale le singole valute cartacee sottintendevano garanzie e salvaguardie di diverso significato.

Bisogna ammettere che il problema monetario quale si presentava all'atto stesso dell'unificazione politica non era dei più semplici. Se si tien conto della complessità del problema stesso e delle difficoltà connesse, anche giudicando col metro delle più moderne conoscenze, bisogna concedere che i nostri nonni fecero in materia di unificazione monetaria un lavoro abbastanza buono. Abbastanza buono soprattutto nel settore dell'unità di conto e della circolazione metallica; meno buono nel settore bancario dove le tendenze unitaristiche non riuscirono a prevalere e si trascinarono avanti incertezze e situazioni gravide di pesanti ipoteche.

Per quanto in particolare riguarda l'unità monetaria fondamentale, in un primo tempo dal 1859 alla metà del 1861 si cercò di contemperare le necessità e gli entusiasmi dell'unificazione con le esigenze delle tradizioni monetarie locali. Questa prima fase

Credito. Il Banco di Napoli e quello di Sicilia però non emettevano allora titoli al portatore e la Banca Toscana di Credito cominciò ad operare effettivamente nel 1863.

di compromesso, espressasi in una numerosa serie di provvedimenti e decreti sia dei vari governi provvisori locali sia del governo centrale culminò nel Regio Decreto del 17 luglio 1861 (n. 452=n. 123 della Raccolta del Regno) che coordinava i vari provvedimenti presi dai governi provvisori in materia monetaria, dava corso legale nelle Province annesse alla *lira nuova di Piemonte* (detta da allora *lira italiana*), ai suoi multipli e sottomultipli di argento, estendeva il corso legale delle monete d'oro piemontesi a quelle sole province ove già in precedenza circolavano monete d'oro, e lasciava provvisoriamente in circolazione le monete dei cessati governi. Poco dopo veniva decretata l'estensione legale delle valute auree a tutte le altre province.

Era evidente peraltro che questo non poteva essere il punto finale di arrivo. Ragioni politiche e ragioni economiche spingevano urgentemente verso una unificazione più completa. Così, dopo studi, discussioni e polemiche, si arrivò alla legge fondamentale del 24 agosto 1862 (n. 788). In base a questa legge: *a*) il sistema monetario italiano era posto su base bimetallica al rapporto legale AU/AR di 1:15,5; *b*) unità monetaria legale del sistema era la lira d'argento da 4,5 grammi di fino corrispondente, per il rapporto legale AU/AR adottato, a grammi 0,29032258 di oro fino; *c*) multipli e sottomultipli erano tutti in rapporto decimo-centesimale con la lira[30].

[30] Nel prospetto di p. 90 ho raccolto i tassi di ragguaglio tra le unità monetarie degli antichi stati e la nuova lira italiana secondo la tariffa annessa al decreto 17 luglio 1861 e successive modifiche. La tariffa ebbe carattere obbligatorio e in base ad essa si prescrisse la voltura delle contabilità e dei rapporti di debito e credito di carattere pubblico.

8. Nelle decisioni che avevano portato alla legge del 1862 c'erano i germi di vari scompigli. S'era discusso a lungo se adottare lo standard monometallico argenteo, oppure quello aureo, oppure quello bimetallico. Le simpatie degli esperti non immuni dal fascino dell'esperienza e della teoria monetaria inglese erano per lo standard aureo. Ma la decisione finale fu per lo standard bimetallico: «le frequenti ed importanti relazioni commerciali che noi abbiamo con la Francia, con la Germania e con altre nazioni che tengono l'argento per moneta legale, le condizioni speciali del credito italiano, per cui i titoli del nostro debito pubblico sono negoziati sui principali mercati ove si usa moneta d'argento, per non accennare altri motivi, renderebbero inopportuna e nociva per ora questa riforma (adozione del tipo aureo), la quale, invece, operata d'accordo con le principali nazioni di Europa, riuscirebbe perfetta e feconda di ottimi risultamenti. Quando avremo rassodato il nostro credito pubblico ed il mercato principale della nostra rendita sarà in Italia, o quando con pra-

Territorio	Anno di rif.to	Unità monetaria locale	Ragguaglio in lire it.
Antiche province	1859	lira nuova di Piemonte	1,00
Province parmensi	1859	lira nuova di Parma	1,00
Province ex-pontificie	1859-61	scudo romano	5,32
Province romane	1870	lira pontificia	1,00
Province toscane	1859	lira toscana	0,84
Province lombarde	1859	fiorino valuta austriaca	2,47
Province venete	1866	fiorino valuta austriaca	2,47
Province meridionali	1860	ducato	4,25

Nelle province modenesi le monete effettive in circolazione erano prevalentemente monete straniere ed in particolare monete austriache. Peraltro nei contratti privati si continuò abbastanza frequentemente a riferirsi all'antica lira di Modena. All'epoca napoleonica, il rapporto tra questa antica lira di Modena e la lira italiana napoleonica era stato fissato a L. it. 0,3838 per una lira antica di Modena (cfr. G. Boccolari, A. Selmi, *Monete e cambi nel ducato di Modena*, pp. 1-10).

tiche presso i governi esteri avremo apparecchiato lo scioglimento della questione, potremo addivenire con sicurezza a questa grande ed utile riforma». Così la relazione Pepoli.

Seguitando pertanto la tradizione bimetallica franco-piemontese, si finì col tener buono anche il rapporto legale AU/AR 1:15,5 che aveva informato dagli inizi del secolo il sistema monetario francese e quello piemontese e che nel 1832 era stato accolto anche dal Belgio e nel 1850 anche dalla Svizzera. Il guaio però era che nel 1862 il rapporto di mercato AU/AR era sceso a 1:15,36[31]. Al rapporto legale di 1:15,5 quindi la moneta argentea veniva sottovalutata e, per la legge di Gresham, sarebbe presto sparita dalla circolazione. L'inconveniente era grave, e per evitarlo, invece di abbassare il rapporto legale adeguandolo a quello di mercato, o invece di abbassare la parità argentea legale della lira, si mantenne il primo a 1:15,5, si mantenne la seconda a 4,5 di fino, ma si coniò la lira con un intrinseco lievemente inferiore alla parità legale. Il pezzo da una lira cioè fu battuto al peso di grammi 5 ed al titolo di 835 millesimi, con un fino quindi di grammi 4,175. I pezzi da L. 2, da cent. 50 e da cent. 20 furono battuti in proporzione all'effettivo contenuto intrinseco del pezzo da una lira. Solo per gli scudi da 5 lire si stabilì un intrinseco proporzionale alla parità teorico-legale della lira: cioè peso grammi 25, titolo 900 millesimi, quindi fino di grammi 22,5 pari a cinque volte la fittizia parità legale della lira (grammi 4,5 di fino). Circa questi scudi di cui si prevedeva la fuga perché sottovalutati rispetto al loro intrinseco dal rapporto legale

[31] Sarà a 15,38 nel 1863, a 15,35 nel 1864 e a 15,46 nel 1865. Cfr. per tutti F. Marconcini, *Vicende dell'oro e dell'argento*, pp. 24 e 62.

AU/AR adottato, lo stato dichiarava di astenersi dalla loro battitura, ma lasciava ai privati la facoltà di farne battere alle zecche pubbliche per eventuali esigenze di particolari negozi.

Il bimetallismo così instaurato era in verità un bimetallismo molto ibrido. Non c'è dubbio che di bimetallismo si poteva ancora parlare solo ed in quanto era prevista la coniazione (per conto dei privati) di questi scudi da L. 5 che soli avrebbero rappresentato «monete piene» d'argento in un dato rapporto con le monete auree. Le altre monete argentee, compreso il pezzo da L. 1, avendo un intrinseco inferiore alla parità legale, venivano ad assumere la natura ed il ruolo di monete divisionarie e fiduciarie: molto logicamente quindi si adottò nei loro riguardi la famosa «regola» della moneta frazionaria che era stata finalmente scoperta agli inizi del secolo ed era stata applicata con successo in Inghilterra dal 1816: si pose cioè un limite massimo al numero dei pezzi da L. 2, L. 1, cent. 50 e cent. 20 che potevano venir coniati; lo stato si impegnava a ricevere illimitatamente questi pezzi garantendo la loro convertibilità con i pezzi superiori; in ogni pagamento fra privati quegli stessi pezzi erano moneta legale sino alla somma di L. 50, cioè a dire nessuno era obbligato ad accettare più di cinquanta lire in pezzi da L. 2, o da L. 1, o da 50 o 20 centesimi.

Questa originale costruzione non era comunque tale da risparmiare al sistema monetario italiano tutta una serie di successive difficoltà del tipo di quelle che fatalmente occorrono ogni qual volta si pretenda di tenere in piedi anche una larva di sistema bimetallico. L'analisi dettagliata di queste difficoltà ci porterebbe lontano dal filo centrale della nostra storia: basti solo ricordare al proposito la convenzione dell'Unione Monetaria Latina del 23 dicembre 1865; la convenzione addizionale dell'UML del 31 gennaio 1874 che fissava un limite massimo alla coniazione degli scudi d'argento; la convenzione del 1878 dell'UML che sospendeva completamente la coniazione degli scudi d'argento; ed infine la convenzione del 6 novembre 1885 che imponeva il ritiro definitivo degli scudi d'argento. Così per gradi successivi, dando l'ostracismo ai pezzi argentei che ancora davano una parvenza di bimetallismo al sistema, si finiva con lo spingere il sistema stesso nella direzione del monometallismo aureo[32].

9. Intanto però cose grosse erano capitate a causa di fattori agenti da tutt'altra direzione. Ricordo qui ancora che esistevano in Italia, al momento dell'unificazione, due banche d'emissione di una certa rilevanza, e cioè la Banca Nazionale Sarda e la Banca Nazionale Toscana; che la moneta cartacea circolante nel paese non doveva superare allora – come vedremo – il 15 per cento della massa dei mezzi di pagamento disponibili; e che infine i biglietti in circolazione erano convertibili in valuta metallica su semplice presentazione secondo le più ortodosse regole bancarie. Così sino al 1866.

Se si vuol capire quella specie di terremoto monetario che scoppiò nel 1866, bisogna prendere in considerazione le condizioni generali economiche e finanziarie del nuovo Regno nei suoi primi sei anni di vita. Io credo che un buon aggettivo per descrivere quelle condizioni sia quello di «disastroso». Il bilancio dello stato accusava disavanzi che arrivavano al 50 per cento della spesa. La bilancia dei pagamenti si reggeva

[32] Sulle vicende accennate nel testo, cfr. con molto maggior dettaglio G. Carboneri, *La circolazione monetaria*, pp. 305-397. Un buon sommario al proposito è anche R. Lefèvre, *La circolazione metallica del Regno d'Italia*, pp. 11-30.

in maniera precaria. Il ricorso al capitale estero – per poter tirare avanti – s'andava allargando in maniera preoccupante. Bisogna ammettere che non mancavano i motivi per un diffuso e grave senso di generale sfiducia. Poi venne una serie di fallimenti nell'Italia settentrionale provocati in gran parte dalla crisi economica internazionale. Quando i segni premonitori di una nuova guerra contro l'Austria si infittirono ed il 30 aprile 1866 fu presentato alla Camera un disegno di legge col quale il governo chiedeva la facoltà di sopperire con mezzi straordinari alle spese per la difesa dello stato, la situazione precipitò. La rendita di stato, già in declino, crollò. I titoli italiani alla borsa di Parigi ebbero la stessa sorte. Il panico si diffuse all'interno del paese. Varie case sospesero i pagamenti e la gente fece ressa agli sportelli degli Istituti di emissione per cambiare i biglietti e ritirare i depositi. La Banca Nazionale vide volatilizzarsi le riserve metalliche. Il governo d'altra parte aveva bisogno di denaro per far fronte alle urgenti spese di guerra. Non c'era via di scampo. E il 1° maggio 1866 il governo emanava il famoso decreto n. 2873 in base al quale mentre si assicurava alla Tesoreria un mutuo di 250 milioni da parte della Banca Nazionale, si dichiarava il corso forzoso dei biglietti della Banca Nazionale stessa e il corso legale dei titoli fiduciari delle altre banche di emissione e dei banchi meridionali.

La manovra fu variamente giudicata. Ci fu chi scrisse che «chi ha conosciuto il povero Scialoia e lo ha visto piangere nel fatale 1° maggio 1866, chi sapeva quanta fosse la nobiltà di quell'animo e l'altezza di quella mente, non ha mai potuto dubitare un istante che, se il corso forzato poteva evitarsi a prezzo di qualunque sacrificio che non fosse la rovina della patria, il grande giureconsulto e l'illustre economista non lo decretava per fermo. Ma il corso forzato era purtroppo divenuto una ineluttabile necessità economica, finanziaria e politica»[33]. E ci fu, di contro, chi, sostenendo che la manovra fosse stata fatta ad uso e beneficio esclusivi della Banca Nazionale, scrisse che «il corso forzoso non fu necessario né economicamente, né finanziariamente, né politicamente»[34]. I contemporanei furono molto divisi tra le due tesi. Oggi noi siamo convinti che il corso forzoso fu una misura necessaria[35]. Qualunque sia il giudizio, sta comunque di fatto che il sistema monetario italiano nel 1866 entrò in regime di corso forzoso: e da allora non ne uscì sostanzialmente più, eccezion fatta per gli inizi del sec. XX quando pur esistendo giuridicamente il corso forzoso di fatto si verificò una situazione di piena convertibilità[36].

[33] G. Boccardo, *Le banche ed il corso forzato*, p. 76.

[34] *Relazione della Commissione parlamentare di inchiesta sul corso forzoso*, Firenze, 1869.

[35] G. Di Nardi, *Le banche di emissione in Italia*, p. 126 e in particolare la bibliografia citata a n. 1 della stessa pagina.

[36] Con la legge del 7 aprile 1881 si preparò la cessazione del corso forzoso: la data poi di cessazione effettiva del corso forzoso stesso e di inizio del cambio dei biglietti in valuta metallica fu fissata al 12 aprile 1883 mediante il Regio Decreto 1 marzo 1883, n. 1218. L'operazione però fondamentalmente fallì. Nell'agosto 1884 l'aggio comparve nuovamente e le banche sospesero di fatto il cambio dei biglietti. «Il corso forzoso tornava in vigore per decisione unilaterale delle banche mentre la legge continuava a riconoscere ai portatori dei biglietti il diritto di riscuoterne il valore in numerario su semplice presentazione agli sportelli delle banche. La prassi adottata dalle banche di ostacolare e di rifiutare il cambio durò a lungo, finché lo stato di fatto da esso creato non fu riconosciuto dalla legge del 10 agosto 1893 che sancì il diritto delle banche a riscuotere l'aggio da chi richiedeva la conversione dei biglietti. Ma prima che la legge fosse intervenuta con questa moratoria, si era verificato un episodio clamoroso: il Banco di Napoli, citato in giudizio dall'industriale Durio di Torino per essersi rifiutato di effettuare il cambio dei propri biglietti, veniva assolto dal Tribunale civile e penale di Torino che dichiarava "la incompetenza

10. Al momento dell'unificazione, la massa dei mezzi di pagamento in Italia era ancora rappresentata in grandissima prevalenza da moneta metallica. Stime attendibili farebbero ritenere che nel 1861 circolassero in Italia circa 1.100 milioni di lire (del tempo) in specie metalliche e poco più di 200 milioni di moneta cartacea, mentre circa 150 milioni fossero rappresentati da moneta scritturale (di cui peraltro circa 100 milioni erano depositi a risparmio). Ciò vuol dire che circa il 75 per cento dei mezzi di pagamento esistenti era ancora rappresentato da moneta metallica.

Questa situazione subì un drastico cambiamento a seguito dell'introduzione del corso forzoso. Nel 1871 le specie metalliche in circolazione erano scese a 534 milioni circa. La moneta cartacea era aumentata a

dell'autorità giudiziaria a statuire in merito alle domande del Durio". Si ebbe in tal modo, come osservò il "Giornale degli Economisti", la dichiarazione del corso forzoso per sentenza del Tribunale» (G. Di Nardi, *Le banche di emissione in Italia*, pp. 348-349).

La legge del 10 agosto 1893 si occupò soprattutto del risanamento degli Istituti di Emissione e della circolazione dei biglietti degli Istituti stessi. Per quanto riguarda la circolazione cartacea: *a*) i biglietti di stato passarono provvisoriamente a corso forzoso (RD 21 febbr. 1894, n. 50) senza obbligo, da parte dello stato, del cambio in valuta metallica; *b*) i biglietti degli Istituti d'Emissione mantennero il corso legale e potevano essere cambiati o in biglietti di stato o in valuta metallica *con le spese del cambio*, cioè dietro pagamento di un aggio. Il corso forzoso veniva così ufficialmente riconosciuto dalla legge.

Il risanamento monetario e lo sviluppo economico del paese dopo il 1896 portarono però alla spontanea scomparsa dell'aggio. Si venne così creando agli inizi del nuovo secolo una situazione esattamente opposta a quella prevalsa tra il 1883 ed il 1893: in quel decennio esisteva ufficialmente un regime di convertibilità ma in pratica si era in regime di corso forzoso; agli inizi del nuovo secolo, con un corso forzoso legalmente in atto il paese ebbe una circolazione fiduciaria di fatto convertibile in oro (cfr. G. Carboneri, *La circolazione monetaria*, pp. 403-404).

Il corso forzoso ritornò ancora di fatto con la prima guerra mondiale.

1.298 milioni. La moneta scritturale aveva raggiunto i 727 milioni. In cifre percentuali cioè della massa dei mezzi di pagamento esistenti nel 1871 la moneta metallica non rappresentava più che circa il 21 per cento, la moneta cartacea rappresentava il 51 per cento e la moneta scritturale il 28 per cento. Da allora il fenomeno fondamentale di lungo periodo è stato quello dell'espansione continua del volume dei mezzi di pagamento e dell'aumento dell'importanza relativa della moneta scritturale rispetto alle altre forme di moneta. Nel 1911, alla vigilia della prima guerra mondiale, il totale dei mezzi di pagamento esistenti nel paese era giunto a circa 10.830 milioni di lire, di cui il 63 per cento era rappresentato da moneta scritturale, il 28 per cento da moneta cartacea e circa il 9 per cento da moneta metallica[37].

Credo opportuno a questo punto mettere in guardia il lettore contro troppo facili paragoni fra i totali globali di mezzi monetari disponibili alle varie date. Anzitutto perché mutarono i confini del paese. I totali citati qui addietro si riferiscono ai confini del tempo. Quali fossero i totali durante tutto il periodo considerato ai confini – diciamo – del 1951 è impossibile stabilire con precisione. Se ci si accontenta di valutazioni induttive molto approssimate si può forse dire che sul territorio del 1951 potevano esistere nel 1861 circa 1.600 milioni di lire e nel 1911 forse 11.000 milioni. Ma il margine di possibile errore in valutazioni del genere supera io credo il 10 per cento.

Comunque anche accettando in via di prima approssimazione dette valutazioni, resta un'altra difficoltà: e cioè che con la trasformazione economica e sociale del paese, nel lungo periodo, anche lo stesso

[37] Per tutto quanto precede cfr. Tab. A3 nell'Appendice III.

significato sostanziale dei vari tipi di moneta mutò profondamente.

11. Torniamo al filo conduttore della nostra storia. Nel 1862 – si è visto prima –, la parità aurea della lira era di grammi 0,29032258 di fino, il che equivale a dire che un grammo d'oro fino valeva L. 3,44. Questo prezzo rimase invariato sino al 1866. L'introduzione del corso forzoso fece comparire un aggio a favore dell'oro, cioè a dire il prezzo dell'oro salì al di sopra della quota di L. 3,44 al grammo. Nel 1873 il prezzo era di L. 3,97 in valuta cartacea. Grazie ad una accurata indagine del nostro Istituto Centrale di Statistica noi siamo in grado di seguire bene le vicende di questo prezzo da quegli anni lontani ad oggi.

Dal 1873 il prezzo dell'oro tende progressivamente a diminuire sino all'abolizione del corso forzoso. Nel 1883 il prezzo è di L. 3,43 al grammo, nel 1884 è di L. 3,42, nel 1885 è di L. 3,44 e nel 1886 è ancora di L. 3,42. L'insuccesso dell'operazione per il ripristino della convertibilità dei biglietti ed il ritorno ad un corso forzoso di fatto riportano il prezzo dell'oro al rialzo. All'indomani della crisi bancaria del 1893, un grammo d'oro si paga L. 3,76. La quota rimane alta durante gli anni dell'impresa etiopica; poi dal 1899 comincia di nuovo a discendere. Il risanamento della circolazione monetaria e lo sviluppo economico generale del paese rafforzano la lira. Tra il 1903 ed il 1910 il prezzo dell'oro fluttua tra le L. 3,40 e le 3,44 al grammo. È il periodo della «carta che fa premio sull'oro»: il periodo che i nostri padri ricordavano con tanta nostalgia.

Tra il 1911 ed il 1914 la lira cede lievemente, ma nel 1914 il prezzo di un grammo d'oro è ancora di L. 3,48.

Nell'insieme tra il 1860 ed il 1914 non si può certo parlare di stabilità monetaria assoluta. Fluttuò il prezzo dell'oro. E fluttuarono anche i prezzi delle merci. Le medie decennali dei prezzi all'ingrosso, facendo base 100 la media del decennio 1900-1909, danno i seguenti indici:

1870-79	:	115
1880-89	:	102
1890-99	:	91
1900-09	:	100

Ma bisogna ammettere che, tutto sommato, le fluttuazioni di lungo periodo furono contenute entro limiti modesti. Per quanto poi in particolare riguarda la parità metallica, bisogna ammettere che, visto nella prospettiva storica delle avventure della lira dal Mille in poi, l'Ottocento rappresentò un secolo di eccezionale stabilità di fondo: agli inizi del sec. XIX la lira italiana napoleonica equivaleva a grammi 0,29032258 di oro fino; nel 1862 la lira del nuovo Regno d'Italia equivaleva a grammi 0,29032258 di oro fino; e nel 1911 la lira equivaleva ancora a grammi 0,29032258 di oro fino.

Epilogo

Lo scoppio della prima guerra mondiale apre clamorosamente una nuova era. Sul cartogramma storico, gli indicatori cominciano a muoversi in maniera frenetica. Mai nei secoli, dai tempi di Carlo Magno, avevano accusato movimenti del genere. Non c'è molto da dire su una storia che tutti noi conosciamo ed abbiamo vissuto. Basti accennare ai punti salienti. Nel 1914 occorrevano L. 3,48 per comperare un grammo d'oro fino. Nel 1921, a seguito dell'inflazione bellica e post-bellica, ne occorrevano 15,68. Tra il 1921 ed il 1926 l'intensità dello svilimento della lira rallentò; nel 1926 un grammo di oro fino valeva L. 17,09. Seguì una breve parentesi deflazionistica: prima per una decisione a sfondo politico che portò nel 1928 il prezzo dell'oro a L. 12,64; poi per gli effetti della crisi mondiale che ridusse ulteriormente il prezzo a L. 11,45 nel 1933. Da allora ricominciò l'ascesa. Nel 1936 la lira venne «allineata» al dollaro, ossia ricondotta alla parità del 1927 (19 lire per dollaro), il che significava una svalutazione del 41 per cento. Intanto venivano istituite imposte straordinarie per rastrellare liquidità, ma il governo non seppe osservare una linea di ortodossia finanziaria. Nel 1938, alla vigilia della seconda guerra mondiale, occorrevano 21,38 lire per acquistare un grammo di oro. Fino all'autunno del 1942, l'effetto inflazionistico della finanza di guerra si manifestò soprattutto nell'accumulazione di liquidità piuttosto che nell'aumento del flusso della spesa del settore privato. I controlli sul volume della spesa di consumo e di investimento agirono con una certa efficacia. Ma ormai era chiaro che la lira era entrata in una fase più che mai burrascosa della sua ormai più che millenaria avventura. Questa fase più recente della storia della lira è succintamente illustrata in un bel saggio di Paolo Baffi (*L'evoluzione monetaria in Italia*). Con l'armistizio, tra il 1943 ed il 1945 il tasso di incremento della circolazione dei biglietti divenne più elevato di quello dei precedenti anni di guerra e anche di quello che si ebbe poi nella inflazione del 1946-47. Il potere di acquisto della lira cadde allora più rapidamente che in qualsiasi altro periodo tra il 1935 ed il 1970. La divisione militare-politica consacrata dalla famigerata «linea gotica» provocò uno sdoppiamento nella vita della lira. A Sud della linea gotica la lira perdette terreno rispetto ai beni ed ai servizi molto più rapidamente che al Nord. Con la riunificazione politica del paese, la lira riacquistò una storia unitaria, ma non meno avventurosa. Come primo effetto della riunificazione si ebbe una caduta del livello dei prezzi nelle regioni centrali e meridionali verso le quotazioni del Nord. Ma nell'insieme del paese, il movimento ascendente dei prezzi riprese con la seconda metà del 1945. Tra il 1945 ed il 1947 la massa monetaria aumentò da 1.234 miliardi a 4.808 miliardi. Il nuovo scivolone della lira ebbe inizio nel maggio 1946 con l'aumento dei prezzi delle azioni e delle valute estere. Due mesi dopo, l'ondata inflazionistica investì i beni di consumo, in corrispondenza con analogo se pur più contenuto movimento scatenato negli Stati Uniti dall'abolizione dei controlli di guerra. Durante i primi mesi del 1947 la Banca d'Italia tentò di richiamare in vita una vecchia disposizione la quale fissava il rapporto massimo tra i depositi ed i capitali delle banche, ma il richiamo della Banca Centrale era troppo lontano dalla nuova realtà e le banche vi prestarono scarsa attenzione. L'espansione del credito continuò. Il prezzo di un grammo d'oro salì da L. 71,53 nel 1944 a L. 646,64 nel 1948. Parallelamente il costo della vita, con indice 1913 = 1, passò da 104 nel 1945 a 211 nel 1948.

Ai primi di giugno del 1947 venne formato il nuovo governo De Gasperi. L'allora Governatore della Banca d'Italia, Luigi Einaudi, entrò nel gabinetto come vice-primo ministro e ministro del Bilancio. Lo affiancava un altro eminente economista, Gustavo del Vecchio, quale ministro del Tesoro. Gente onesta, della vecchia borghesia; gente che aveva idee chiare in testa, che aveva preparazione tecnica, che sapeva anteporre il vero interesse pubblico alla facile demagogia e spendaccioneria populiste. L'annuncio del programma finanziario del nuovo governo accelerò la caduta dei corsi dei titoli azionari e delle valute. Nella sua prima riunione, il Comitato dei ministri incaricato dell'indirizzo generale della politica del credito introdusse un nuovo sistema di riserve obbligatorie per le banche. La manovra ebbe successo anzitutto per la sua validità tecnica e poi anche per altre condizioni che si erano venute gradualmente sviluppando durante il processo inflazionistico.

Tra il 1948 ed il 1961, ad onta di scossoni provocati da eventi quali la guerra di Corea (1950-51) e dalla crisi di Suez (1956), la lira conobbe una pausa di prosperosa tranquillità. Il prezzo di un grammo di oro che si aggirava sulle 703 lire nel 1950 era ancora sullo stesso livello dieci anni dopo. Alla fine degli anni Cinquanta, la lira aveva il sostegno di oltre due miliardi di dollari di riserve valutarie. Il periodo tra il 1948 ed il 1961 fu il periodo del «miracolo italiano» e tra i tanti miracolati c'era anche la lira.

I miracoli hanno un grosso svantaggio: capitano di rado e durano relativamente poco.

Tra il 1961 ed il 1970 lo sviluppo economico del paese continuò sorretto soprattutto dallo sviluppo del settore industriale. Nel complesso dell'industria manifatturiera il valore aggiunto calcolato a prezzi costanti crebbe al saggio medio annuo di circa il 7 per cento contro circa l'8 per cento del decennio precedente. Ma dietro la facciata superficialmente ancora brillante si erano aperte gravi incrinature.

Lo sviluppo economico del periodo del «miracolo» aveva avuto un certo carattere caotico che lasciò in eredità pesanti problemi al periodo successivo. Masse di gente si erano trasferite dalle campagne alle città e dal Sud al Nord senza una adeguata preparazione psico-culturale e senza adeguata assistenza e divennero un pericoloso elemento di instabilità politico-sociale. Mancarono adeguati investimenti sociali e riforme di struttura. Problemi del genere sono comuni a tutti i paesi che sperimentano una Rivoluzione Industriale: ma mentre nell'Inghilterra e nella Francia dell'Ottocento si presentarono e furono risolti nel corso di oltre un secolo, in Italia si presentarono concentrati nel corso di un ventennio e non furono risolti. La situazione fu tanto più grave in Italia perché l'amministrazione pubblica rimase quella che era, cioè di stampo e di efficienza borboniche. La classe politica si dimostrò fondamentalmente impreparata e cinica. Il sindacato operaio le sottrasse via via più potere ma non si dimostrò né più preparato né più lungimirante. Anni di slogan incentrati sul tema della lotta di classe instillarono sentimenti di odio e di rancore che impedirono quella cooperazione tra i vari gruppi sociali che è alla base di uno sviluppo ordinato e civile. Sarebbe un grave errore considerare la storia della moneta soltanto sulla base di elementi tecnici: la storia di una moneta riflette la storia civile oltre che la storia economica di un popolo.

Gli incrementi salariali tra il 1961 ed il 1970 presentarono notevoli diversità da settore a settore, ma nel complesso si può affermare che l'aumento dei salari fu superiore all'aumento della produttività. Alla lunga questa disparità provocò squilibri tra costi e prezzi. Ne derivò una diffusa situazione di dissesto che, in combinazione con un clima di conflittualità e di sfiducia, pesò negativamente sull'attività di investimento. Negli anni 1970 e 1971, nel complesso dell'economia italiana, la quota del reddito destinata agli investimenti in macchinari ed attrezzature fu la più bassa nell'ambito della Comunità Europea, con esclusione del Regno Unito e dell'Irlanda. La spesa statale continuò a dilatarsi, ma l'azione pubblica fu più determinata da facile demagogia che da ragionato calcolo economico e da efficiente amministrazione per cui si verificò un forte aumento dei consumi pubblici mentre mancò una efficace azione nel campo degli investimenti.

Nell'industria manifatturiera il rapporto fra capitale di rischio e passività finanziarie calcolato per il complesso delle imprese pubbliche e private discese dal 47 per cento alla fine del 1963 al 32 per cento alla fine del 1970. Ormai, in un clima di sfiducia, si puntava apertamente su ulteriori scivoloni della lira. Nella sua Relazione a termine dell'anno 1971 il Governatore della Banca d'Italia parlava apertamente di «disordine del sistema produttivo e di quello monetario», avvertiva che «né l'impulso della spesa pubblica né l'espansione creditizia avrebbero restituito vigore all'economia se non si fossero raggiunti incrementi nella produttività» e concludeva citando parole pronunciate nel 1762 da Cesare Beccaria a proposito di «disordine del sistema monetario»:

nella maggior parte degli uomini manca il vigore per rimontare ai principi grandi e universali e di scomporre con analisi le mal combinate idee; altri si fanno gioco dell'umana debolezza e colla facile superiorità di alcuni termini non volgari costituiscono un commercio di errori fondato sulla docilità di molti e sull'impostura di alcuni.

Le parole dell'illustre Governatore venivano applaudite, ma i suoi consigli scarsamente seguiti. Intanto la gravità della situazione italiana veniva ad essere accentuata dal progressivo deterioramento nella situazione economica e monetaria internazionali. Una ondata inflazionistica mondiale travolse un paese dopo l'altro, portò tra l'altro alla dichiarazione di inconvertibilità del dollaro (15 agosto 1971) e allo scardinamento dell'ordinamento monetario internazionale creato dagli accordi di Bretton Woods. Gli avvenimenti scombussolarono non solo i banchieri ma anche gli economisti che non si raccapezzavano più di fronte ad una situazione pericolosa e paradossale caratterizzata contemporaneamente da inflazione e ristagno. La crisi del petrolio ed il massiccio trasferimento di potere di acquisto nelle mani dei produttori di petrolio vennero a complicare ed a confondere ulteriormente le cose.

Da una posizione di forza agli inizi degli anni Sessanta la lira precipitò in una situazione di estrema debolezza nella prima metà degli anni Settanta e per sostenerla si dovette ricorrere a massicci aiuti finanziari dall'estero. Nel 1973 e nel 1974 la lira raggiunse tra le varie monete europee un poco invidiabile primato di svalutazione. Nella primavera del 1975 il prezzo dell'oro raggiunse la quota di quasi L. 3.500 al grammo e il prezzo dell'argento quella di circa L. 90 al grammo. La lira si è talmente svalutata nel corso dei secoli che noi dobbiamo computare con cifre di migliaia, milioni e miliardi. Negli scambi il pezzo da una lira è ormai del tutto scomparso. Già nell'aprile del 1968 un alto funzionario mi scriveva al proposito: «Quanto ai pezzi metallici da 1 lira, di diritto, nell'ultimo Supplemento straordinario alla "Gazzetta Ufficiale", risultano coniati 100 milioni di pezzi del tipo in lega "Italma" ai sensi del decreto presidenziale del 31.12.1951 ed emessi 99.120.050 pezzi ai sensi del decreto ministeriale n. 212991 del 2.8.1954. Nelle casse del Tesoro ne residuano pertanto solo 879.950. Di fatto non ne circola neanche uno. Dicono che anni fa siano stati incettati da fabbricanti di bottoni, come materia prima molto a buon mercato per la loro attività».

La lira è tornata ad essere un fantasma, ma un fantasma col piede di carta.

Appendici

Appendice prima

Note metodologiche

1. Un documento del 1375 ci fa sapere che a quei tempi in Lombardia con circa 30 lire una persona poteva mangiare, vestirsi e pagare l'alloggio per un anno. Pochi anni più tardi un accurato cronista calcolava che una famiglia benestante spendesse per il proprio mantenimento una media di circa 50 lire all'anno per persona. La cifra fornita dal cronista comprende però oltre alle spese per vitto, alloggio e vestiario anche le spese per le tasse e le imposte, il servitorame, il ronzino (l'automobile del tempo) e le varie. Tenendo conto di questo fatto e tenendo altresì conto del fatto che il documento del 1375 si riferisce alle spese di un uomo comune mentre il cronista si riferisce alle spese di una famiglia molto agiata («certe pauci sunt qui talibus expensis possint componere»), bisogna ammettere che le due testimonianze concordano abbastanza bene. E la conclusione è che nella pianura padana alla fine del Trecento una singola persona con 30 lire poteva pagarsi vitto, vestiario e alloggio e con 50 lire poteva vivere riccamente per un anno intero.

Circa duecentocinquant'anni più tardi, cioè ai primi del sec. XVII, sempre in Lombardia, per vivere decentemente non dovevano occorrere meno di 500 lire all'anno. Nel 1957 per mantenersi su un certo livello di agiatezza bisognava spendere in media un milione di lire all'anno per persona.

Raffronti del genere sono molto adatti per colpire la fantasia e far riflettere sullo spettacolare fenomeno dell'inflazione secolare. Ma possono servire a misurare il fenomeno stesso?

2. La misurazione delle variazioni del potere d'acquisto di una moneta lungo periodi di tempo secolari e plurisecolari è una delle più ardue imprese dell'economia applicata: un continuo trabocchetto alla logica, alla precisione ed al buon senso.

Il potere d'acquisto, cioè il valore di una moneta, è rappresentato da ciò che quella moneta può comperare tra i beni ed i servizi disponibili sul mercato. Pertanto uno dei modi più semplici per misurare le variazioni del potere d'acquisto dall'anno *A* all'anno *B* è quello di vedere quante unità monetarie occorrono per comperare un certo «insieme» di beni e servizi nell'anno *A* e quante unità occorrono per comperare un «insieme» *equivalente* di beni e servizi nell'anno *B*.

Fin qui tutto può parer molto semplice. Ma le cose si dimostrano estremamente complicate quando si tratta di scegliere i due «insiemi» *equivalenti* di beni e di servizi rispettivamente per l'anno *A* e per l'anno *B*. Se l'anno *A* e l'anno *B* non sono molto distanti tra loro, le difficoltà non sono enormi. Ma se tra l'anno *A* e l'anno *B* intercorrono secoli o addirittura millenni, le difficoltà diventano insuperabili. Supponiamo di avere il prezzo in moneta corrente nell'anno 1955 di un insieme di beni e servizi che oggi la gente comunemente acquista, cioè, pane, carne, frutta, vino, stoffe, alloggio, carbone, libri, luce elettrica, automobile, benzina, spettacoli cinematografici, radiotelevisori, e così via. Se vogliamo far dei calcoli sulla variazione del potere d'acquisto della lira dal 1938 al 1955 basta indagare quanto costava nel 1938 lo stesso «insieme» di beni e servizi (in adatte proporzioni) di cui conosciamo il prezzo nel 1955. Ma se il raffronto lo vogliamo fare con il 1355, la cosa diventa oltremodo ardua. Cosa mettiamo per il 1355 nel «cestello» (così gli statistici chiamano l'«insieme») dei beni e dei servizi al posto dell'automobile, della benzina, dello spettacolo cinematografico e del radiotelevisore? Anche quando nel «cestello» mettiamo merci apparentemente identiche è difficile dire se mettiamo effettivamente la stessa cosa. Oggi, per esempio noi comperiamo lo zafferano e lo usiamo per condire il risotto. Nel Trecento si comperava pure lo zafferano, ma le donne lo usavano per tingersi i capelli, i farmacisti per preparare abortivi e afrodisiaci, gli industriali per tingere le sete, i pittori per dipingere. Lo zafferano per l'uomo del Trecento era una cosa diversa di quel che sia per l'uomo d'oggi. Lo stesso dicasi per il pepe, per il riso, per lo zucchero, e così via. Anche la diversità dei metodi di produzione modifica sostanzialmente la natura dei beni. Un libro scritto a mano prima della invenzione della stampa *è* una cosa essenzialmente diversa da un libro stampato moderno.

Quando noi diciamo che alla fine del Trecento in Lombardia una persona poteva vivere «riccamente» con 50 lire all'anno mentre a noi oggi per vivere «riccamente» occorre più di un milione di lire all'anno, il raffronto può a prima vista apparire sensato, ma ad un più attento esame risulta decisamente viziato: viziato dal fatto che noi confrontiamo due cose diverse, il «vivere riccamente» del Trecento essendo una cosa assolutamente diversa dal «vivere riccamente» dei nostri tempi. E noi non veniamo messi in grado di sapere quanto dell'aumento da 50 a 1.000.000 di lire sia dovuto allo slittamento della lira e quanto al diverso livello e alla diversa struttura dei bisogni dell'uomo.

Il problema è di quelli che non ammettono una soluzione precisa. Come disse Lord Keynes «non ci si può illudere di poter mettere come sostituti equivalenti i gladiatori al posto del cinema o gli schiavi al posto delle automobili».

3. A questo punto della complicata vicenda è opportuno prendere in considerazione due altri personaggi: l'oro e l'argento. Per secoli e secoli le monete furono materialmente composte da uno o l'altro di questi due metalli eventualmente mischiati con rame o qualche altro materiale. Nei tempi più recenti poi, l'unità monetaria, anche quando cartacea o scritturale, fu in un modo o nell'altro ancorata o ragguagliata ad una certa quantità di metallo fino. L'idea dell'oro e dell'argento è inestricabilmente legata all'idea di moneta e sono fermamente convinto che molti dei lettori a questo punto si saranno domandati se tutte le difficoltà cui si è accennato nei due paragrafi precedenti non potrebbero venir superate se soltanto ci si prendesse la briga di calcolare l'equivalente aureo o argenteo della moneta attraverso i secoli.

Per non creare confusioni o illusioni al riguardo, è opportuno chiarire che vi sono qui due rapporti da considerare: *a*) tra la moneta da una parte e l'oro e l'argento dall'altra; *b*) tra l'oro e l'argento da una parte ed i beni ed i servizi forniti dal mercato dall'altra. Sia il rapporto *a* che il rapporto *b* non furono mai – almeno su periodi secolari – rapporti stabili. L'unità monetaria – nel nostro caso la lira – non riuscì mai a corrispondere ad un peso di oro (o di argento) fisso e costante attraverso i secoli della sua storia. Per ragioni che si sono accennate proprio in questo libro, il rapporto tra lira e oro (o argento) andò continuamente aumentando nel tempo, cioè a dire una lira corrispose ad un sempre minor peso di oro (o di argento). D'altra parte anche il rapporto tra l'oro (o l'argento) ed i beni ed i servizi offerti sul mercato non è stato mai un rapporto costante. Cioè a dire, anche se la moneta fosse sempre stata composta o rappresentata da una sempre identica e costante quantità di oro (o di argento), i prezzi dei beni e dei servizi (e non solo i prezzi di singoli beni o di specifici gruppi di beni o di specifici servizi, ma anche il cosiddetto livello medio generale dei prezzi) sarebbero stati pur sempre instabili. Nonostante tante illusioni nutrite durante i secoli, il potere d'acquisto dell'oro (o dell'argento) non è un'entità sacramentalmente immutabile. Se ne accorsero già i nostri nonni dell'età aurea del gold standard. Sul piano storico poi se ne possono dare esempi a non finire. Verso il 1550 a Firenze con un grammo d'oro si comperavano circa 7 dozzine di uova. Nel 1955 con un grammo d'oro se ne comperavano sì e no due dozzine e mezza. A Milano verso il 1440 con un grammo d'oro si pagavano quasi due giornate di lavoro di operai specializzati. Nel 1955 con un grammo d'oro non se ne paga nemmeno una, e c'è da tener conto che la giornata lavorativa è molto più breve oggi che nel Quattrocento. Alla fine del Trecento a Pavia con meno di 200 grammi d'oro si poteva comperare una bella schiava; nel 1955 con la stessa quantità d'oro si paga sì e no il servizio di un anno di una poco servizievole cameriera.

Riassumendo, noi ci troviamo di fronte a tre variabili:

a) il rapporto tra l'unità monetaria e l'oro (o l'argento);

b) il rapporto tra l'oro (o l'argento) e i beni ed i servizi;

c) il rapporto tra l'unità monetaria e i beni ed i servizi.

4. Le complicazioni non sono comunque finite. Il rapporto *a*, cioè il rapporto tra l'unità monetaria e l'oro (o l'argento) si configura in tre differenti maniere: α) la quantità di metallo fino (oro o argento) contenuto nella moneta *M* quando questa è una moneta metallica; β) la quantità di metallo fino (oro o argento) che la moneta *M* può acquistare; γ) la quantità di metallo fino (oro o argento) contenuto in una certa quantità di moneta *X* che la moneta *M* può comperare. Ciascuno di questi tre rapporti ha un significato e quindi un nome suo proprio: α è il cosiddetto intrinseco fino della moneta; β rappresenta il potere d'acquisto della moneta rispetto all'oro (o all'argento); γ è la parità metallica calcolata sul cambio con un'altra moneta. Il valore di α, β, γ non è necessariamente identico. Nei secoli precedenti il XIX per esempio α tendeva ad essere inferiore di β e tanto più alto era il costo di coniazione della moneta e più alti erano i diritti di signoraggio tanto più grande era la differenza tra α e β. Così pure β può risultare superiore a γ e tanto più la moneta *X* che si prende a paragone per il computo della parità è una moneta ricercata (per cui il cambio può riflettere un certo aggio a favore della moneta stessa) tanto più grande sarà la differenza.

Il calcolo di α o di β o di γ può comunque essere tentato solo a determinate condizioni. Il calcolo di α ha senso soltanto se: 1) si tratta di una moneta metallica; 2) la lega della moneta non è molto bassa (a meno di poter stabilire il valore del metallo mischiato al metallo nobile); 3) si tratta di una «moneta-piena» e non di una «moneta-segno». Circa il calcolo di β c'è da osservare che spesso nel corso della storia vi fu sui vari mercati un doppio prezzo dell'oro (o dell'argento): e cioè un prezzo legale e un prezzo di mercato differenti l'uno dall'altro. In tali casi il calcolo di β è significativo soltanto se fondato sul prezzo di mercato. Circa il calcolo di γ esso ha senso a condizione che: 1) α di X sia valutato rispettando le condizioni di cui qui sopra per il calcolo di α di M; 2) il cambio tra M e X sia un cambio di mercato.

Se queste condizioni sono osservate, non v'è difficoltà teorica del calcolo di α, β e γ. Per il calcolo invece di quel che si è chiamato prima il rapporto tra l'oro (o l'argento) e i beni e i servizi (cioè il potere d'acquisto dell'oro e dell'argento), sorgono di nuovo tutte quelle insormontabili difficoltà teoriche cui si è accennato qui addietro nel paragrafo 2 di questa Appendice a proposito del potere d'acquisto della moneta in termini di beni e servizi.

5. Fin qui, i problemi teorici. Ad essi vanno aggiunti i problemi e le difficoltà di ordine pratico. Per i secoli precedenti il XIX, i dati numerici di carattere economico sono rari, saltuari, rozzi, spesso inattendibili: colpa del tempo che ha distrutto molti documenti e colpa degli uomini di allora che non avevano per il fatto economico quell'interesse sistematico che abbiamo noi oggi. Più lontani sono i secoli cui ci rivolgiamo e più deficiente troviamo la documentazione e silenziose le fonti. In particolare per quel che riguarda i problemi trattati in questo libro, si può dire che:

I) i dati circa i prezzi e salari sono estremamente rari per i secoli precedenti il XVI: a quelli che sopravvivono manca poi in genere la continuità, l'organicità e l'omogeneità. Ancora per i secoli XVI, XVII e XVIII se si vuol fare una storia dei prezzi e dei salari bisogna sacrificare molto all'esattezza statistica;

II) circa il rapporto tra unità monetaria e l'oro (o l'argento), serie di prezzi di metallo in verga, fino al secolo XIX, si conoscono, ma solo in modo saltuario e disorganico e solo per taluni centri. In genere poi i dati disponibili si riferiscono a prezzi legali o di zecca e non a prezzi di mercato. Gli unici elementi di cui si può disporre con una certa continuità e sistematicità per la moneta dell'Italia centro-settentrionale da Carlo Magno alla Rivoluzione Francese sono α e γ: α grazie alle raccolte numismatiche; γ grazie ai corsi dei cambi delle unità monetarie correnti con le cosiddette «monete grosse» (fiorini, zecchini, scudi, ecc.): corsi dei cambi di cui si è conservata sistematica documentazione quasi per ogni mercato dell'Italia centro-settentrionale a partire dalla seconda metà del Duecento.

Queste circostanze di ordine pratico e le esigenze di carattere teorico cui si è accennato prima hanno condizionato l'indagine che sta alla base di questo libro. Per questo è parso utile richiamarle qui sia pure in maniera estremamente superficiale e schematica.

Appendice seconda

Note metrologiche

1. La prima unità ponderale cui si è fatto riferimento agli inizi di questo libro è stata la libbra romana. L'origine ultima di questa unità si perde nella notte dei tempi, e molto oscure rimangono pure le sue prime e più lontane vicende. Sappiamo però con certezza che con la grande riforma monetaria del 269 a.C. alla libbra fu attribuito un peso preciso e la libbra stessa divenne l'unità fondamentale con riferimento alla quale si stabiliva il peso legale delle varie specie monetali.

Quale fu dunque il peso della libbra romana dopo la riforma del 269 a.C.? Gli studiosi che si sono occupati della questione sono concordi nel ritenere che tale peso dovesse superare di poco 320 dei nostri grammi, ma sulla equivalenza *esatta* le opinioni sono contrastanti. I giudizi variano dai 321 ai 327 grammi. Riconsiderando l'intera questione, Philip Grierson ritiene che la libbra romana pesasse sui 325 grammi ma che, allo stato presente delle nostre conoscenze, non ci sono elementi sufficienti per discostarsi dall'opinione finora più correntemente accettata, quella cioè di una equivalenza di circa 327 grammi[1].

[1] Ph. Grierson, *Weight and Coinage*, pp. XII-XIV. Cfr. anche Nissen, *Metrologia greca e romana*, pp. 96 e 133.

2. Un'atmosfera di maggiore incertezza circonda la libbra che uscì dall'ultima riforma monetaria e ponderale carolingica. Le Blanc riteneva che la libbra carolingica corrispondesse a «12 de nos onces, poids de marc»[2], cioè a dire 367,129 dei nostri grammi. La tesi del Le Blanc fu accettata per lungo tempo e da molti studiosi[3], ma oggi è considerata inaccettabile. Guerard la confutò con solidi argomenti[4] e, dopo un accurato studio di numerosi denari, concluse che il denaro carolingico tipo, quale uscì dalla ultima riforma di Carlo Magno, doveva pesare grani 32 (cioè grammi 1,699)[5], e che perciò la libbra doveva pesare grammi 407,92[6]. Diversi numismatici – tra cui, degli italiani, il Promis[7] ed il Brambilla[8] – seguirono e confermarono le conclusioni del Guerard, ma il consenso non fu unanime e vi fu chi avanzò l'ipotesi che la libbra carolingica equivalesse a grammi 428,317[9], chi la fece uguale a grammi 433,41636[10], chi a grammi 436,80[11], chi a grammi 467,724[12], chi a grammi 489,50[13] e chi addirittura a grammi 491,179[14].

[2] F. Le Blanc, *Traité historique*, p. 96.

[3] Tra cui per esempio H. Dannenberg, *Die deutschen Münzen*, t. I, p. 11. L. Blancard, *La pile de Charlemagne*, pp. 609-613, ritiene un peso di circa 360 grammi.

[4] B. Guerard, *Du système monétaire des Francs*, pp. 416 e 423.

[5] B. Guerard, *Du système monétaire des Francs*, p. 416.

[6] B. Guerard, *Du système monétaire des Francs*, pp. 422, 423 e 428.

[7] D. Promis, *Monete dei romani Pontefici*, p. 47.

[8] C. Brambilla, *Monete di Pavia*, p. 56.

[9] V. Capobianchi, *Pesi proporzionali*, pp. 106-107.

[10] S. Fossati, *De ratione nummorum*, p. 80.

[11] A. Blanchet, *Monnaies frappées en Gaule*, p. 361.

[12] C. Desimoni, *La décroissance graduelle du denier*, p. 78.

[13] P. Rocca, *Sistema metrico e numismatico dei Merovingi*, p. 54.

[14] M. Prou, *Les monnaies carolingiennes*, p. XLIV.

Queste differenze derivano talune da differenza di interpretazione di documenti scritti o di antichi pesi rinvenuti, la maggior parte invece dal fatto che i vari studiosi hanno in genere calcolato induttivamente il peso della libbra moltiplicando per duecentoquaranta volte il peso del denaro e per far ciò taluni studiosi assunsero come peso del denaro il peso medio dei denari analizzati, altri assunsero il peso massimo e altri il peso più frequente.

Secondo le più recenti indagini, Carlo Magno attuò una serie di riforme del sistema ponderale a partire dal 789 e la libbra che risultò da queste riforme corrispose con tutta probabilità a circa 409 dei nostri grammi[15]. In ogni caso c'è da dire poi che pretendere di determinare il peso della libbra carolingica al grammo e alla frazione di grammo è fondamentalmente antistorico perché a quei tempi non esistevano strumenti di precisione che permettessero la esatta giustezza dei pesi e delle pesature né soprattutto esisteva una mentalità che desse origine o facesse osservare queste cose.

3. Per quanto riguarda la storia dei pesi delle epoche successive, anche essa rimane avvolta in un fitto mistero. Tutto quel che noi sappiamo con una certa precisione è il valore delle antiche unità ponderali al momento della introduzione del sistema metrico decimale, cioè sul finire del sec. XVIII[16]. Allora la gente – autorità, studiosi e uomini d'affari – si preoccupò

[15] Ph. Grierson, *Money and Coinage under Charlemagne*, pp. 529-30. Cfr. anche P. Naster, *Trouvaille de monnaies carolingiennes*, pp. 221-223.

[16] Per un breve riassunto della storia delle origini e dell'introduzione del sistema metrico-decimale cfr. A. Tacchini, *La metrologia universale*, pp. 1-16.

attivamente di stabilire l'esatta corrispondenza tra le vecchie e le nuove unità. Sulle equivalenze allora stabilite furono poi pubblicati, nel corso del sec. XIX, numerosi manuali quali il Martini, il Malavasi, il Sismondi, il Guidi, ecc. ecc. ai quali solitamente gli studiosi si rifanno. Bisogna avvertire però che queste opere – anche quelle che vanno per la maggiore come il Martini – dovrebbero venir usate con cautela perché le inesattezze non vi mancano: talvolta dovute ad errori veri e propri, sovente derivate invece da arbitrari arrotondamenti dei valori delle unità più basse che provocano poi sensibili alterazioni nei valori delle multiple più alte. In genere è consigliabile perciò controllare i dati con quelli riportati nelle pubblicazioni ufficiali del tempo. Per comodità del lettore ho raccolto qui di seguito le equivalenze metrologiche – derivate dalle fonti più attendibili – per le antiche unità ponderali delle cinque zecche più importanti dell'Italia centro-settentrionale. È da sottolineare che qui si tratta appunto di pesi di zecca.

Firenze[17]:	1 libbra	= 12 once	= grammi	339,50000
	1 oncia	= 24 denari	= »	28,29167
	1 denaro	= 24 grani	= »	1,17882
	1 grano	=	»	0,04912
Genova[18]:	1 libbra sottile	= 12 once	= grammi	316,75000
	1 marco	= 9 once	= »	237,56250
	1 oncia	= 24 denari	= »	26,39583
	1 denaro	= 24 grani	= »	1,09983
	1 grano	=	»	0,04583

[17] L'equivalenza per la libbra è tratta dalle *Tavole di ragguaglio... già in uso nelle varie Provincie del Regno* (ediz. uff. 1877), p. 291.

[18] Cfr. *Tableaux comparatifs des anciennes mesures du dept. de Gênes*, p. 17 e P. Rocca, *Pesi e misure antiche di Genova*, pp. 110 e 117.

Milano[19]:	1 marco	= 8 once	=	grammi	234,99730
	1 oncia	= 24 denari	=	»	29,37466
	1 denaro	= 24 grani	=	»	1,22394
	1 grano	= 24 granetti	=	»	0,05100
	1 granetto	=		»	0,00212
Torino[20]:	1 marco	= 8 once	=	grammi	245,91985
	1 oncia	= 24 denari	=	»	30,73998
	1 denaro	= 24 grani	=	»	1,28083
	1 grano	= 24 granotti	=	»	0,05337
	1 granotto	= 24 granottini	=	»	0,00222
	1 granottino	=		»	0,00009
Venezia[21]:	1 libbra grossa	= 2 marchi	=	grammi	476,99872
	1 marco	= 8 once	=	»	238,49936
	1 oncia	= 24 denari	=	»	29,81242
	1 denaro	= 6 carati	=	»	1,24218
	1 carato	= 4 grani	=	»	0,20703
	1 grano	=		»	0,5176

Naturalmente non è detto che per tutti i secoli precedenti il XVIII il valore dei vari marchi o delle varie once sia rimasto sempre invariato. Dai documenti anzi trapela, sia pur assai raramente, qualche velato accenno a ritocchi o modifiche subiti dai pesi e dalle misure allora in uso. Purtroppo però la storia di queste modifiche non è mai stata fatta e rimane avvolta – salvo rare eccezioni – nel più fitto mistero. Perciò noi, ogni volta che si voglia tradurre in pesi moderni unità ponderali antiche, siamo costretti a far uso, in via di prima approssima-

[19] *Tavole di ragguaglio... della Repubblica Italiana* (1803). La divisione del grano in granetti non figura in queste *Tavole* ma figura nelle *Tavole di ragguaglio... già in uso nelle varie Provincie del Regno* (ediz. uff. 1877), p. 430.

[20] M. Dho, *Guida pratica*, p. 50 e *Tavole di ragguaglio... degli Stati di S.M. in Terraferma*, p. 28. Le equivalenze citate sono quelle comunemente accolte dopo il 1818. Prima di tale data si era erroneamente stabilita l'eguaglianza di un marco con 245,9 grammi.

[21] *Tavole di ragguaglio... del Regno d'Italia* (1810), pp. X e 834.

zione, delle equivalenze stabilite alla fine del sec. XVIII nella speranza tacita che le modifiche subite dai vari pesi nel corso del Medioevo e dei primi secoli dell'età moderna non siano state né molte né sensibili.

4. Anche le unità usate per le misurazioni della lega furono sino alla fine del sec. XVIII diverse da quelle moderne. Oggi noi misuriamo le leghe in *millesimi*. Nei secoli precedenti il XIX invece si usava, per le leghe d'oro, far riferimento a *ventiquattresimi*, e per le leghe d'argento a *dodicesimi*, ciascun dodicesimo suddividendosi a sua volta in *ventiquattresimi*.

L'unità ventiquattresimale usata per le paste d'oro era il carato: «24 carati» significava purezza assoluta, cioè quel che noi oggi definiamo «1.000 mill.». Il seguente prospetto fornisce il ragguaglio tra carati e millesimi:

Carati	=	Millesimi	Carati	=	Millesimi
1		41,667	13		541,667
2		83,333	14		583,333
3		125,000	15		625,000
4		166,667	16		666,667
5		208,333	17		708,333
6		250,000	18		750,000
7		291,667	19		791,667
8		333,333	20		833,333
9		375,000	21		875,000
10		416,667	22		916,667
11		458,333	23		958,333
12		500,000	24		1.000,000

L'unità *duodecimale* cui si faceva riferimento per le leghe argentee era il *denaro* ed il suo sottomultiplo ventiquattresimale era il *grano* (24 *grani* = 1 *denaro*)[22].

[22] Talvolta però si chiamava «oncia» l'unità duodecimale, nel qual caso il sottomultiplo ventiquattresimale veniva chiamato «dena-

Con «12 denari» si intendeva purezza assoluta. Il rapporto tra *denari*, *grani* ed i nostri *millesimi* è indicato dal seguente prospetto:

Denari	= Millesimi	Grani	= Millesimi	Grani	= Millesimi
1	83,333	1	3,472	13	45,139
2	166,667	2	6,944	14	48,611
3	250,000	3	10,417	15	52,083
4	333,333	4	13,889	16	55,556
5	416,667	5	17,361	17	59,028
6	500,000	6	20,833	18	62,500
7	583,333	7	24,306	19	65,972
8	666,667	8	27,778	20	69,444
9	750,000	9	31,250	21	72,917
10	833,333	10	34,722	22	76,389
11	916,667	11	38,194	23	79,861
12	1.000,000	12	41,667	24	83,333

Talvolta la lega era determinata invece che qualificando la proporzione di fino contenuta nella pasta, riferendosi alla quantità di metallo vile. In tali casi si parlava di *peggio*: cioè una pasta era *x* denari di *peggio* per oncia o a *x* once (o carati) di *peggio* per marco. Se noi sappiamo quale fosse nel sistema metrologico locale il numero di denari entranti in un'oncia o il numero di once (o di carati) entranti in un marco, la valutazione della lega in millesimi si effettua facilmente con una semplice equazione proporzionale[23].

ro» (cfr. per esempio il passo di G. Cordero di San Quintino riportato qui addietro nel cap. I, nota 21).

[23] A Venezia per esempio si usava esprimere il *peggio* in carati per marco considerando che un marco contenesse 1.152 carati. Una «*Informatione*» settecentesca conservata all'Archivio di Stato di Venezia, *Provv. agli ori e argenti*, «orefici et altra arte in oro», b. 1371, fornisce le seguenti indicazioni:

«L'oro fin di tutta perfetione s'intende di esser carati 24 come cosa perfetta.

Per la valutazione esatta del peso e della lega di una moneta quando si abbiano da valutare questi dati sulla base di documenti scritti quali ordinanze, appalti e registri di zecca, ecc. è necessario naturalmente tener conto anche della tolleranza legale stabilita sia per il peso che per la lega. Nei documenti antichi la tolleranza viene indicata col nome di *rimedio*.

L'oro che si disse (leggi: dice) de carati 23 sono pèso (leggi: peggio) de fin per marca carati 48.

L'oro che si disse de carati 22 sono pèso de fin per marca carati 96 et son al sazo della tabela venetiana, al qual sazo l'Arte degli orefici lavorano li suoi lavori di detta bontà.

L'oro a carati	21	sono pèso de fin per marca carati	144
»	20	»	192
»	19	»	240
»	18	»	288
»	17	»	336
»	16	»	384
»	15	»	432
»	14	»	480
»	13	»	528
»	12	»	576

Il qual oro sono di mettà; et sono di mesa marca.

L'oro di tutta perfetione è detto popolarmente oro di zecchino».

Appendice terza

Tabelle statistiche

TAB. A1. *Parità aurea e parità argentea delle varie lire nel periodo 1252-1500*

Lira di	Periodo considerato	Moneta aurea di cui si considera il cambio con *a*	Cambio medio corrente nel periodo *b* tra *a* e *c*	Parità aurea di *a* calcolata in base al cambio *d*	Rapporto di scambio medio approssimativo nel periodo *b* tra AU e AR	Parità argentea di *a*
a	*b*	*c*	*d*	*e*	*f*	*g = e·f*
	anni	nome del pezzo	lire e centesimi di lira	grammi di oro fino	unità di AR per 1 unità di AU	grammi di argento fino
Asti	1252	fiorino			10	
	1315-1325	»	2,0	1,75	13,5	23,6
	1390-1400	»	3,8	0,92	10	9,2
	1490-1500	»	16,1	0,22	11	2,4
Milano	1252	fiorino	0,5	7,00	10	70,0
	1315-1325	»	1,5	2,33	13,5	31,5
	1390-1400	»	1,7	2,06	10	20,6
	1490-1500	»	4,5	0,78	11	8,6
Genova	1252	fiorino	0,5	7,00	10	70,0
	1315-1325	»	1,2	2,92	13,5	39,4
	1390-1400	»	1,2	2,92	10	29,2
	1490-1500	»	3,0	1,17	11	12,8
Venezia	1252	ducato		2,00	10	20,0
	1315-1325	»	3,2	1,09	13,5	14,8
	1390-1400	»	4,6	0,76	10	7,6
	1490-1500	»	6,2	0,56	11	6,2
Firenze	1252	fiorino	1,0	3,50	10	35,0
	1315-1325	»	3,1	1,13	13,5	15,2
	1390-1400	»	3,8	0,92	10	9,2
	1490-1500	»	6,7	0,52	11	5,7

Questa tabella è fondata sui dati derivati da C.M. Cipolla, *Studi di storia della moneta*, integrati per Asti con i dati forniti da D. Promis, *Monete dei Reali di Savoia*, t. II, pp. 6-42; per Venezia 1252 con le fonti citate qui addietro nella nota 16 del cap. II; per Firenze 1390-1400 con i dati contenuti in un registro dell'epoca conservato nell'Archivio di Stato di Firenze, *Miscellanea repubblicana*, busta 33, int. 2.

La lira di Milano cui si fa riferimento è sempre la cosiddetta «*lira di imperiali*».

La parità argentea di cui alla colonna *g* è stata ottenuta moltiplicando i dati della colonna *e* per i corrispettivi dati della colonna *f*. Eventuali discrepanze sono imputabili agli arrotondamenti.

Quando è stato possibile confrontare i dati ottenuti nella colonna *g* con dati derivati con metodi più diretti si è riscontrata una notevole concordanza: cfr. per esempio la parità riportata nella colonna *g* per Milano 1490-1500 e per Genova 1490-1500 con la parità calcolata sulla base dei prezzi correnti dell'argento in C.M. Cipolla, *Argento tedesco e monete genovesi*, p. 107.

TAB. A2. *Parità aurea e parità argentea delle varie lire nel periodo 1550-1700*

Lira di	Periodo considerato	Moneta aurea di cui si considera il cambio con *a*	Cambio medio corrente nel periodo *b* tra *a* e *c*	Parità aurea di *a* calcolata in base al cambio *d*	Rapporto di scambio medio approssimativo nel periodo *b* tra AU e AR	Parità argentea di *a*
a	*b*	*c*	*d*	*e*	*f*	*g = e·f*
	anni	nome del pezzo	lire e centesimi di lira	grammi di oro fino	unità di AR per 1 unità di AU	grammi di argento fino
Torino	1562	scudo d'oro	3,0	1,00	11,5	11,5
	1690-1700	zecchino	9,0	0,39	15	5,8
Milano	1545-1555	scudo imper.	5,6	0,54	11	5,9
	1615-1625	doppia	15,9	0,38	13	4,9
	1690-1700	»	23,5	0,26	15	3,9
Genova	1545-1555	scudo 5 stampe	3,4	0,88	11	9,7
	1615-1625	»	5,6	0,55	13	7,1
	1700	zecchino	10,6	0,33	15	4,9
Venezia	1545-1555	zecchino	7,7	0,45	11	5,0
	1615-1625	»	13,0	0,27	13	3,5
	1690-1700	»	17,5	0,20	15	3,0
Firenze	1556	scudo	7,6	0,41	11	4,5
	1711-1712	zecchino	13,2	0,26	15	3,9

Circa i dati originari su cui è stata costruita questa tabella, è opportuno distinguere tra I) i dati relativi agli intrinseci metallici delle monete di cui alla colonna *c* e II) i dati relativi ai cambi di cui alla colonna *d*. Le fonti cui si sono attinti i dati sono:

Torino: I) D. Promis, *Le monete dei Reali di Savoia*, t. I, p. 483 (scudo, fino gr. 3,01; per lo zecchino cfr. Venezia); II) D. Promis, *Le monete dei Reali di*

Savoia, t. I, p. 199 e t. II, p. 70; V. Saraceno, *Il corso delle monete*, pp. 99 ss.

Milano: I) F. Bellati, *Tariffa delle monete*, t. I (mscr, in Bibl. Naz. Braid. Milano, sez. mscr. AH. XI. 7) decreto del duca di Sessa del 15 luglio 1563 (scudo imperiale, fino gr. 3,04); F. Argelati, *De Monetis*, t. III, p. 25 e t. III *app.* p. 31 (doppia d'oro, fino gr. 6,04-6,08); II) F. Bellati, *Tariffa delle monete*, cit., alle date 1546, 1549, 1552 e 1557; A. De Maddalena, *Prezzi e aspetti di mercato*, pp. 151-153.

Genova: I) U. Meroni, *Declarationes*, p. IX e D. Spinola, *Sommario*, p. 52 n. 58 e p. 54 (scudo 5 stampe, fino prima del 1569 gr. 3,08, dopo il 1569 gr. 3,06; per zecchino cfr. Venezia); II) F. Argelati, *De Monetis*, t. III, p. 21 (per il cambio del periodo 1690-1700 devo il dato alla cortesia del dr. Sensi la cui tesi di laurea ho avuto occasione di citare nel corso dell'opera).

Venezia: I) N. Papadopoli, *Le monete di Venezia*, t. II, p. 751 e t. III, p. 1004; II) N. Papadopoli, *loc. cit.* integrato con G. Mandich, *Formule monetarie*, p. 681 e con Archivio di Stato di Venezia, *Arch. not.* b. 645, r. 2, c. 76v.; *Provv. Zecca*, cod. 18 bis, p. 348; *Misc. Greg.* b. 23, n. 15; *Arch. Grimani*, Libro conti L. Grimani (7 luglio 1544); *Avogaria di Comun*, b. 151, c. 21, ecc.

Firenze: I) A. Galeotti, *Le monete del Granducato di Toscana*, p. 44 (scudo, fino gr. 3,11); II) I. Orsini, *Delle monete dei Granduchi*, p. 111 e A. Galeotti, *Le monete del Granducato di Toscana*, p. 44 e p. 293 n. 2.

Come si è già detto per la Tab. A1, la parità argentea di cui alla colonna *g* è stata ottenuta moltiplicando i dati della colonna *e* per i corrispettivi dati della colonna *f*. Eventuali discrepanze sono imputabili agli arrotondamenti. Per quasi tutti i dati riferiti nella colonna *g* ho effettuato controlli calcolando le stesse parità direttamente sul cambio con monete grosse d'ar-

TAB. A3. *Mezzi di pagamento in Italia dal 1861 al 1971*

Anni	Moneta metallica (milioni di lire)			Moneta cartacea (milioni di lire)				Moneta scritturale (milioni di lire)			Totale complessivo (milioni di lire)
	a contenuto pieno	divisionaria	totale	biglietti di banca ed altri	biglietti di stato	vaglia, assegni e titoli affini	totale	c/c e depositi moneta	quasi moneta	totale	
1861	800	300	1.100	200	–	10	210	50	100	150	1.500
1871	302	232	534	599	629	70	1.298	329	398	727	2.559
1881	637	240	877	736	940	110	1.786	759	811	1.570	4.233
1891	787	281	1.068	1.122	342	170	1.634	1.075	1.511	2.586	5.288
1901	450	666	1.116	1.154	452	250	1.856	1.381	2.225	3.606	6.578
1911	300	659	959	2.194	485	350	3.029	2.401	4.440	6.841	10.829
1921	–	442	442	19.209	2.267	2.600	24.076	8.581	15.677	24.258	48.776
1931	–	2.138	2.138	14.295	–	1.297	15.592	24.116	43.260	67.376	85.106
1941	–	1.161	1.161	49.609	4.150	6.327	60.086	48.696	97.196	145.892	207.139
1951	–	2.276	2.276	1.291.843	10.531	154.930	1.457.304	1.699.506	1.958.623	3.658.129	5.117.709
1961	–	89.661	89.661	2.779.229	–	334.965	3.114.194	5.982.905	8.665.095	14.648.000	17.851.855
1971	–	232.900	232.900	7.281.200	76.500	691.500	8.049.200	30.450.100	24.642.000	55.092.100	63.374.200

Nota: I dati si riferiscono ai confini del paese alle date indicate. I valori sono espressi in milioni di lire del tempo. I dati relativi al 1861 sono tutti arrotondati. Discrepanze tra i totali parziali e il totale generale vanno imputate per detto anno agli arrotondamenti.

gento, circolanti allora come monete piene. I risultati hanno sempre confermato i dati citati qui nella colonna g: le differenze sono sempre risultate di entità trascurabile.

Per la *moneta metallica* i dati riportati nella tabella comprendono le monete di emissione a tutto il 31 dicembre, le giacenze di cassa del Tesoro e delle banche (legali o ad altro titolo), mentre non comprendono le specie esportate o importate, le fusioni e il tesoreggiamento privato. Sotto la dizione *monete metalliche a contenuto pieno* si intendono le monete d'oro e le monete d'argento a 900 millesimi (scudi). Per il 1861 il dato rappresenta le stime ufficiali della circolazione di monete (sia a base decimale che a base non decimale) degli antichi stati. Dal 1871 i dati si riferiscono alle monete (a base decimale) emesse dalle zecche del paese. I dati nel 1901 e nel 1911 rappresentano l'ammontare presunto delle emissioni precedenti. Sotto la dizione *moneta metallica divisionaria* il dato del 1861 rappresenta le stime ufficiali della moneta cosiddetta eroso-mista e di rame degli antichi stati ancora in circolazione. Dal 1871 al 1891 i dati comprendono le monete d'argento a 835 millesimi e di bronzo. I dati del 1941 comprendono anche i pezzi di acmonital. I dati del 1951 comprendono soltanto i pezzi di italma.

Per la *moneta cartacea*, salvo diverse indicazioni, i dati della tabella si riferiscono a biglietti e altri titoli a fine d'anno, e comprendono le giacenze di cassa e le eventuali riserve di biglietti del Tesoro e di altre banche (legali o ad altro titolo). Per quanto in particolare riguarda i dati della colonna *biglietti di banca ed altri*, tali dati comprendono per l'anno 1871 quindici milioni di buoni cassa delle banche popolari, un milione di buoni agrari e di altre banche e cinque milioni di buoni emessi da ditte e persone private. I *biglietti di stato* rappresentano fino al 1874 mutui in biglietti della Banca Nazionale; dal 1874 al 1880 biglietti del consorzio di emissione; dal 1881 biglietti a corso legale con copertura metallica. Circa la colonna *vaglia, assegni e titoli affini* va osservato che il dato del 1861 comprende solo i biglietti all'ordine della Banca Nazionale Sarda, in quanto la carta apodissaria dei banchi meridionali è compresa – data la sua funzione di quel momento – nel dato relativo alle banche di emissione. Dal 1871 al 1911 i dati rappresentano stime effettuate in base alle situazioni delle aziende di credito: comprendono vaglia, chèques e titoli di credito dei banchi meridionali stilati all'ordine.

Circa la *moneta scritturale* va osservato che i dati della colonna *conti correnti e depositi moneta* rappresentano i conti correnti e i depositi presso le banche di emissione (dal 1861 depositi fruttiferi e disponibili; dal 1901 debiti a vista, esclusi i vaglia e i conti liberi delle banche), le società di credito ordinario (fino al 1921 sono comprese tutte le banche in forma di società per azioni; dal 1931 i banchi meridionali, gli altri istituti di credito di diritto pubblico, le banche di interesse nazionale e tutte le banche di credito ordinario), le banche cooperative e popolari (le casse rurali e artigianali vengono comprese in questo gruppo solo fino al 1891), le casse di risparmio (per gli anni dal 1941 al 1971 vengono compresi in questo gruppo anche i monti di pietà di prima categoria), le casse postali (di cui, oltre i biglietti e buoni fruttiferi, vengono inclusi nel computo per gli anni 1941-1971 anche i conti correnti postali). La colonna *quasi moneta* rappresenta i depositi a risparmio e vincolati.

TAB. A4. *Prezzi dell'oro e indici dei prezzi dell'oro, dei prezzi all'ingrosso e del costo della vita in Italia dal 1871 al 1974*

Anni	Prezzo dell'oro in Italia Lire per gr.	Numeri indici: 1913 = 1		
		Prezzo dell'oro in Italia	Prezzi all'ingrosso	Costo della vita
1871	3,61	1,034	0,913	0,868
1872	3,73	1,069	0,991	0,981
1873	3,97	1,137	1,051	1,040
1874	3,81	1,093	1,049	1,065
1875	3,68	1,055	0,929	0,912
1876	3,69	1,057	0,900	0,965
1877	3,74	1,072	1,021	1,004
1878	3,75	1,074	0,989	0,967
1879	3,79	1,088	0,928	0,955
1880	3,70	1,061	0,933	0,990
1881	3,48	0,996	0,873	0,926
1882	3,50	1,002	0,896	0,904
1883	3,43	0,983	0,839	0,875
1884	3,42	0,979	0,804	0,858
1885	3,44	0,985	0,847	0,877
1886	3,42	0,979	0,852	0,876
1887	3,46	0,992	0,794	0,874
1888	3,46	0,991	0,808	0,885
1889	3,44	0,987	0,854	0,900
1890	3,48	0,996	0,876	0,932
1891	3,48	0,998	0,853	0,929
1892	3,52	1,010	0,810	0,921
1893	3,69	1,059	0,760	0,901
1894	3,76	1,078	0,738	0,897
1895	3,58	1,027	0,776	0,892
1896	3,66	1,050	0,782	0,888
1897	3,58	1,027	0,766	0,886
1898	3,69	1,059	0,787	0,892
1899	3,67	1,051	0,808	0,878
1900	3,64	1,042	0,845	0,882
1901	3,56	1,019	0,841	0,883
1902	3,45	0,989	0,813	0,877
1903	3,41	0,977	0,806	0,903
1904	3,41	0,977	0,770	0,914
1905	3,40	0,973	0,803	0,915
1906	3,43	0,983	0,833	0,932
1907	3,44	0,985	0,898	0,976
1908	3,40	0,973	0,874	0,966
1909	3,41	0,977	0,881	0,939
1910	3,44	0,985	0,882	0,965
1911	3,44	0,987	0,953	0,989
1912	3,46	0,992	1,028	0,998
1913	3,49	1,000	1,000	1,000
1914	3,48	0,996	0,958	1,000

TAB. A4. *(segue)*

Anni	Prezzo dell'oro in Italia Lire per gr.	Numeri indici: 1913 = 1		
		Prezzo dell'oro in Italia	Prezzi all'ingrosso	Costo della vita
1915	4,03	1,154	1,273	1,070
1916	4,37	1,251	1,847	1,339
1917	4,92	1,411	2,743	1,894
1918	5,22	1,495	4,129	2,641
1919	5,82	1,669	4,501	2,681
1920	14,05	4,027	5,907	3,523
1921	15,68	4,493	5,411	4,168
1922	14,08	4,036	5,447	4,143
1923	14,46	4,145	5,499	4,119
1924	15,28	4,381	5,466	4,264
1925	16,67	4,779	6,127	4,790
1926	17,09	4,899	6,254	5,167
1927	13,10	3,754	5,255	4,724
1928	12,64	3,623	5,080	4,378
1929	12,69	3,636	4,846	4,448
1930	12,69	3,636	4,338	4,307
1931	12,73	3,650	3,785	3,891
1932	12,94	3,709	3,535	3,789
1933	11,45	3,281	3,220	3,565
1934	13,13	3,764	3,149	3,381
1935	13,64	3,909	3,464	3,429
1936	15,93	4,567	3,880	3,688
1937	21,38	6,128	4,526	4,037
1938	21,38	6,128	4,841	4,347
1939	21,64	6,202	5,050	4,539
1940	22,28	6,386	5,893	5,297
1941	21,80	6,247	6,574	6,129
1942	21,39	6,131	7,386	7,084
1943	21,38	6,128	11,079	11,880
1944	71,53	20,503	41,544	53,794
1945	112,53	32,253	99,710	103,980
1946	245,26	70,582	139,614	122,716
1947	329,05	94,314	249,747	198,875
1948	646,64	185,341	263,496	210,569
1949	664,84	190,556	250,231	213,655
1950	703,05	201,509	237,064	210,786
1951	703,16	201,542	270,176	231,260
1952	703,20	201,551	255,121	241,085
1953	703,18	201,549	254,153	245,779
1954	703,11	201,525	256,234	252,387
1955	703,13	201,532	257,541	259,472
1956	703,14	201,535	260,446	272,383
1957	703,21	201,555	263,012	277,642
1958	703,05	201,504	258,413	291,002
1959	698,65	200,243	250,715	289,773

TAB. A4. *(segue)*

Anni	Prezzo dell'oro in Italia Lire per gr.	Numeri indici: 1913 = 1		
		Prezzo dell'oro in Italia	Prezzi all'ingrosso	Costo della vita
1960	698,47	200,191	253,039	297,390
1961	698,74	200,258	253,572	305,985
1962	698,51	200,207	261,317	323,927
1963	699,38	200,456	274,872	343,927
1964	702,53	201,359	284,070	366,263
1965	703,06	201,511	288,669	382,174
1966	702,64	201,391	293,026	389,823
1967	702,25	201,279	292,445	397,619
1968	808,58	231,755	293,607	402,687
1969	842,17	241,383	305,031	413,992
1970	743,15	213,002	327,300	435,042
1971	855,37	245,167	338,434	456,794
1972	1189,26	320,183	352,183	482,461
1973	1880,03	537,814	412,066	532,491
1974	3482,07	859,731	579,976	636,031

Fonte: Dati Istat, «Bollettino mensile».

TAB. A5. *Numeri indici dei prezzi all'ingrosso, del costo della vita e del potere d'acquisto della lira dal 1901 al 1974*

Anni	Numeri indici (1938 = 1)			Potere d'acquisto della lira rispetto alla media degli indici (1938 = 1)
	Prezzi all'ingrosso	Costo della vita	Media aritmetica	
a	*b*	*c*	*d*	*e*=1: *d*
1901	0,17	0,20	0,19	5,2631
1902	0,17	0,20	0,19	5,2631
1903	0,17	0,21	0,19	5,2631
1904	0,16	0,21	0,19	5,2631
1905	0,17	0,21	0,19	5,2631
1906	0,17	0,21	0,19	5,2631
1907	0,19	0,23	0,21	4,7619
1908	0,18	0,22	0,20	5,0000
1909	0,18	0,22	0,20	5,0000
1910	0,18	0,22	0,20	5,0000
1911	0,20	0,23	0,22	4,5454
1912	0,21	0,23	0,22	4,5454
1913	0,21	0,23	0,22	4,5454
1914	0,20	0,23	0,22	4,5454
1915	0,26	0,25	0,26	3,8461
1916	0,38	0,31	0,35	2,8571
1917	0,57	0,44	0,51	1,9607
1918	0,85	0,61	0,73	1,3698
1919	0,93	0,62	0,78	1,2820
1920	1,22	0,81	1,02	0,9804
1921	1,12	0,96	1,04	0,9615
1922	1,13	0,95	1,04	0,9615
1923	1,14	0,95	1,05	0,9524
1924	1,13	0,98	1,06	0,9434
1925	1,27	1,10	1,19	0,8403
1926	1,29	1,19	1,24	0,8065
1927	1,09	1,09	1,09	0,9174
1928	1,05	1,01	1,03	0,9709
1929	1,00	1,02	1,01	0,9901
1930	0,90	0,99	0,95	1,0526
1931	0,78	0,90	0,84	1,1904
1932	0,73	0,87	0,80	1,2500
1933	0,67	0,82	0,75	1,3333
1934	0,65	0,78	0,72	1,3888
1935	0,72	0,79	0,76	1,3157
1936	0,80	0,85	0,83	1,2048
1937	0,94	0,93	0,94	1,0638
1938	1,00	1,00	1,00	1,0000
1939	1,04	1,04	1,04	0,9615
1940	1,22	1,22	1,22	0,8197
1941	1,36	1,41	1,39	0,7194
1942	1,53	1,63	1,58	0,6329

TAB. A5. *(segue)*

Anni	Numeri indici (1938 = 1)			Potere d'acquisto della lira rispetto alla media degli indici (1938 = 1)
	Prezzi all'ingrosso	Costo della vita	Media aritmetica	
a	*b*	*c*	*d*	*e* = 1: *d*
1943	2,29	2,73	2,51	0,3984
1944	8,58	12,15	10,37	0,0964
1945	20,60	23,92	22,26	0,0449
1946	28,84	28,23	28,54	0,0350
1947	51,59	45,75	48,67	0,0205
1948	54,43	48,44	51,44	0,0194
1949	51,69	49,15	50,42	0,0198
1950	48,97	48,49	48,73	0,0205
1951	55,81	53,20	54,51	0,0183
1952	52,70	55,46	54,08	0,0185
1953	52,50	56,54	54,52	0,0183
1954	52,93	58,06	55,50	0,0180
1955	53,20	59,69	56,45	0,0177
1956	53,80	62,66	58,23	0,0172
1957	54,33	63,87	59,10	0,0169
1958	53,38	66,94	60,16	0,0166
1959	51,79	66,66	59,23	0,0169
1960	52,27	68,41	60,34	0,0166
1961	52,38	70,39	61,38	0,0163
1962	53,98	74,52	64,25	0,0156
1963	56,78	79,12	67,95	0,0147
1964	58,68	84,26	71,47	0,0140
1965	59,63	87,92	73,78	0,0136
1966	60,53	89,68	75,10	0,0133
1967	60,41	91,47	75,94	0,0132
1968	60,65	92,64	76,66	0,0130
1969	63,01	95,24	79,12	0,0126
1970	67,61	100,08	83,86	0,0119
1971	69,91	105,08	87,50	0,0114
1972	72,75	110,99	91,87	0,0109
1973	85,12	122,50	103,81	0,0096
1974	119,77	146,31	133,04	0,0075

Nota: I dati delle colonne *b* e *c* sono derivati dalle pubblicazioni ufficiali dell'Istituto Centrale di Statistica. La colonna *d* rappresenta la media aritmetica dei dati delle colonne *b* e *c*, cioè la media aritmetica degli indici dei prezzi all'ingrosso e del costo della vita. I dati della colonna *e* rappresentano il reciproco dei dati della colonna *d*, cioè tendono a rappresentare un indice del potere d'acquisto della lira.

TAB. A6. *Cambi in lire del franco, del dollaro e della sterlina: 1860-1890, 1945-1974*

Anno	Franco	Dollaro	Sterlina
1860		5,18	
1861		5,18	
1862		5,18	
1863	99,58	5,18	25,15
1864	99,33	5,18	25,07
1865	99,75	5,18	25,14
1866	104,85	5,49	26,75
1867	109,43	5,55	27,48
1868	110,80	5,67	27,80
1869	104,05	5,37	26,22
1870	107,24	5,40	26,92
1871	104,44	5,43	26,92
1872	108,09	5,61	27,70
1873	112,44	5,97	28,62
1874	110,95	5,74	28,–
1875	106,96	5,54	27,01
1876	107,52	5,55	27,17
1877	108,96	5,63	27,24
1878	108,75	5,64	27,32
1879	110,17	5,71	27,88
1880	108,34	5,57	27,39
1881	100,28	5,23	25,40
1882	101,26	5,26	25,55
1883	99,15	5,16	25,03
1884	100,–	5,14	25,23
1885	100,38	5,17	25,38
1886	100,19	5,14	25,31
1887	100,82	5,21	25,54
1888	100,98	5,20	25,57
1889	100,67	5,18	25,42
1890	101,15	5,23	25,54
1945	2,02	100,00	400,00
1946	0,84	225,00	907,31
1947	1,89	584,16	1982,00
1948	2,21	574,67	1880,64
1949	1,81	626,19	2317,25
1950	1,81	624,78	1749,39
1951	1,78	624,88	1749,66
1952	1,78	624,91	1749,74
1953	1,78	624,90	1749,71
1954	1,78	624,83	1749,53
1955	1,79	624,85	1750,28
1956	1,78	624,86	1752,00
1957	1,78	624,93	1759,30
1958	1,48	624,77	1744,54
1959	1,27	620,79	1743,68
1960	126,59	620,71	1742,74

TAB. A6. *(segue)*

Anno	Franco	Dollaro	Sterlina
1961	126,61	620,95	1740,01
1962	126,69	620,75	1742,93
1963	126,94	621,54	1739,94
1964	127,41	624,36	1743,05
1965	127,48	624,79	1746,78
1966	127,09	624,33	1744,06
1967	126,85	624,07	1741,26
1968	125,91	623,34	1492,05
1969	112,77	627,28	1499,51
1970	113,45	627,07	1502,50
1971	118,91	594,60	1584,19
1972	115,71	583,41	1460,09
1973	121,92	616,15	1457,03
1974	132,46	658,89	1408,02

Nota: Per il periodo 1863-1865 i dati si riferiscono alle quotazioni all'inizio e alla fine di ciascun anno.

Bibliografia

Bibliografia

Qui di seguito vengono elencati, con indicazione bibliografica completa, soltanto i lavori cui si è fatto riferimento nel corso del libro. La seguente lista non va quindi considerata come saggio bibliografico. Il lettore che desiderasse ulteriori indicazioni su opere relative alla storia della moneta in Italia può ricorrere agli ottimi repertori bibliografici di V. Promis, *Tavole sinottiche delle monete battute in Italia o da Italiani all'estero dal secolo VII a tutto l'anno 1868*, Torino, 1869, sez. V, pp. XLVII-LXXIX; F. & E. Gnecchi, *Saggio di bibliografia numismatica delle zecche italiane medievali e moderne*, Milano, 1889; Ph. Grierson, *Coins and Medals: A Select Bibliography*, London, 1954 (per l'Italia, pp. 48-52).

I. Storia della moneta

1. *Opere generali*

Argelati F. (ed.), *De monetis Italiae variorum illustrium virorum dissertationes*, Milano, 1750-1759.

Benaven J.M., *Le caissier italien*, Lyon, 1787.

Blanchet A., Dieudonné A., *Manuel de numismatique française*, t. I: (Blanchet A.) *Monnaies frappées en Gaule depuis les origines jusqu'à Hugues Capet*, Paris, 1912; t. II (Dieudonné A.) *Monnaies royales françaises depuis Hugues Capet jusqu'à la Révolution*, Paris, 1916.

Brooke G.C., *English Coins from the Seventh Century to the Present Day*, London, 1932.

Carli G.R., *Delle monete e dell'instituzione delle zecche d'Italia*, Mantova-Lucca, 1754-1760.

Cipolla C.M., *Studi di storia della moneta: i movimenti dei cambi in Italia dal sec. XIII al XV*, Pavia, 1948.
Cipolla C.M., *Moneta e civiltà mediterranea*, Venezia, 1957.
Cipolla C.M., *Appunti per una nuova storia della moneta nell'alto medioevo*, in *Settimane di Studio del Centro Italiano di Studi sull'alto medioevo*, vol. 8, Spoleto, 1961.
Cipolla C.M., *Currency Depreciation in Medieval Europe*, in «The Economic History Review», sez. II, vol. XV (1963).
Dannenberg H., *Die deutschen Münzen der sächsischen und fränkischen Kaiserzeit*, Berlin, 1876.
Del Mar A., *A History of the Monetary Systems*, New York, 1903.
Desimoni C., *La décroissance graduelle du denier de la fin du XI au commencement du XIII siècle*, in *Mélanges de numismatique*, serie I, t. III (1878), pp. 52-79.
Desimoni C., *La moneta e il rapporto dell'oro all'argento*, in *Memorie della R. Accademia dei Lincei. Classe scienze morali, storiche e filologiche*, serie V, t. 3, parte I (1895), pp. 3-56.
Einaudi L., *Teoria della moneta immaginaria nel tempo da Carlomagno alla Rivoluzione Francese*, in «Rivista di storia economica», 1 (1936), pp. 1-35.
Feaveryear A.E., *The Pound Sterling: a History of English Money*, Oxford-London, 1932.
Ferrara F., *Della moneta e dei suoi surrogati*, introd. in *Biblioteca dell'economista*, serie II, voll. 5 e 6 (Torino, 1857).
Grierson Ph., *Cronologia delle riforme monetarie di Carlo Magno*, in «Rivista Italiana di Numismatica», vol. 2, ser. 5, t. 56 (1954), pp. 65-79.
Grierson Ph., *Mint Output in the Tenth Century*, in «The Economic History Review», serie II, t. 9 (1957), pp. 462-466.
Grierson Ph., *Money and Coinage under Charlemagne*, in *Karl der Grösse*, Düsseldorf, 1965, vol. I.

Grierson Ph., *Numismatics*, London-Oxford, 1975.
Guerard B., *Du système monétaire des Francs sous les deux premières races*, in «Revue de la numismatique française», 2 (1837), pp. 406-440.
Hamilton E.J., *American Treasure and the Price Revolution in Spain*, Cambridge, Mass., 1934.
Le Blanc F., *Traité historique des monnayes de France*, Amsterdam, 1692.
Lopez R.S., *Back to Gold, 1252*, in «The Economic History Review», serie II, t. 9 (1956), pp. 219-240.
Luschin von Ebengreuth A., *Allgemeine Münzkunde und Geldgeschichte des Mittelalters und neueren Zeit*, München-Berlin, 1926.
Martinori E., *La moneta: vocabolario generale*, Roma, 1915.
Mikhalevskii F.I., *Ocherki istorii deneg u denezhnogo obraschcheniia*, Mosca, 1948.
Montanari G., *La zecca in consulta di stato (1683)*, in *Economisti del Cinque e Seicento* (ed. A. Graziani), Bari, 1913, pp. 237-379.
Naster P., *Trouvaille de monnaies carolingiennes à Zelzate*, in «Revue belge de numismatique et de sigillographie», 96 (1950), pp. 208-224.
Oman C., *The Coinage of England*, Oxford, 1931.
Prou M., *Catalogue des monnaies françaises de la Bibliothèque Nationale*, t. I: *Les monnaies mérovingiennes*, Paris, 1892; t. II: *Les monnaies carolingiennes*, Paris, 1896.
Ruding R., *Annals of the Coinage of Great Britain and its Dependencies* (3ª ediz.), London, 1840.
Sedillot R., *Le franc, histoire d'une monnaie des origines à nos jours*, Paris, 1953.
Soetber A., *Edelmetallproduktion und Wertverhältniss zwischen Gold und Silber seit der Entdeckung Amerika's bis zur Gegenvart*, in Dr. A. Petermanns Mittheilungen aus Justus Perthes' Geographischer Anstalt, Ergänzungsheft 57, Gotha, 1879.
Zanetti G.A. (ed.), *Nuova raccolta delle monete e zecche d'Italia*, Bologna, 1775-1789.

2. *Monete e zecche italiane dalla fine del sec. VIII alla fine del sec. XVIII*

a) Piemonte e Savoia

Chiaudano M., *La riforma monetaria di Emanuele Filiberto*, in *Lo stato sabaudo al tempo di Emanuele Filiberto*, t. III (Biblioteca Società Storica Subalpina 109, Torino, 1928), pp. 177-477.
Fossati A., *Elementi per uno studio del corso e dell'abbassamento delle monete d'oro sotto Carlo Emanuele I*, in *Carlo Emanuele I – Miscellanea*, t. I (Biblioteca Società Storica Subalpina 120, Torino, 1930), pp. 49-92.
Praj G., *La moneta piemontese ai tempi di Vittorio Amedeo I e di Carlo Emanuele II (1630-1675)*, in «Bollettino storico bibliografico subalpino», 40 (1938), pp. 221-327.
Promis D., *Monete dei Reali di Savoia*, Torino, 1841.
Saraceno V., *Il corso delle monete seguìto negli Stati di SS. RM. il Re di Sardegna*, Torino, 1782.

b) Milano e Pavia

Biondelli B., *La zecca e le monete di Milano*, Milano, 1869.
Brambilla C., *Monete di Pavia*, Pavia, 1883.
Cipolla C.M., *Les mouvements monétaires dans l'état de Milan (1580-1700)*, Paris, 1952.
Meroni V., *Cremona fedelissima*, Cremona, 1951.
Mulazzani G., *Studi economici sulle monete di Milano*, in «Rivista Italiana di Numismatica», 1 (1888), pp. 41-72.
Repossi L., *Milano e la sua zecca*, Torino, 1877.
Vianello C.A. (ed.), *La riforma monetaria in Lombardia nella seconda metà del Settecento*, Milano, 1939.

c) Venezia, Verona e Treviso

Buenger Robbert L., *The Venetian Money Market 1150-1229*, in «Studi Veneziani», 13 (1971).
Cessi R., *Problemi monetari veneziani fino a tutto il sec. XIV*, Padova, 1937.
Grierson Ph., *La moneta veneziana nell'economia mediterranea del Trecento e Quattrocento*, in *La Civiltà Veneziana del Quattrocento*, Venezia, 1957.
Lane F.C., *Le vecchie monete di conto veneziane ed il ritorno all'oro*, in «Atti dell'Ist. Veneto di Scienze, Lettere ed Arti», vol. CXVII (1958-59).
Luzzatto G., *L'oro e l'argento nella politica monetaria veneziana dei secoli XIII-XIV*, in *Studi di storia economica veneziana*, Padova, 1954, pp. 259-270.
Mandich G., *Formule monetarie veneziane del periodo 1619-1650*, in «Il Risparmio», 5 (1957), pp. 634-682.
Murari O., *Denari veronesi di un ripostiglio del secolo XII*, in «Numismatica», 17-18 (1951-1952), pp. 19-27.
Murari O., *I presunti mezzi denari veronesi dell'imperatore Ottone I*, in «Rivista Italiana di Numismatica», vol. VI, ser. V, t. LX (1958).
Murari O., *La moneta veronese nel periodo comunale*, in «Annali della Facoltà di Economia e Commercio in Verona», ser. I, vol. II (1965-66).
Padovan V., *Le monete dei veneziani*, Venezia, 1881.
Papadopoli N., *Le monete di Venezia*, Venezia, 1893-1919.
Perini Q., *Le monete di Verona*, Rovereto, 1902.
Perini Q., *Le monete di Treviso*, Rovereto, 1904.
Stella A., *Politica ed economia nel territorio Trentino Tirolese dal XIII al XVIII secolo*, Padova, 1958.

d) Firenze, Lucca, Pisa e Siena

Bernocchi N., *Le monete della Repubblica Fiorentina*, Firenze, 1974.

Castellani A., *Nuovi testi fiorentini del Dugento*, Firenze, 1952, voce «Fiorino», t. II, pp. 869-942.
Cordero di San Quintino G., *Della zecca e delle monete degli antichi marchesi di Toscana*, in *Memorie e documenti per servire alla storia di Lucca*, t. IX, parte I (Lucca, 1860), pp. 63-104.
Galeotti A., *Le monete del Granducato di Toscana*, Livorno, 1929.
Herlihy D., *Pisan Coinage and the Monetary Development of Tuscany 1150-1250*, in «American Numismatic Society», Museum Notes VI (New York, 1954), pp. 143-168.
Massagli D., *Della zecca e delle monete di Lucca nei secoli di mezzo*, in *Memorie e documenti per servire alla storia di Lucca*, t. XI, parte II (Lucca, 1860), pp. 1-222.
Orsini I., *Storia delle monete dei Granduchi di Toscana della casa de' Medici e di quelle dell'Augustissimo Imperatore Francesco di Lorena come Granduca di Toscana*, Firenze, 1756.
Promis D., *Monete della Repubblica di Siena*, Torino, 1848.
Vettori F., *Il fiorino d'oro antico illustrato*, Firenze, 1738.

e) Genova

Belgrano L.T., *Illustrazione del Registro Arcivescovile*, in «Atti Società Ligure di Storia Patria», 2 (1871), pp. 247-600 (le pagine 589-600 relative alla storia della moneta genovese furono scritte da C. Desimoni).
Casaretto P.F., *La moneta genovese in confronto con le altre valute mediterranee nei secoli XII e XIII*, in «Atti Società Ligure di Storia Patria», 55 (1928), pp. 1-225.
Chiaudano M., *La moneta di Genova nel secolo XII*, in *Studi in onore di A. Sapori*, Milano, 1957, t. I, pp. 187-214.
Cipolla C.M., *Argento tedesco e monete genovesi alla fine del Quattrocento*, in «Rivista Italiana di Numismatica», vol. 4, serie 5, num. 58 (1956), pp. 100-107.

Desimoni C., *Tavole dei valori in lire antiche e in lire italiane delle principali monete d'oro e d'argento genovesi*, in L.T. Belgrano, *Della vita privata dei genovesi*, Genova, 1875, pp. 506-532.
Desimoni C., *Sui denari minuti della zecca genovese*, in «Giornale Ligustico di archeologia, storia e letteratura», 9 (1882), pp. 209-226.
Desimoni C., *Le prime monete d'argento della zecca di Genova ed il loro valore (1139-1493)*, in «Atti Società Ligure di Storia Patria», 19 (1887), pp. 177-223.
Desimoni C., *Tavole descrittive delle monete della zecca di Genova dal 1139 al 1814*, in «Atti Società Ligure di Storia Patria», 22 (1890), pp. I-LXXII, 1-319.
Meroni U. (ed.), *Declarationes valoris monetarum per officiales officii monetarum civitatis Janue sedentes in cecha pro tribunali ad bancum iuris*, Mantova, 1953.
Spinola D., *Sommario di quello che si contiene nelli due libri rossi della moneta* (ed. U. Meroni), Mantova, 1953.

f) Varie

AA.VV., *Le zecche minori toscane fino al XIV secolo*, Pistoia, 1967.
Cordero di San Quintino G., *Cenni intorno al commercio dei Lucchesi coi Genovesi nel XII e XIII secolo con alcune ricerche sul valore delle monete colle quali a quei tempi si contrattava presso di quelle nazioni*, in «Atti R. Accademia Lucchese di Scienze, Lettere ed Arti», 10 (1840), pp. 55-117.
Crespellani A., *La zecca di Modena nei periodi comunale ed estense*, Modena, 1884.
Falconi P., *Le monete piacentine*, Piacenza, 1914-1920.
Lisini A., *Le monete e le zecche di Volterra, Montieri, Berignone e Casole*, in «Rivista Italiana di Numismatica», 22 (1909), pp. 253-302 e 439-467.

Mazzi A., *La convenzione monetaria del 1254 e il denaro imperiale di Bergamo nel sec. XIII*, Bergamo, 1882.
Murari O., *Le monete di Bergamo: nuove varianti nei denari*, in «Italia numismatica», 8 (1957), pp. 25-28 e 34-36.
Promis D., *Monete dei romani pontefici avanti il Mille*, Torino, 1858.
Salvioni G.B., *La moneta bolognese e la traduzione italiana del Savigny*, in «Atti e memorie della deputazione di storia patria per le provincie di Romagna», serie 3, t. 12, pp. 140-170; 295-329.

3. *La moneta italiana dal periodo napoleonico ad oggi*

Baffi P., *L'evoluzione monetaria italiana dall'economia di guerra alla convertibilità (1935-1958)*, in *Studi sulla moneta*, Milano, 1965.
Barberi B., *Cambio e parità economica della lira*, in «Annali di statistica», serie VIII, vol. 1 (1947), pp. 1-36.
Boccardo G., *Le banche ed il corso forzato*, Roma, 1879.
Boccolari G., Selmi A., *Monete e cambi nel ducato di Modena dal 1819 al 1859*, in «Archivio Economico dell'Unificazione Italiana», 3-4 (1956), fasc. 3.
Carboneri G., *La circolazione monetaria nei diversi stati*, vol. I: *Monete e biglietti in Italia dalla Rivoluzione Francese ai nostri giorni*, Roma, 1915.
Di Nardi G., *Le banche di emissione in Italia nel sec. XIX*, Torino, 1953.
Felloni G., *Monete e zecche negli Stati Sabaudi dal 1816 al 1860*, in «Archivio Economico dell'Unificazione Italiana», 2 (1956), fasc. 2.
Lefèvre R., *La circolazione metallica del Regno d'Italia (1862-1930)*, Roma, 1931.
Nelkenbrecher J. Chr., *Nuovo manuale di monete, pesi, misure, corsi di cambio, fondi pubblici...* (trad. it. sull'ediz. francese curata dal Deschamps), Milano, 1847-51.

Parenti G., *Monete e cambi nel Granducato di Toscana dal 1825 al 1859*, in «Archivio Economico dell'Unificazione Italiana», 2 (1956), fasc. 1.

Supino C., *Storia della circolazione cartacea in Italia (dal 1860 al 1928)*, Milano, 1929.

Tucci U., *Le monete del Regno Lombardo-Veneto dal 1815 al 1866*, in «Archivio Economico dell'Unificazione Italiana», 2 (1956), fasc. 3.

II. Metrologia

Blancard L., *Sur les notations pondérales des patères d'Avignon et de Bernay et la livre romaine*, in «Bulletin monumentale», serie V, t. 11 (49° della collez.) (1883), pp. 55-83.

Blancard L., *La pile de Charlemagne: étude sur l'origine et les poids des deniers neufs et de la livre de Charlemagne*, in «Annuaire de la Société de numismatique», 1887, pp. 595-638.

Bockh A., *Metrologische Untersuchungen über Gewichte, Münzfüsse und Masse des Altertums*, Berlin, 1838.

Capobianchi V., *Pesi proporzionali desunti dai documenti della libbra romana, merovingia e di Carlo Magno*, in «Rivista Italiana di Numismatica», 5 (1892), pp. 79-114.

Dho M., *Guida pratica del sistema metrico decimale ed itinerario dei Regi Stati*, Torino, 1847.

Fossati S., *De ratione nummorum, ponderum et mensurarum in Galliis sub primae et secundae stirpis regibus*, in «Atti Accademia delle Scienze di Torino», serie 2, t. 5 (1842), pp. 39-159.

Grierson Ph., *Weight and Coinage*, in «Numismatic Chronicle», ser. VII, vol. IV (1964).

Guilhiermoz P., *Note sur les poids du moyen âge*, in *Bibliothèque de l'École des Chartes*, c. 67 (1906), pp. 161-233 e 402-450.

Hultsch F.C., *Griechische und Römische Metrologie*, Berlin, 1882.

Martini A., *Manuale di metrologia*, Torino, 1883.

Naville L., *Fragments de métrologie antique*, in «Revue suisse de numismatique», 22 (1920), pp. 42-60.

Naville L., *La livre romaine et le denier de la loi salique*, in «Revue suisse de numismatique», 22 (1920), pp. 257-263.

Nissen F., *Metrologia greca e romana* (trad. it. sulla 2ª ediz. tedesca del 1892 in *Biblioteca di storia economica*, ed. V. Pareto, t. III, Milano, 1915).

Rocca P., *Pesi e misure antiche di Genova e del Genovesato*, Genova, 1871.

Rocca P., *Sul sistema metrico e numismatico dei merovingi riformato da Carlo Magno*, Crema, 1889.

Tableaux comparatifs des anciennes mesures du département de Gènes avec les mesures métriques de l'empire, par la commission des poids et mesures de ce département, Genova, 1811.

Tacchini A., *La metrologia universale ed il codice metrico internazionale*, Milano, 1895.

Tavole di ragguaglio fra le nuove e le antiche misure e fra i nuovi e gli antichi pesi della Repubblica Italiana pubblicate per ordine del Governo, Milano, 1803.

Tavole di ragguaglio fra le nuove e le antiche misure e fra i nuovi e gli antichi pesi del Regno d'Italia pubblicate per ordine del Governo, Milano, 1805.

Tavole di ragguaglio degli antichi pesi e misure degli Stati di S.M. in terraferma coi pesi e misure del sistema metrico decimale, Torino, 1849.

Tavole di ragguaglio dei pesi e delle misure già in uso nelle varie Provincie del Regno col sistema metrico decimale, approvate con D.R. 20 maggio 1877, n. 3836 (ed. ufficiale), Roma, 1877.

III. Varie

Bollea L.C., *Documenti degli archivi di Pavia relativi alla storia di Voghera* (Biblioteca Società Storica Subalpina 46), Pinerolo, 1909.

Cecchetti B., *Saggio sui prezzi delle vettovaglie e di altre merci in Venezia nei secoli XII-XIX*, in «Atti R. Istituto Veneto di Scienze, Lettere ed Arti», serie IV, t. 3 (1874), pp. 1465-1491.
Cipolla C.M., *The Decline of Italy: the Case of a Fully Matured Economy*, in «The Economic History Review», serie II, vol. 5 (1952), pp. 178-187.
Cipolla C.M., *L'economia milanese: i movimenti economici generali (1350-1500)*, in *Storia di Milano* (ed. Treccani), t. VIII, Milano, 1957.
Cipolla C.M., *La prétendue révolution des prix: réflexions sur l'expérience italienne*, in «Annales: économies, sociétés, civilisations», 10 (1955), pp. 513-516.
Colombo A., *Cartario di Vigevano e del suo comitato* (Biblioteca Società Storica Subalpina 128), Torino, 1933.
De Maddalena A., *Prezzi e aspetti di mercato in Milano durante il sec. XVII*, Milano, 1949.
Fanfani A., *Indagini sulla rivoluzione dei prezzi*, Milano, 1940.
Fumagalli A., *Le vicende di Milano durante la guerra con Federico I Imperatore* (ristampa), Milano, 1854.
Gualazzini U., *Rapporti fra capitale e lavoro nelle industrie tessili lombarde del Medioevo*, Torino, 1932.
Haberler G., *Fattori monetari e reali e stabilità economica*, in «Moneta e credito», 9 (1956), pp. 119-135.
Marconcini F., *Vicende dell'oro e dell'argento dalle premesse storiche alla liquidazione della Unione monetaria latina (1803-1925)*, Milano, 1929.
Mueller K.O. (ed.), *Welthandelsbräuche (1480-1540)* (Deutsche Handelsakten des Mittelalters und der Neuzeit 5), Stuttgart-Berlin, 1934.
Nef J.U., *Silver Production in Central Europe (1450-1518)*, in «Journal of Political Economy», 49 (1941), pp. 575-591.
Parenti G., *Prime ricerche sulla rivoluzione dei prezzi in Firenze*, Firenze, 1939.
Pfaff V., *Die Einnahmen der römischen Kurie am Ende des*

12 Jahrhunderts, in «Vierteljahrschrift für Sozial- und Wirtschaftsgeschichte», 40 (1953), pp. 97-118.

Roberti M., *Milano capitale napoleonica: la formazione di uno stato moderno (1796-1814)*, Milano, 1947.

Solmi A., *L'amministrazione finanziaria nel Regno Italico nell'alto medioevo*, in «Bollettino Società Pavese di Storia Patria», 31 (1931), pp. 5-288.

Tiraboschi G., *Storia dell'augusta Badia di San Silvestro di Nonantola*, Modena, 1785.

Zobi A., *Manuale storico delle massime e degli ordinamenti economici in Toscana*, Firenze, 1847.

Finito di stampare
nel mese di settembre 2026
presso Rotomail Italia S.p.A. – Vignate (MI)